Vietnamese chopper pilots were asked to evacuate the dead and wounded but refused to come because of the dark, the rain, and possible Viet Cong fire. At Captain Beng's request and using the ARVN radio net, I called the American helicopter unit in Saigon and requested a medical evacuation. I told the pilots there were Viet Cong near the landing zone and about the torrential rains. Within an hour, using a radio beacon as a guide, two choppers landed in the dark and rain, loaded twelve wounded and four dead, and lifted off to Saigon. I knew that some of the wounded would not live through the night.

Before they departed, I spoke briefly with the pilots. They were calm and professional. One of them asked, "Are you the only American with these ARVN?"

The other said, "We can get you out of here. Ride back to Saigon with us." It was a tempting invitation, but I could not accept it under those circumstances.

LOST IN TRANSLATION

VIETNAM
A Combat Advisor's Story

Martin J. Dockery

PRESIDIO
PRESS

BALLANTINE BOOKS • NEW YORK

A Presidio Press Book
Published by The Random House Publishing Group

www.presidiopress.com

Library of Congress Control Number: 2004092174

ISBN 0-89141-851-2

Map by Meridian Mapping

Manufactured in the United States of America

First Hardcover Edition: July 2003
First Mass Market Edition: June 2004

OPM   10   9   8   7   6   5   4   3   2   1

This book is dedicated to my sons,
Martin Patrick Dockery and Timothy Li Dockery.

'Dockery was junior to you,
Wasn't he?' said the Dean. 'His son's here now.'
Death-suited, visitant, I nod. 'And do
You keep in touch with ____' Or remember how
Black-gowned, unbreakfasted, and still half-tight
We used to stand before that desk, to give
'Our version' of 'these incidents last night'?
I try the door of where I used to live . . .

—"Dockery and Son,"
Philip Larkin

CONTENTS

Acknowledgments xi
Preface xiii
Map xviii
1. Early Lessons 1
2. A Volunteer 8
3. The Participants 25
4. In the Field 43
5. The Cement Plant 94
6. Delta Life 119
7. Back to the USA 164
8. Reflections 192
9. Return to Vietnam 208
Afterword 223
Appendix A: Myths 230
Appendix B: Role of the Advisor 234
Appendix C: Dos and Don'ts 238
Appendix D: Tips to Advisors 247

ACKNOWLEDGMENTS

This book is not a scholarly work or a comprehensive history. There are no footnotes. It is a memoir based primarily on my recollection of events that occurred when I was a combat advisor in Vietnam in 1962–63. It is only my story.

Although I read numerous books and articles for background information and general reference, I alone am responsible for any errors in this book. I am particularly indebted to the following sources: Lawrence M. Baskir and William A. Strauss, *Chance and Circumstance: The Draft, the War, and the Vietnam Generation* (Knopf, 1978); Bernard B. Fall, *Street Without Joy* (Schocken Books, 1961); Frances Fitzgerald, *Fire in the Lake* (Atlantic, Little Brown, 1973); Richard A. Gabriel and Paul L. Savage, *Crisis in Command* (Hill and Wang, 1978); Gerald Hickey, *Village in Vietnam* (Yale, 1964); Stanley Karnow, *Vietnam: A History* (Viking, 1983); Robert S. McNamara, *In Retrospect* (Random House, 1995); Neil Sheehan, *A Bright Shining Lie: John Paul Vann and America in Vietnam* (Random House, 1999); *Readings in Guerrilla Warfare* (U.S. Army Special Warfare School, 1960); *Book of Instructions for U.S. Military Advisors to South Vietnam* (MAAG, Vietnam, 1962); and various U.S. Army field manuals.

Many people helped me by commenting on the entire manuscript. Some of them read several drafts. They made valuable suggestions that improved each page of this book.

More important, their frequent encouragement gave me the courage to finish. The following people critiqued my work: Brother Alois, Lisa Blitman, Virginia Bress, Rev. Edward Byington, Alan Clark, Whitney Clark, Rev. Barry Connerton, Richard Crystal, Cathy Disbrow, Emmett Dockery (Vietnam Veteran), Karen Dockery, Una Dockery, Mike Gillen, Ed Hellwig, Alan Klavins (Vietnam veteran), Michel Kramer, James Lap, Jane Leventhall, Eileen Matthews, Mark Matthews, Bobby McDonald, Cathy L. McDonald, Jenny Ordish, Olive Ordish, Roger Ordish, Lois O'Reilly, Monsignor Daniel Peake, Jeremy Putley, Rob Schwartz, and David Young (Vietnam veteran).

Mike Blackwell (Vietnam veteran), my good friend and army buddy, assisted me in many ways. He helped organize the material and suggested revisions and new topics. Mike reined in my philosophical musings and corrected inaccuracies. I gratefully acknowledge that his suggestions made this book better. Likewise, I am indebted to Jeff Curry for his encouragement and helpful comments and suggestions.

I could not have written this book without the help of Kotie Cannon, a loyal and dedicated friend. Not only did she transcribe my confusing handwritten paragraphs into error-free typewritten copy, she endured innumerable drafts and revisions with good cheer. I thank you, Kotie.

My editor, Bob Kane (Vietnam veteran), and my copy editor, Barbara Feller-Roth, worked hard to turn my manuscript into a book. I appreciate their professionalism and their help.

Finally I thank my wife, Meliora, and my sons, Martin and Tim, for their significant contributions to this book and for their patience during the past four years.

PREFACE

Next to the birth of my sons, Vietnam has been the defining experience of my life; it has impacted me profoundly. Not a day goes by that I do not think about Vietnam and my experiences there. I am not referring to flashbacks or nightmares but rather to recollections and ruminations. I am not visited by ghosts, and I have no devils to exorcise. But I do remember and I vividly recall those experiences every day. Even now I recollect with clarity the sounds, smells, and vistas of that place and its people. My tour of duty in Vietnam was marked by isolation, frustration, and danger. Nevertheless, Vietnam transported me. I want my sons and anyone interested in that phase of U.S. history to know about these events that have so shaped my life.

This is primarily an account of my assignment as a combat advisor to a South Vietnamese infantry battalion. That is the crux of my story. It is an old tale from an old war, but I think it is relevant and instructive today. Some events from my life and army service prior to and after Vietnam are included to put the story into context. The events and episodes described reveal a lucky and at times foolish young man—indeed, at times a young man bounding from near disaster to near disaster.

I lived and fought with a South Vietnamese infantry unit. Much of the time, I was isolated from other Americans and was usually the only American soldier with these Vietnamese soldiers. This experience gave me a point of view shared by only a few Vietnam veterans and is a factor in the story I tell and the opinions I relate. Most field advisors in 1963 had experiences similar to mine. The thousands of U.S. combat troops who came after me had different experiences and faced perhaps greater dangers. They have their own stories and opinions.

Heraclitus, a Greek philosopher, believed that war was the father of everything. He may have been right. Although my individual experiences in Vietnam were "sound and fury signifying nothing," collectively they were not inconsequential. They added up to something greater. There was a process at work during this period. The cumulative effect of these events was to turn an immature and insecure person into someone capable, confident, and caring. That is how I see myself today. We all grow up; the Vietnam War was the period during which I matured.

Although my character was tested, I was fortunate and came home a stronger person. I learned that my limitations were fewer than I had thought. But there were things I could not accomplish as an advisor; there were so many things that I and other advisors were simply not capable of doing. Maybe those who sent us to Vietnam knew this, but I suspect they did not; we were all well trained, highly motivated, and dedicated, but oh so naive, uninformed, and inexperienced.

These pages reveal contradictions between my values and my conduct, but only fiction can portray a man without contradictions. For the most part, I have not written about the awful or the barbaric. I tried to avoid the fault common to old soldiers: The more distant the event, the more heroic one becomes. I recognize, however, that nostalgia for a time in my life long past stalks these pages.

If there is a recurring theme to be found in this book, I suppose it is that the advisor program failed in Vietnam. It failed because, from the outset, cultural differences and the reality of human nature undermined the goal of forging the South Vietnam armed forces into an effective force against the Viet Cong, who were the surrogates for the communist government of North Vietnam. The Americans who served as advisors did their best and persevered under trying circumstances, but we did not succeed. And in the end, American military intervention failed. Although we had the tools, we did not understand the forces at work or the dynamics of nationalism. Even if we had understood, South Vietnam was a loser from the beginning because of endemic corruption and lack of reform. Those of us on the ground—the combat advisors—in 1962–63 came to know these things and wonder at the naiveté and unrealistic goals of the Washington policy makers.

My purpose in writing this book is to share my experiences, crow a little, and vent too. This is not about closure; my hope is that by putting all of this in writing, I can make some sense of it. After thirty-eight years, I have the perspective to view my Vietnam experience in its relative importance to my life. I hope those who read these pages will enjoy them, find them interesting, and learn something new about the American experience in Vietnam. There are realities and truths within these pages that should be considered by those men who send other men to war.

This book is a collection of anecdotes that cumulatively describe an experience and an environment. It is not a war story per se; it belongs to a larger, less defined genus of soldiers' stories. There are no descriptions of daylong battles or heroic action. I do not write like Kipling, Churchill, Caputo, or Herr. I write like the lawyer I became after the war: terse, direct, and nonfloral.

This work is not intended to be a broad analysis of the Vietnam War, its causes and mistakes. Notwithstanding, I have included short passages on the history and religions of Vietnam so that the roots of Vietnamese nationalism can be understood in the context of this conflict. The passages describing the Cold War are intended to explain why the United States went to war in Vietnam. The purpose of the nonmilitary biographical information is to provide background for my acts and decisions.

I have related this story with dates and place names when I am certain they are accurate. In 1999 my mother gave me sixty-two letters that I wrote to my parents from Vietnam. I kept a diary while I was there. Entries were not made daily. The entries that were made were cryptic and have little meaning to me today. The diary is really no more than a memo book that records incomplete information about troop movements, operations, and body counts. Alas, it contains no reflections.

Unless otherwise noted, the photographs included in this book were taken in 1962 and 1963. The letters, the diary, and the photographs helped me verify my memories as well as date and place some of the events described here. I have included anecdotes and situations not mentioned in the letters or the diary, and in those instances I relied on my memory. But I can assure the reader that I have not added pieces of the past that did not exist. The names Colonel Ted, Legionnaire Michael, and Captain Smith, which appear in this book, are fictitious, but the anecdotes describe actual happenings. All of these experiences have been recorded as I remember them without conscious embellishments or distortions.

I hope that reading this book will prove to be an enlightening experience in a little-studied and much-misunderstood aspect of the Vietnam War.

MJD
Rye, New York
December 2001

LOST IN
TRANSLATION

One

EARLY LESSONS

Draw from others the lesson that may profit yourself.
—Anon.

Family My parents were part of the American immigrant experience. They came to the United States from Ireland in 1927. Their formal education was limited, but they understood its importance. Religion, education, family, truth, and country (both old and new) were important to them, so they passed on these values to their seven children. I was the third child and the first male. I graduated from Catholic grammar and high schools in White Plains, New York, and from Boston College. My family and these schools formed my character and prepared me, for better or worse, for what followed.

Dad kept a tavern, Dockery's Restaurant, at 11 West 31st Street in New York City for forty-two years before retiring in 1975 at age seventy-five. He was the vice commandant of the 1st Roscommon Battalion of the Irish Republican Army (IRA) and was imprisoned during Ireland's fight for independence. He told me he had nothing against the English people. The guards treated him well, but the government of England was another matter. He kept a donation jar on the bar for the Saint Francis Bread Line on 35th Street and one behind the bar for the IRA. My mom and dad fed, clothed, sheltered, and educated seven children with the tavern profits. Dad took the 6:10 A.M. train to New York City six days a week "to catch the early birds," those wanting a drink before work. He returned home tired and sober at 10 P.M. each evening. Advice he gave me when I was young showed he had qualms about his business: "Sure 'n' I sell the poison, but I don't want ye drinking it." At the time, I did not understand his concern. I know now. John Barleycorn is fun but not a friend. Do not invite him home. He will not leave on his own.

My father was proud to be Irish and proud of his adoptive country. "Martin," he once said to me, "this is really the land of opportunity. In the Old Country I couldn't have provided for and educated all of ye. And ye and yer brothers and sisters have opportunities here that wouldn't be possible for ye over there." As a thirteen-year-old, I told him I wanted to have a tavern when I grew up. He rested his hand on my arm, looked me in the eye, and said: "Tavern work is okay for an immigrant boy like me; twelve hours a day on your feet is okay for me, but not for my son. Ye go to school and stay there. Do something with yer brain. It will be better for ye and you'll feel better about yerself too." I wish I had accumulated enough experiences, a past, to ask the questions of my dad that come to mind today.

Diversity Training As a young person my world included whites and blacks—"coloreds" back then—as well as Catholics, Protestants, and Jews, and Irish and Italians. In those days you weren't called an Irish American or an Italian American. You were simply Irish or Italian. My parents taught us tolerance and understanding and judging people by what they did and not by their race, religion, or ethnicity. They had felt the sting of discrimination when they arrived in the United States. At that time it was not uncommon for the last line in published job advertisements to read, "Irish need not apply." When I was old enough to understand, my mom told me why the Irish were not sought as employees. In 1927 alcohol was a problem for the Irish; my mom, in her honesty, said that was why it was difficult for the Irish to get jobs. I have memories of lessonlike talks dealing with slavery, lynchings, and Jim Crow laws. Other times her talks were about the mistreatment of Jews by Christians and how that was wrong. She used the plight of the Irish under English rule and as U.S. immigrants as examples of prejudice. My parents also taught me by example how to treat people, the best way to teach.

My father cut the grass on Sunday afternoons. I was six and wanted to help but was not strong enough to push the lawn mower by myself. One Sunday we pushed it together, he from the back with his hands next to mine on the mower handle. We cut the whole lawn that way. It must have been painfully slow for him.

As we were mowing the lawn, a car pulled to the curb across the street. Three people emerged and approached my dad. A woman introduced herself and said she was a real estate agent. She was showing houses in the neighborhood to the couple with her and they wanted to know whether any Jews lived close by. My father and I stood there behind the lawn mower, with me in front, his hands on mine. My father's answer burned itself into my young mind so that today I can still hear him responding: "Some Jews are good neighbors and some Jews are bad neighbors, just like Christians. That's all I'm saying." After the people left, he explained to me what had happened and why it was wrong for them to ask those questions and think like that. I asked, "What's a real estate agent?" and "What's a Jew?" These are old questions from a young person. In answer to the second question, my dad said something like it's a different religion and they believe in different things than we do, but we are all the same in God's eyes.

Dad went to work every day. Mom raised, fed, and clothed us. She cleaned the house and dealt with teachers, priests, doctors, groceries, and schoolwork. Clean clothes for nine, meals for eight twice a day, seven lunch bags on school days, and supervision, supervision, and supervision seven days a week—that was my mom's lot. All this was hard for her, but she shepherded us through the pitfalls of youth and schooling.

Breakfast and supper were eaten in the kitchen around a big table. The food was hot and good, and we ate everything in sight. Fourteen quarts of milk, two dozen eggs, and a pound of butter were delivered three times a week. At the evening meal she would make a point of asking each of us what we had done that day, where we had been and with whom. During one supper when I was ten, I answered that after school I was playing ball on the street with Barry and Steve Levine, our neighbors. Then as an aside I said, "Barry Levine's a kike." Within seconds, mom dragged me by my hair over to the sink and pushed a bar of soap in my mouth. All this while she called me a "little Hitler" and asked, "Where did you hear that word? Who did you hear it from?" With tears streaming down my cheeks and soap bubbles coming out of my mouth, I said I didn't know what the word meant but that Steve Levine had called his brother, Barry, a "kike" while we were playing ball that afternoon. Mom was taken aback. Her initial reaction was out of character. She always was caring and reasonable with us. Gamely, she said it was a hateful word and did not care where I had heard it; I was not to use it again. That evening before my bedtime, she said she was sorry about the soap and should have let me explain first, but prejudice and hateful words made her angry.

ROTC When I started at Boston College in 1956, I enrolled in the Reserve Officers' Training Corps, commonly known as ROTC, with the purpose of spending two years in the army as an officer. I was hoping to fulfill my military obligation while at the same time gaining experience that would be useful upon return to civilian life. The ROTC program required one class a week for four years plus summer camp after my junior year.

After graduating in 1960 from Boston College, where I studied philosophy, economics, and theology, I received a reserve commission as a U.S. Army second lieutenant of infantry. Officer Infantry Orientation School and Paratrooper School at Fort Benning, Georgia, preceded my assignment to Fort Knox, Kentucky.

Sensitivity Training I was a late bloomer, both academically and emotionally. I was not particularly susceptible to the attitudes, feelings, or circumstances of others. My mom and sisters endeavored to teach me to be sensitive. They tried hard, but I never mastered it.

Paratrooper School consisted of one month of strenuous physical conditioning and instruction in the techniques of parachute jumping from an airplane and the niceties of landing on the ground unhurt. Graduation occurred after five jumps from 1,200 feet. I was proud of completing the course and sent my parents a recording of the paratrooper song. I thought they would like to share in my accomplishment and the humor of the song. Alas, I was insensitive again. My mom was horrified, and my sisters roundly criticized me for sending the recording home. "Blood on the Risers" is a song about the fate of a paratrooper whose parachute fails to open. The last eight lines of the song are:

There was blood upon the risers, there were brains upon
    the chute
Intestines were a-dangling from his paratrooper's boots,
They picked him up, still in his chute, and poured him
    from his boots.
He ain't gonna jump no more.
Gory, gory, what a helluva way to die,
Gory, gory, what a helluva way to die,
Gory, gory, what a helluva way to die,
He ain't gonna jump no more.

There was something about the song that upset Mom. This lesson in sensitivity was not lost on me. The letters I wrote to my parents from Vietnam were devoid of hardship, danger, and combat. They touched on politics, weather, food, geography, and religion. I was learning to be sensitive, incrementally. Still am.

Fort Knox Recruit training is probably the worst assignment a second lieutenant can receive, and that was my assignment. I learned that I would be training recruits at Fort Knox for the balance of my two-year military commitment. Caring for and training inductees was not appealing. After eight weeks the recruits leave for other training at other posts and the eight-week cycle begins again, ad infinitum. Regular army (career) officers were not assigned to recruit training; they received choice postings. Not so with reserve officers.

I remember Fort Knox as a large, sprawling, dreary place. The barracks, bachelor officers' quarters, and classrooms available for recruit training were built in 1942 and were made of wood and tar paper. The army, with hope, called them temporary buildings; they are probably in use today. In cold weather, coal furnaces in hundreds of temporary buildings spread soot everywhere. Skin, clothes, cars, and indeed the sky were darkened with coal soot. Snow quickly turned black.

Senior officers have great tolerance for the mistakes and poor judgment of lieutenants. They let them learn in peacetime when their errors are not costly. And always the senior officers tell the lieutenants, "Ask your sergeants what to do and follow their advice. They know, they have the experience." Newly commissioned second lieutenants do not come to the army fully formed leaders of men. Only with training and experience do the judgment and maturity necessary for leadership develop. Mistakes are part of the process and, in most cases, a harmless and valuable learning tool. Junior officers test the patience and require the understanding and guidance of their commanders and sergeants. All of these things were true in my case. Fort Knox is where I learned what was expected of a young officer and what kind of conduct and values were essential for successful leadership.

Two

A VOLUNTEER

If a man will make a purchase of a chance
he must abide by the consequences.
—SIR RICHARD RICHARDS

Mind-set Any discussion of the U.S. involvement in Vietnam should begin with an understanding of the mind-set in America that had existed since the end of World War II. It is paramount for an understanding of U.S. motives. The country was involved in an intense competition, at all levels, in all fields, with the champions of communism. The Soviet Union and China, allies during World War II, were now our enemies. It was a fierce, protracted struggle in a time of great fear and uncertainty. Most Americans were aware of this conflict and many were touched by fear. I was. Grade schools across America held nuclear bomb drills. I remember them. Children were taught in school what to do if the Soviets dropped atom bombs on us. "Get under your desk," the teachers said. For the survivors of a nuclear attack, the government stockpiled food, water, and equipment in basements of public and private buildings. Signs with nuclear symbols were affixed to buildings notifying the public that survival stores were in the basement. New York State encouraged citizens to build atom bomb shelters in their backyards or basements, and many people did. Ethicists discussed the morality of letting a neighbor into your shelter if, by doing so, there would not be enough food for your family.

The great fear was of communism. It combined an attractive doctrine, a calculated use of power, and an unusual stay-

8

ing power. Americans thought that it was a force unparalleled in history and a global movement that was intent on overthrowing one noncommunist government after another. Our leaders believed that we were involved in a desperate struggle with enemies who swore to bury us, and we were not winning. These leaders grew up during the 1920s and 1930s and had participated, in one way or another, in World War II. They remembered the losses and felt the pain, and they believed that the appeasement of Hitler led to World War II. They were determined that it would not happen again.

This was the challenge America and its leaders faced, and in time most of its people accepted the fact that we were in a fierce contest against a determined foe intent on destroying us. The United States decided on a policy of containment to stop the communist advance.

The Soviets and the Chinese had developed a theory of guerrilla warfare earlier, and they had better trained and more organized forces for its implementation than did the United States to counteract it. To our dismay we learned that guerrilla warfare was a successful way to wage war for small, ill-equipped forces fighting against great odds. Moscow and Beijing were supporting armed coups and guerrilla movements in third-world countries and had done so in the past. In Indochina, French soldiers had been engaged by guerrillas for eight years, and the French troops were defeated by them and conventional forces at Dien Bien Phu. In Algeria, an estimated 30,000 rebels engaged 500,000 French troops; in Cuba, Fidel Castro's small invasion force eventually brought the downfall of the Cuban government, which had a 43,000-man army.

In the early 1960s, communism was waging a political and military struggle for control, first of South Vietnam and then, many believed, all of Southeast Asia. Cambodia, Laos, Thailand, Burma, and Malaysia might fall one by one, like dominoes. The United States believed we had to meet the communist challenge wherever it occurred because our freedom and way of life were ultimately at stake. That is the reason we were willing to help South Vietnam, which had a noncommunist, authoritarian government, defend itself. It was thought to be in our own interest.

When our ally South Vietnam was confronted with a communist-supported guerrilla war and we were faced with the prospect of another fallen domino, the United States committed itself, gradually and with forethought, to the military defense of South Vietnam. Our leaders believed that to do otherwise would be an appeasement of communism. And so did I. The prize in this contest was Vietnam. Beneath all is the land. What we did not comprehend was the passionate determination of the Vietnamese, communists and noncommunists alike, to free Vietnam from foreign domination.

One aspect of the U.S. commitment was to send army officers as advisors to the South Vietnam armed forces. In 1962 I was part of that commitment and was assigned as an advisor to a South Vietnamese infantry battalion.

Your Time Will Come At Fort Knox I became friends with my suite mate, Mike Blackwell, a 1959 Boston College graduate. We detested what we were doing (recruit training) and wanted a challenging and adventurous assignment. The press was full of coverage of the war between the government of South Vietnam and the Viet Cong. Aware that American officers were being assigned as advisors to the South Vietnam armed forces, and with frightfully little soul searching, Mike and I volunteered for service in Vietnam. We did not want to miss this adventure. Concerned that all the Viet Cong would be dead before we got there, we arranged a three-day pass and went to the Officers' Personnel Division at the Pentagon to volunteer in person. After a number of separate interviews, we were told, "You are fine young infantry officers, have great motivations, and will go places, but not to Vietnam; you're too young and inexperienced in the army. Go back to Fort Knox. Learn soldiering. Only a few of the senior, experienced officers are eligible for Vietnam. Your time will come."

We were disappointed to return to Fort Knox, but three weeks later, out of the blue, to our everlasting surprise, we received orders to Vietnam via Fort Bragg, North Carolina, and the Army Language School in Monterey, California. Our military service, which had been extended for one year, would now include a tour of duty in Vietnam. Our trip to the Pentagon, it seems, had actually been successful.

On April 18 I wrote to my parents about my assignment. To lessen their concern, I told them I would be an intelligence officer, which was not true:

> Yesterday I received orders from the Department of the Army. On the 3rd of June I will leave Ft. Knox and report to Ft. Bragg, N.C. At Bragg I will receive four weeks of intelligence training and from there I will report to the Presidio, in Monterey, California. After six weeks of a special language course there, I will be sent to Saigon, Vietnam. My job in Saigon will be Corps Intelligence Officer.

> I was surprised because they told me they weren't sending young officers. I'm not sorry about the assignment, nor am I upset about spending another year in the Army. My adjusted ETS (Estimated Time of Separation) is now December 1963.

> I welcome the idea of traveling and experiencing new things. I can't easily imagine myself settling down, not yet. I sincerely believe that I will benefit by this assignment, maybe some of this restlessness will disappear.

> I will be home for about a week at the end of May.

* * *

I was young. I got what I wished for. The future stretched before me without limit and was unknown. I was thrilled.

Advisor Training   We were to be in a class of fifty junior officers, each trained as an advisor to the South Vietnamese Army. At the time, I thought the training program was excellent. We studied the language and military tactics, weapons, explosives, and radio usage. We also read about the history of Vietnam and its culture. Bernard Fall's *Street Without Joy,* which chronicles the Vietnamese communist (Viet Minh) defeat of the French in the 1950s, was required reading.

We were instructed on how to deal with our counterparts, the Vietnamese officers to whom we would be assigned as advisors. It was made clear that in order to accomplish our mission, we had to establish a relationship of mutual respect and trust, a rapport, with our counterparts, and much of the instruction focused on the common-sense aspects of this goal.

The training at the Army Language School consisted of six forty-five-minute classes five days a week. It was a basic six-week introductory course; all other courses at the school were thirty-six weeks or more. Each class had seven students and was taught by a different Vietnamese national. Beginning with the first class on the first day, no English was spoken. In the evenings we listened to language tapes. The Vietnamese we learned was limited to what would help us in our role as advisors. The only exception was that for some strange, inexplicable reason, we were taught the Vietnamese word for igloo, *ham chua dan*. This should have been a tip-off that the training was imperfect. We were not taught the words for compassion or mercy. We learned enough Vietnamese to perform our job and live among the Vietnamese. I was not taught how to read or write Vietnamese, but I did learn the basics and in time I could speak the language.

Although I expected that these courses would give me meaningful insight into the Vietnamese mind, politics, and culture, that was not the case. Unfortunately, we Americans had still not figured these things out twelve years later when we were hauling people off the embassy roof out to carriers in the South China Sea. The instructors were well intentioned, and a lot of the material was informative, but a great deal of the cultural information was silly and useless. Appendix A is an example of cultural information taken from the course material presented to my class. It shows how shallow and superficial our understanding of the Vietnamese culture was. This material was taught to advisors who were at that time, according to the army, "our best and brightest."

When I left Fort Bragg, I thought I had received a tutorial covering all I would need to know about the Vietnamese culture. I was wrong. Soon after beginning my assignment, I realized that I had received only an introduction, and a lot of what I was taught was incorrect or mythical. How could it have been otherwise? The U.S. Army knew little about Vietnam, as did other Americans and the U.S. government. By the end of my tour, I had learned a great deal about Vietnam and the Vietnamese culture, but I learned it by living there—the only way anyone can truly understand a culture.

Jesuit Lunch During predeparture leave I traveled to Boston. I had lunch in the Jesuit dining room at Boston College with four of my former teachers. Proudly I told them where I was going. My teachers raised the issue of the morality of our government's policy toward Vietnam and my role. They asked me to justify in moral terms my decision to volunteer. They asked important questions: "Why, Martin?" and "Martin, what have you done?"

The truth is that I had never considered my decision in moral terms. These Jesuits voiced their disappointment that I had volunteered without considering whether or not the war was immoral. Implicit in their criticism and demeanor was their judgment that the war was not just. They were upset. It amazes me today that I made the decision to volunteer for

Vietnam without considering the morality of the war or my decision to be part of it. I had been taught at home and in school to ask whether my actions were right or wrong and to examine in moral terms what I was going to do and why and to whom. At that time I believed there was a bright line between right and wrong.

The Jesuits should not have questioned their role as teachers. Textbooks and lectures are no substitute for experience, and experience alone leads to wisdom. Alas, notwithstanding what and how we are taught, mostly we learn only facts and theories in school.

I was not committed to a cause. To paraphrase Muhammad Ali, I had no enmity toward these little people. So why did I volunteer? The answer is that I asked to go to Vietnam for the excitement and adventure it promised. Although I knew that even a bird has to land, I was not ready to take on the challenge of civilian life, at least not until I had been tested. I wanted to be in the arena. I wanted a grand adventure. And so it was.

Diplomat at Large We were issued "official" U.S. passports. Mine had printed on it: "The Bearer Is Abroad On An Official Assignment For the United States Government." To be twenty-three years of age and abroad on an official assignment of the U.S. government was exhilarating. No one explained why a diplomatic passport was necessary, so we conjectured that either some treaty prohibited U.S. soldiers from being in Vietnam, or it was thought we would be treated better as captured diplomats than as captured soldiers.

At the end of August 1962, the fifty junior officers from Fort Bragg and Monterey assembled at Travis Air Force Base, in Fairfield, California, for departure. We flew a total of thirty-two hours in a propeller plane with web seats and little noise insulation. Arrival in Saigon was on September 2, after night stopovers in Hawaii, Guam, and Manila. As the plane neared the coast of Vietnam, I could make out the features of the land, tree-covered mountains partially hidden by clouds, coastal plains, and everywhere a beautiful, deep green.

I was extremely confident and determined. I was an American. I was young, healthy, and well trained (I thought), and I believed in our mission and our country's righteousness. America had won every other war, and I was sure we would win this one too.

As we boarded the bus that was to take us from Tan Son Nhat airport to our quarters in Saigon, the driver explained that the bus windows were covered with chicken wire to keep out grenades. The seriousness of my situation became apparent to me when we passed the French military cemetery, full of row after row of white crosses marking the graves of soldiers killed during what the Vietnamese referred to as the French War. Those soldiers were expended by France in the pursuit of colonial riches. None of us had any idea then of the human expenditure that America would ultimately make in Vietnam.

Saigon was an armed camp, with soldiers and police on every corner and the roads patrolled by soldiers in jeeps. Ready response troops were kept at central locations. I was added to this arsenal. Whether in uniform or civilian clothes, I carried a gun until I left Vietnam on August 28, 1963.

Our first week was spent in Saigon, where we were given equipment and attended cultural and medical lectures. The lecturers knew that we were assigned to live with Vietnamese soldiers for the next year, and we were warned about "going native." The medical lecture was given by a colonel who advised us not to drink untreated water, eat uncooked food, or sleep with local women. That was great advice. He cautioned against the unavoidable. The colonel should have been a general.

We were issued a medical/survival kit. It contained bandages, salves, antibiotics, and a bottle of orange primoquin tablets, a malaria prophylactic. Taken each week on the same day, primoquin would prevent malaria. But it provided protection only if taken as directed. It proved to be far more difficult than I thought it would be to follow such simple instructions. Days and weeks merged as events overshadowed schedules, and simple forgetfulness accounted for numerous missed dosages. The kit also contained salt tablets, a knife, a fishing line and hooks, a piece of aluminum for signaling with reflected sunlight, and waterproof matches—all useful if we were separated from our unit and were trying to evade the Cong. All of us also received a South Vietnamese photo ID card and were told to show it if requested by Vietnamese officials.

The *Book of Instructions for U.S. Military Advisors to the 42nd Tactical Zone IV Corps, South Vietnam,* was given to advisors. Prominently marked on each page was the security classification "Confidential." The book was a good effort and contained what was known or believed at that time, but in no way did it prepare me for what lay ahead.

With one exception the equipment issued to us was useful and practical. The M-2 carbine, which weighed six pounds, was not fully automatic, which meant that each shot required a trigger squeeze. The gun did not provide enough firepower for my liking.

Equipment included two sets of lightweight green fatigues, a bush hat (a soft hat with a wide brim, which one could shape to express one's character and/or block the sun), and jungle boots. The boots were made of canvas and leather with a treaded rubber sole, which contained an embedded steel plate that ran from toe to heel for protection from foot traps, the dreaded *punji* stakes. Each boot had two metal-rimmed holes midboot, a half inch above the sole line. These grommets allowed the foot to breathe and water to exit. After a soldier walked through water, the first five steps on dry land would send streams of water shooting out each side of each boot. A line of soldiers exiting water appeared comical.

The Australian bush hat was issued to advisors early in the war and was a favorite of all. Over time, most advisors adapted their issued uniforms to their own fancy. Bright insignias of rank, white name tags, and brass buckles, ludicrous in the field, quickly gave way to darkened or camouflaged identifiers. Many advisors, myself included, often wore the plain black shirt of the peasants when on operations.

There were 12,000 U.S. military advisors in Vietnam when I arrived in September 1962. Of this number, 2,000 were field combat advisors assigned to various Vietnamese military units. The rest were assigned to advisory or support positions in Saigon and other major cities.

A Little History The Vietnamese are not Chinese. Although for thousands of years their language, religion, and philosophy were influenced by the Chinese, the Vietnamese developed their own cultural and national identity and a separate nation. The Chinese conquered Vietnam in 100 B.C. and ruled for the next thousand years. The Vietnamese fiercely resisted Chinese rule, and in the process developed a strong sense of nationalism. They are formidable in the defense of their homeland.

The area that we know as Vietnam developed into separate kingdoms, one in the north and one in the south. These entities fought a forty-five-year bloody war in the seventeenth century. The animosity between the people of the north and the people of the south evident during that time is common in Vietnam today.

After a thousand years of war, immigration, and political consolidation, Vietnam became unified for the first time in 1802, but unification lasted only a few years. The country was not united again until 1975.

In order to understand fully the underlying tensions affecting Vietnam in 1962, it would be necessary to analyze the impact of French colonial rule. That is beyond the scope of this work, but there is no doubt that the policies of France during the colonial period made for a difficult and, ultimately, losing struggle against the Viet Minh, a communist-controlled patriotic group formed in 1941 by Ho Chi Minh. Beginning in the 1850s, the French gradually took control of the economy and government of Vietnam. In 1880 Vietnam, Cambodia, and Laos, collectively known as French Indochina, became colonies of France. Vietnamese nationalism motivated activism and violence from the beginning of French rule. Many Vietnamese believed that conflict and armed resistance were the only ways to rid their country of the French.

At one point during World War II, the United States supported Ho Chi Minh and the Viet Minh against the Japanese occupiers but abandoned them in return for French support of U.S. policy in postwar Europe. After World War II, the Viet Minh and other Vietnamese nationalists wanted independence from France. The ensuing war with the French ended with the surrender of more than 10,000 French troops to the Viet Minh at Dien Bien Phu. The Geneva Accords of 1954 provided that until such time as unifying elections were held, the country would be split in half at the seventeenth parallel, between the communists in the north and the American-supported noncommunists in the south.

Although the Viet Minh came to the 1954 peace talks in a strong position, they reluctantly agreed to a partitioned country. China and Vietnam were historic enemies who shared a common border, and China did not want a strong, unified Vietnam as its neighbor. This was not satisfactory to the Vietnamese communists, but they had no acceptable choice and were forced to comply with their allies' wishes. The Geneva Accords provided that an election would be held in the north and the south within two years to vote on unification. Neither the United States nor the government of South Vietnam endorsed the peace agreement because they thought the Accords would result in a united, communist-ruled Vietnam. Fearing the communists would not allow a free election in the north, and weak from internal problems, President Ngo Dinh Diem of South Vietnam, with the tacit agreement of the United States, refused to hold elections. When the elections to unify Vietnam continued to be postponed, the leadership in Hanoi founded the National Liberation Front (NLF) and through this organization they conducted the war in the south. What had been a war between the French and the Vietnamese now became a war between Vietnamese, a civil war. However, it was a revolutionary war as well. It was a continuation of the nationalist wars for independence from foreign domination, first against the Chinese and then against the French and Americans.

France had lost the war and Vietnam was no longer its colony. In the north the French were forced to leave and their property was confiscated. This didn't happen in the south, where the French were allowed to keep their property and businesses. They stayed, and this gave the people further reason to identify Diem and his government with foreigners.

The peasants in the south, who had begun to believe that they would soon own land, saw the old landlords reclaim their land after the Geneva Accords. They were frustrated that the old land ownership system was not going to change. The lack of land reform and the corruption at all levels of the South Vietnamese government helped the Viet Cong. By 1963 South Vietnam was faced with a desperate situation. The Viet Cong had become entrenched throughout the south and were strong. They controlled large segments of the population and the countryside. Throughout the country they had informers, agents, and sympathizers in the government as well as in the military.

During the French period, many Vietnamese became

Roman Catholics, either out of religious conviction or self-interest. The Buddhist majority identified the Catholic Vietnamese with the French and considered them as agents of France. During the French colonial period, Catholics were given preference in the schools and in government jobs. When the country was partitioned in 1954, approximately one million mostly Catholic refugees moved to the south to escape communism. The United States encouraged and financed the move in order to provide support in the south for an anticommunist government. Among the Catholics who were in the south in 1954 was President Ngo Dinh Diem. He, with the active support of the United States, formed a government consisting of his family, friends, and supporters. He was president; his brother Ngo Dinh Nhu was an influential advisor; and another brother, Ngo Dinh Thuc, was a powerful Vietnamese Roman Catholic archbishop. Diem's sister-in-law Madame Nhu held successive government positions. She was recklessly blunt, and her public statements drew hostile criticism in the western media to herself and the South Vietnamese government.

District and province chiefs, and military officers, were Diem's people. He appointed them. Assembly members, although elected by the people, were generally under his control. The government was a dictatorship in the form of a democracy. It was not popular with the people because they were being ruled by Catholics who had moved from the north and because the government was repressive and corrupt.

The Cambodian Problem During the 1800s the French colonized and consolidated their control of Indochina. By administrative fiat, France created new borders for Vietnam, Cambodia, and Laos that were different from the former ones. These were ancient countries; in the case of Vietnam and Cambodia, they had fought since the 1700s for control of the delta, with the Vietnamese eventually winning. Vietnam's claim to thousands of square miles of delta land still claimed by Cambodia was validated by the French-drawn border. The loss of land angered the Cambodians then and it angers them now.

The Vietnamese delta has a large Cambodian population. Cambodians have a larger bone structure, darker skin, and different ethnic origins than the Vietnamese. Animosity and suspicion between these people has existed for centuries. This enmity complicated the South Vietnamese government's effort to win all the people to its side.

Religions The religious life of most Vietnamese is centered around the teachings of Buddhism, Confucianism, and Taoism. About 55 percent of the population consider themselves Buddhist. Confucianism, Taoism, and Caodaism account for approximately 28 percent of the people. Catholics and the Cao Dai and Hoa Hao sects make up about 13 percent of the population. However, ancestor worship and animism coexist harmoniously with other religions. The Vietnamese believe that ancestors can intercede with the gods and spirits on their behalf. Almost every home, regardless of the religion of those living there, maintains an ancestral altar with prayer sticks and offerings of flowers, food, and drink.

Cao Dai and Hoa Hao, both founded in the twentieth century, are indigenous religions that incorporate elements of Christianity, Buddhism, ancestor worship, and western ideas. Their philosophies are complex. Diem viewed these religions as potential political rivals because of their centralized authoritarian hierarchy and paramilitary units. A multitude of saints are embraced by the Cao Dai, including Joan of Arc, Lenin, Victor Hugo, Napoleon, Shakespeare, Churchill, and Sun Yat-sen. The Cao Dai priests are celibate and are able to communicate with their ancestors through seances.

Hoa Hao is a spiritualist religion based on personal faith and abstinence from alcohol, opium, and gambling. The Hoa

Hao are puritanical. They preach a rigid morality and hostility to social pleasures.

The South Vietnamese government believed that it had to prepare for and deal with three different internal military threats: the Viet Cong, the Hoa Hao, and the Cao Dai. Although not as dangerous as the Viet Cong, both the Cao Dai and the Hoa Hao had formidable military capabilities, and although they were anti–Viet Cong, they were also antigovernment. The government had to accommodate them in order to deal with the greater Viet Cong threat. Frequently these armed religious bodies attempted to expand their autonomy while the government was trying to deal with the Viet Cong threat. On occasion, this resulted in government military action against the Cao Dai or the Hoa Hao until these religions agreed to return to the original protocols. This worked in the Viet Cong's favor, both politically and militarily. Many delta villages were exclusively of one religion. Operations conducted near Cao Dai, Hoa Hao, or Catholic villages were considered less dangerous than those near Buddhist villages because the Cao Dai, Hoa Hao, and Catholics were staunchly anticommunist.

During what the Vietnamese government of today refers to as the American War of Destruction, the major religious groups sought to achieve independence from government control and enhance their relative positions by alternating between contesting and cooperating with the South Vietnamese government. Monitoring these religious affairs was a distraction that interfered with the government's pursuit of the Viet Cong.

The Buddhists were basically anticommunist except for agents and provocateurs in their ranks. However, Diem's open favoritism toward Catholics alienated the Buddhists, who during 1963 actively opposed him and eventually contributed to his downfall. In June 1963 a Buddhist monk burned himself to death in protest of Diem's government. On a main street in Saigon he poured gasoline over himself and lit a match, but not before notifying the press of the where, when, and why of his act. True to form, Madame Nhu combatively called the self-incineration "a Buddhist barbecue" and was quoted as saying, "Let them burn, and we shall clap our hands." Press reports of this suicide and of her remarks, and the publication of the shockingly vivid photographs, caused widespread antigovernment street protests and worldwide condemnation of the United States and South Vietnam.

The Vietnamese Language The fact that the Vietnamese language is difficult for Westerners to master limited my ability to be effective as an advisor. Vocabulary appears simple to learn because every word is one syllable, and only one Vietnamese word has more than six letters. Words with more than one syllable have been westernized. For example, in Vietnamese, Vietnam is "Viet Nam" and Saigon is "Sai Gon."

The form of verbs in Vietnamese does not change according to tense or person. Words are added to a sentence to indicate tense, plurality, and questions. At times the context determines the tense, or sometimes adverbs indicate time; for example, *da* means past action and *se* means future action. The grammar is logical and not difficult to learn. However, the problem for me and most others who wish to learn the language is that Vietnamese is tonal, which means that a word's meaning is determined by the pitch at which it is pronounced. For me the tones were bewilderingly alike. Complicating the learning process is the fact that there are six tones in the north but only five in the south. Different rising and falling tones indicated by diacritical marks above and below individual letters impart different meanings to the identical arrangement of letters. Thus the same word can have many different meanings. The word *ta* has different meanings depending on the frequency, loudness, and intensity of the spoken word. The pitch determines whether *ta* means we or us, dozen, flap, 100 kilograms, describe, or worn out. To make it more confusing, there is a northern, a middle, and a southern accent. Few advisors mastered the language, and we were often hopelessly baffled and frequently misunderstood.

Although I did not master the language, I was good enough not to need an interpreter. I could understand almost everything and could make myself understood, but generally only if I and the person with whom I was talking established eye contact and knew the topic of the conversation. Nevertheless, not a day went by that I did not find certain situations confusing. I was never entirely certain of what I was being told or what was happening. Most times, being in the dark was of no consequence. But it was frustrating and at times embarrassing. A country's language is a window to the people and their culture. Advisors did not really know the Vietnamese language, and for the most part Vietnamese did not know English. We were strangers, one to the other.

Three

THE PARTICIPANTS

Oft expectation fails, and most oft there
Where most it promises.
—SHAKESPEARE, All's Well That Ends Well

Role of the Advisor The mission of the U.S. advisor to units of the Army of the Republic of Vietnam (ARVN) was expressed in different terms by different commands. The mission statement that follows was designed to express what the U.S. Advisory Group, IV Corps, felt to be the reason that advisors were in Vietnam:

> To represent the United States of America in South Vietnam; to perform assigned and implied duties in such a way as to further the best interest of the United States of America; to advise and assist officials of the Government and/or members of the Armed Forces of South Vietnam in performance of their duties and in the defense of this Country against communism; and to conduct one's self personally in such a way as to bring respect for and credit to the Armed Forces of the United States of America.

This was a noble and honorable mission, but it ended badly. In time it was obvious that our expectations had exceeded our capabilities. The mission was just not possible.

An advisor program of the size and scope of what was intended for Vietnam had never before been undertaken by the U.S. Army. It was a new role for the U.S. soldier. And I was one of the first. The U.S. Army had a pretty clear idea of what

25

the role of an advisor should be, and thought it knew how the job should be performed. Appendices B, C, and D provide a good overview of what the U.S. Army thought it knew about the advisor job in 1962. Appendix B describes the *Role of the Advisor.* Appendix C is a list of *Dos and Don'ts.* Appendix D enumerates *Tips to Advisors.*

These recommendations by inexperienced staff officers contain many well-meaning and many totally incongruous points—dark humor when the Vietnamese officers would not accept any of my suggestions and at times would not even talk to me. After all these years I am still trying to figure out what was meant by the warning in *Tips to Advisors:* "Avoid making recommendations that lead to decisions." Although well meaning, the points were often not relevant to the real world of the combat advisor.

It quickly became apparent to field advisors that much of this information was laughable. The authors of these directives were doing the best they could. But they were trying to develop a theoretical modus operandi based, I believe, upon little experience or observation. At that time, the United States had few, if any, people in command situations who knew what advisors did or how to make them effective. The authors must have borrowed heavily from the military manuals of former colonial powers, which perhaps explains why the tone of the directives is one of noblesse oblige and the "white man's burden."

At battalion level, an advisor team was supposed to consist of a U.S. captain, a first lieutenant, and one senior noncommissioned officer. The rationale for the staffing was threefold. First, a captain would advise the commander, a Vietnamese officer of equal rank, and thus prevent the Vietnamese captain from losing face. The advisor lieutenant would interface with the Vietnamese company commanders, who were also lieutenants. The advisor team did not include designated counterparts for platoon leaders. In theory, the

U.S. noncommissioned officer would relate to the senior Vietnamese noncommissioned officers. Because of his wealth of military knowledge and experience, the U.S. non-commissioned officer could advise not only the Vietnamese of equal rank on an equal basis, but also the American officers, as he would in an all-U.S. situation. Another practical reason for more than one U.S. advisor with a unit was to give the advisors another American to talk to, so their performance would not be adversely affected by isolation and insecurity. Finally, and not incidentally, the rationale for the staffing was for mutual support and protection under the most dire of circumstances.

Notwithstanding the above, many advisor teams were not staffed as I have described. My advisor "team" wasn't really a team at all, and that affected my mission adversely. I was the only American with the battalion for much of my tour. Twice, U.S. captains were assigned to the battalion. The first, who was there when I arrived, spent several months with me before being reassigned to the advisor team at the ARVN's 21st Division headquarters at Can Tho. The second captain stayed for three weeks; he became sick and was hospitalized. The noncommissioned advisor, who asked out after one month, was reassigned to Saigon.

The Viet Cong A guerrilla fighter is an efficient combat weapon. He is a great deal more selective, more mobile, and cheaper than modern weapons. One guerrilla can effectively tie down or dissipate the usefulness of many conventional soldiers. The Viet Cong was a small guerrilla force pitted against as many as fifteen government soldiers for every one of its own.

The Viet Cong (which translates as Vietnamese communists) were recruited from the local population and consisted of men and women, both young and old. Due to the appeal of nationalism and a desire of the people to be free of the repressive Diem regime, the Viet Cong (an updated version of the Viet Minh) had no recruiting problems. Many Vietnamese found the Viet Cong ideology attractive because it offered land and other reforms as well as a way to rid their country of foreign dominance. It was a national movement that viewed Diem's government as a surrogate for the French and/or the Americans. The Viet Cong were formidable foes because they had self-confidence, were motivated by nationalism, and had an iron discipline. They also possessed an excellent military intelligence–gathering apparatus and knowledge of government activities from their civilian and military contacts. The Viet Cong lived off the land and were maintained by a significant, but indeterminate, segment of the people. Supplies carried down the Ho Chi Minh Trail from North Vietnam supplemented local support. The trail was not a single track but a network of six or seven north-south routes that ran through Laos, Cambodia, and South Vietnam.

The Viet Cong were ingenious. When they could not capture or buy what was needed, they made it from recycled military and civilian goods. I brought home three souvenirs, taken from dead Viet Cong after engagements, which are examples of their ingenuity. The first, a two-handed war machete, is the work of a master craftsman. It is thirty-four inches long, five inches of carved wooden handle, and twenty-nine inches of three-inch-wide steel blade. It is encased in a wooden sheath, painted blue. The second, a ten-inch-long cannon with a tripod and a firing device activated by rope, is crude but effective. Packed with powder, then with metal and glass bits, it was pointed down a trail and fired by rope when South Vietnamese soldiers were in range. The third, a Viet Cong flag, is a work of art. It is hand sewn and made from three pieces of different colored cloth. I had it framed and hung it in my living room above the fireplace; it lasted for one day until spousal disapproval forced its removal to the basement. I also brought home an inexplicable dream, which I relate later in this book.

The Viet Cong had combat hamlets, hospitals, schools, and training centers. Their sympathizers were numerous. The peasantry provided them with support, either willingly or through forced taxation. In 1963 there were thousands of Viet Cong in the delta: at least 4,000 in a main force (full time and well equipped), 6,000 regional guerrillas, and thousands of village militia. They operated in battalion, platoon, company, and squad strength. They did not use the roads. They had no trucks, tanks, or air support; other than mortars, they had no artillery. But they ruled the night. In darkness they assembled for operations on foot and dispersed afterward to the villages and countryside.

The Viet Cong in 1963 had a presence in most rural villages and hamlets; they engaged in military disruption of the countrywide local administration and the sabotage of economic development programs. They harassed the government by collecting and destroying the photo identification cards issued to the peasants by the government, promoting demonstrations, stopping buses and giving lectures to the passengers, and encouraging people to defy the authorities. They were ruthless, cunning, and able. Their tactics included murdering local mayors, teachers, youth leaders, police officers, and militiamen. The peasants, for the most part, feared, loathed, and rejected the barbarism of the Viet Cong.

The purpose of these activities was to cause the South Vietnamese government, in its effort to defeat the Viet Cong, to impose harsh and restrictive measures on the population. That is exactly what happened. In response to Viet Cong successes, government measures became more and more repressive. Although the government officials were aware that the Viet Cong were attempting to alienate the people from the government, they did not know how to counter the Viet Cong without harsh measures that affected the people. The ARVN was reminded frequently to behave properly toward civilians and provide assistance when possible. Government policy was to act in ways that would "win the hearts and minds of the people." The slogan was no more than a cliché. Policy notwithstanding, the ARVN and other government agencies acted in ways to ensure their own safety and survival first and foremost, then to enrich themselves. These actions either directly or indirectly affected the civilian populace adversely and hurt the government's cause. For the Viet Cong, their success in alienating the people from the government was far more important than the killing of ARVN soldiers. Without reforms, and faced with the unenviable choice of equally oppressive rulers, a large number of peasants helped both sides. They were uncommitted. They informed on, provided food for, and paid taxes to both the Viet Cong and the South Vietnamese government. When the peasants saw the Viet Cong winning, they stopped supporting the government.

Twelve main-force Viet Cong battalions operated in the delta in 1963. Main-force battalions were hard-core Viet Cong ideologues. They were the primary Viet Cong fighting forces, often large enough and well enough equipped to participate in direct attacks on large Vietnamese installations and units. The Viet Cong, like all armies, kept its strength secret. The number of Viet Cong in each battalion was not known by the South Vietnamese government, but it was believed that the number was smaller than in government battalions. The battalions were named and numbered in order to confuse and deceive. Naming a battalion the 510th Liberation Battalion didn't mean there were 509 lower numbered liberation battalions. Indeed, there may have been no other liberation battalions. Such numbers were also chosen for their numerological potency.

Cambodia, Laos, and remote mountainous areas, inland jungles, and extensive mangrove swamp forests along the South Vietnam coast afforded the Viet Cong natural safe havens and bases of operation. Mangrove trees are saltwater tolerant. They grow in soft mud on interlocking roots above the ground with stems that reach heights of forty feet. The dense overhead canopy and intertwined roots make the mangrove swamps dark, humid, and difficult to traverse, but not so difficult that the Viet Cong could not use them as base camps and staging areas for attacks.

The communists had a variety of French, Japanese, Chinese, and Soviet weapons. They also had U.S. weapons and supplies that had been captured from the ARVN or purchased on the black market. Advisors believed that province chiefs, district chiefs, and the ARVN were selling supplies to the Viet Cong that the United States was giving to them.

Usually the Viet Cong limited their activity to attacks against strategic hamlets and civil guard and self-defense corps forts. They restricted, and in many areas controlled, the use and security of roads and waterways. Generally, contact with the ARVN was avoided (many advisors thought by mutual consent), but if circumstances were favorable they would attack. The ARVN was most vulnerable when it was on the move, whether by road convoy or in the field. The Viet Cong were dedicated to unifying Vietnam and ridding it of foreign influence. They had a stronger conviction than the ARVN, and I soon came to realize that the Viet Cong were winners.

The South Vietnamese Military The South Vietnamese defense force consisted of many different units, including the ARVN, provincial forces, district forces, rangers, airborne units, naval forces, the air force, and intelligence units. The ARVN consisted of regular army personnel and draftees. The civil guard and self-defense corps were units organized at province level under the province chief and at district level under the district chief. The civil guard was formed into units capable of limited mobility. The self-defense corps consisted of village militia, poorly equipped and usually stationed in small mud forts.

The ARVN was, theoretically, totally mobile and had the best, most modern equipment. It was modeled on the U.S. Army and structured as a modern western force. Advisors learned early on of its poor leadership, lack of tactical imagination, poor cross-country maneuverability, clumsy logistics, and lack of motivation. Advisors came to understand that the ARVN could not cope with guerrilla warfare against the Viet Cong, a highly motivated, nationalist force.

The ARVN soldiers were, for the most part, young and uneducated. They were conscripted from the countryside by the South Vietnamese government. Both sides of this civil war replenished their forces from the same pool of boys, boys who before being impressed either watched water buffalo or worked in the rice paddies. They were teenagers with no experience outside their villages. Needless to say, either because of ideology or happenstance, family members ended up on opposite sides of the war, often against their wishes. As in the United States, many of the wealthy and well connected stayed out of the army. Vietnamese cities were full of draft-age males, either deserters or those who were exempt for some reason or other. Although in theory ARVN soldiers had to serve three years, in reality their service was indefinite. There was some formal training. Discipline was infrequent but harsh. They were not committed or well led. Men in the ARVN were not soldiers to be feared by other soldiers.

It is the custom in Vietnam for young male friends to hold hands in public. It has no homosexual connotation. In the field, soldiers held their buddies' hand. Laden with equipment and rifles, they walked hand in hand down jungle paths in search of the Viet Cong. Tactically, this was not wise.

The officers and noncommissioned officers were generally career soldiers, but there were numerous senior officers whose only qualification was loyalty to President Diem. Promotion to senior positions was not on merit but went to officers who were trusted friends or connected to Diem's family.

Frequently the officers were incompetent and corrupt. Often they were politically motivated, ineffectual, cowardly, or infamously all three. The ARVN soldiers performed their role even in the face of their officers' incompetence, sometimes with success.

As dangerous as incompetent officers were to their soldiers, more menacing were incompetent and self-serving politicians and government officials, because their decisions could be crucial and far reaching. They were removed in both time and place from the consequences that their decisions brought to soldiers. Their person was not at risk, and even if they were held accountable at some distant point in time, the consequences to them, in comparison to soldiers, would be minor. During the Vietnam War, both South Vietnam and the United States had their share of incompetent and self-serving politicians and government officials.

New Weapons Military weapons development and replacement were costly and took years. Weapons that proved effective, practical, durable, and reliable were not changed unless enemies developed better weapons. Then the cycle of weapon design, testing, manufacturing, and training was undertaken. The weapons used by American infantry soldiers during World War II and Korea were still in use in the early 1960s. The United States supplied the ARVN with its standard small-arms weapons, including the M-1 rifle, the M-2 carbine, the .30-caliber machine gun, the M-2 Browning automatic rifle, the M-60 mortar, the 3.5-inch rocket launcher, and the M-1 grenade. M stands for model.

During the 1950s, communist countries equipped their soldiers and communist guerrillas worldwide with small-arms weapons that were superior to U.S. weapons. In response, the United States developed new weapons and tested them in real combat situations in Vietnam during the early 1960s. One of these, the Armalite AR-15 rifle, was eventually redesignated the M-16 rifle. Two hundred twenty of these rifles were field tested by the ARVN for six months in 1963. The M-16 rifle differed from the M-1 rifle in many ways; it was lighter and shorter, had a twenty-round magazine, and could be fired fully automatic, and its bullets tumbled on impact. A tumbling bullet causes larger, more severe wounds. The worse the wound, the less likely the casualty will return to the battlefield and the more resources will be expended caring for him.

Another U.S. weapon that was field tested in Vietnam was the M-79 grenade launcher. It is breech loaded, has a single, short barrel with a 3-inch muzzle, has a range of 100 meters, and fires a 40mm round which explodes on impact. My battalion received four M-79s in January 1963, one for each company. Initially the officers insisted on keeping the M-79s with them, but that was not effective because the officers were always in the rear. Eventually the launchers were given to the soldiers, who made good use of them up front.

In 1965 when U.S. Marines landed on the beaches of Vietnam, they were supplied with the M-14 rifle and the M-79 grenade launcher, which had been proven reliable and durable under combat conditions years earlier. However, the M-14 was exchanged for the "improved" M-16, which, it soon became apparent, had mechanical problems. Many good men died before the problems were corrected. Both of these weapons are still standard equipment in the U.S. Army today.

2d Battalion The fifty young officers who had trained together at Fort Bragg and Monterey received assignments to various locations in Vietnam. Except for my friend Mike Blackwell, whom I once met in Saigon, I never saw any of these people again. I received my assignment as a field combat advisor to the ARVN commander of the 2d Battalion, 33d Regiment, 21st Infantry Division. Mike received a similar assignment to an infantry battalion of the 7th Infantry Division, which was headquartered in the delta city of My

Tho. None of us had any idea of what to expect. Yes, we were combat battalion advisors, but we did not know what that meant or what our working and living conditions would be like. We got what we had volunteered for.

A handwritten list of 2d Battalion officers was presented to me upon my arrival by my counterpart, Captain Beng, the battalion commander. The 2d Battalion had a complement of 500 men, organized in four companies of 125 men each. When I left eight months later, there were less than 400 men. Combat, sickness, and desertion (to the Viet Cong and to home villages) accounted for the reduction in force.

Foreshadowing The headquarters of the 21st Infantry Division was in Can Tho. The city was and still is the cultural, economic, political, and transportation center of the Mekong Delta. Americans were assigned as advisors to the division headquarters. Nearly a hundred advisors and support personnel lived at a compound located in a former rice paddy. Wood bungalows with plastic roofs lined the compound street. These small houses were built on cement block pilings to keep them dry during the rainy season. Gun positions and barbed wire atop mud walls surrounded the compound. There were sleeping quarters, offices, a game room, and a bar. A laundry service was available. I decided it didn't look too bad and I could handle it. However, I spent only three nights during my year in Vietnam at the compound, and the night of my arrival was not one of them.

On the day of my arrival, a U.S. sergeant met me at the Can Tho airport and took me to meet the U.S. colonel in charge of the division U.S. advisory team. I received a briefing about ARVN and Viet Cong troop strengths and was told to stay in touch, then I was dropped off at the 21st Division headquarters. The colonel's words "stay in touch" should have alerted me to the isolation I was to experience. I spent the night at a safe house anxiously awaiting the dawn and the start of my assignment. My room that night had a rotating ceiling fan and was home to insect-eating lizards (geckos), which walked on the ceiling. The geckos hunted insects with a well-developed tongue. They hunted all night long and made a croaking noise like a squeaky bedspring.

The Vietnamese soldiers stationed in the yard provided security for the house. They were also responsible for the monthly feeding of a python, which was twenty feet long and twenty inches in diameter. It was kept in an eight- by eight-by fifteen-foot cage situated under a large tree in the yard. Pushed through the cage at various heights were tree limbs, around which the python lay curled.

Early the next morning the yard filled with people; it was feeding time. Men and women, soldiers and police waited in anticipation. Children pushed to the front. A chicken was placed in the cage. The people knew what was going to happen; the python and the chicken knew too. The python quickly uncurled and dropped to the cage floor. The chicken scurried around in desperation doing three-foot vertical leaps. It was over quickly. The excitement abated and the satisfied crowd dispersed. It should have crossed my mind that I, about to go to a new job in new surroundings to meet a foe whose strength I could not gauge, might be consumed by these people and this country. During the next twelve months, I would meet the unusual and surprising at every step.

Captain Beng It was impossible for Americans, myself included, to understand well the Vietnamese or their war. Whereas I had known little but security and good times, their lives moved from uncertainty to danger.

Captain Beng, the Vietnamese officer to whom I was assigned as an advisor, was forty-five years old, had been in the army for twenty-five years, and had fought against the French, Japanese, Viet Minh, and Viet Cong. He spoke no English and had never been outside Vietnam. Trim and five foot four, he strutted, a little wide at the knees. Unless on an operation, he sported a swagger stick. I was an unwanted burden for this man. He had to provide me with a jeep, driver, and bodyguard. He had to house and feed me and was responsible for my safety and well-being. Although we did not share the command of the battalion, Captain Beng was expected to listen to my suggestions and consult with me prior to and during operations. I could call in air strikes and medevac helicopters through American channels. I had access to my superiors and, through them, his superiors.

Because I was an American, Captain Beng knew that I had and would continue to have advantages he did not have and could never have. There was a wide chasm between his experience and mine, and his questions made me aware of the gap: "Does your father have a house? A car? A television? Did you go to university? Did your sisters go to school? What religion are you? How much do you make? How did you become an officer? How long have you been in the army? How old are you?"

I was twenty-three years old, with a high energy level, and I knew I could change the way the ARVN did things. I was determined to show them how to do it the correct way. In the field Captain Beng was overly cautious and preferred to react to what happened around him rather than take the initiative. I was a lieutenant; he was a captain. I had little military and no combat experience; he had twenty-five years of both. He lost face with his fellow officers because of my lower rank and younger age. Yet he was expected to listen to and occasionally take my advice.

I started out being circumspect. I waited until we were alone and put my advice in the form of questions. I was being sensitive. I did not want to undermine his authority by telling him what to do in front of his soldiers. I asked him, "Why are we walking through a rice paddy where we can be shot at from the tree line and where we have no cover? Why don't we walk in the tree line where we cannot be seen from afar? Why is the battalion walking in a single file? Why don't we have flankers out to protect us from ambush? Why don't you put the point fifty yards ahead of the battalion and not just at the head of the line of march? Why don't you put listening posts around the camp at night? Should you inspect the guards? The camp? The equipment? The outhouse is full; should it be moved?"

Often he bridled at my suggestions. He was a proud man, and he resented my presence and the fact that he would be held accountable if anything happened to me. He was patient; but when he did not want to hear any more, he would stop talking to me. When he stopped talking to me, the other officers also stopped. At such times body language sufficed. After a couple of days of silence, talk would start anew. *Tips to Advisors* (Appendix D) did not address this situation.

Captain Beng knew what had to be done; he just did not do it. He would listen to me with his eyes fixed on a spot over my left shoulder. When I was finished he would smile, nod, mumble something, and walk away. He knew I did not approve of how he soldiered. My questions were criticism from a junior and not acceptable to him. His rejection of my advice and his manner of doing so eventually convinced me that my approach was wrong. I became increasingly less sensitive and more and more confrontational. I would tell him to do things, demand that he do things, in front of the soldiers. He would raise his voice and I would raise mine. I always got his attention when I thundered at him in English. I had the advantage then. Anyway, few of my suggestions were ever taken. When he did take one, he always followed it by an elaborate demonstration of thankfulness. The subtleties of the Vietnamese language escaped me, but contempt and satire are part of the universal language. The writers of the manuals for advisors had not envisioned the kind of relationship I had with Captain Beng or the relationships that other field advisors had with their counterparts. In most situations those that developed between advisor and counterpart were bizarre by any conventional military standards, and almost never reached the level of effectiveness anticipated by the theorists. My relationship with Captain Beng was not the vital rapport that I was expected to establish in order to accomplish my mission.

The fact that U.S. Army lieutenants are trained to move to the sound of battle and lead from the front where they can influence the situation added to our problem. I was trained to close with the enemy, shoot them, and get it over with. Whenever possible the battalion officers stayed in the rear away from combat. Captain Beng and his officers wanted to avoid combat so as to have as few casualties as possible. Beng wanted to minimize his losses, because he would be criticized for taking casualties.

Our relationship was defined by a mutual ambivalence. We needed each other to get the job done, but we had reservations about each other's commitment, abilities, and motives. I would have preferred not to have to work through him, and he, I am sure, felt the same about me. This shared ambivalence was not unique to us. In time, it came to characterize the overall relationship between the governments of South Vietnam and the United States.

The war had been going on long before I got there, and Captain Beng did not know when it would be over for him. I knew to the very day when it would be over for me. Sooner or later I would go home, but he would remain in the middle of a war. This reality affected both of us and our relationship. It affected how we did our jobs.

I was raised in a culture where directness is expected. His culture valued indirectness. Captain Beng and his officers would avoid saying no or disagreeing. When they said yes, it could mean, "Yes, I agree" or it could mean, "Yes, I hear you." Initially, I was never sure whether they had agreed to a particular course of action or not. Later, I knew that regardless of the words Captain Beng spoke in response to my suggestions, he would not accept my advice.

To be fair to Beng, maybe my advice and suggestions were wrong. It is possible that under those conditions and during those times and based on his twenty-five years of combat experience, the U.S. Army solution did not make any sense. I suppose he told his superiors that my advice was foolish and I was a nuisance. Maybe he thought the U.S. Army had sent a boy to do a man's job. Maybe so. Furthermore, he could not be seen to be abdicating his authority to me. To do so would have swiftly impaired his ability to command the battalion. The soldiers, his peers, and the populace would have questioned his credibility.

Before long I realized that I really was not an advisor, in the common understanding of the word, and my government knew that, or should have known it, when they sent me. I was informed by the reality. I was just an observer, there to wave the American flag. The advisor program was not a demonstration of American power. It was something quite different, something symbolic. I was there to show the North Vietnamese, Soviets, and Chinese that the United States, by putting its men in harm's way, was serious about preventing a communist takeover of South Vietnam. We were telling them, how can you doubt our resolve and expect to prevail if we are willing at this early stage to sacrifice our young men?

In some ways I was an aide to Captain Beng in charge of expediting resources, supplies, and materials (all from U.S. sources) to the battalion. My most useful function was to generate air support, whether for troop movement, resupply, medevac, or combat support for troops in contact with the enemy. Most of the available air assets were American, and coordination was always through me. But I was not willing to accept the role of Captain Beng's aide. There were things I knew that ARVN could benefit from, and I was determined to keep trying to convey them.

Friendly Fire One morning while moving companies on line across a large expanse of rice paddies, Captain Beng was unable to get the attention of the company commander on his left. He was not in sight, and either the radio was not working or the commander was not paying attention. In frustration and to get his attention, Captain Beng fired his weapon in that company's direction. He got their attention all right, but they thought the Viet Cong were shooting at them, so they returned fire. What followed was a brief but intense exchange of fire between the headquarters company and the other company. Bullets filled the air. I hugged the dirt. Somehow, it ended after several frightening minutes and somehow no one was wounded. Beng was all smiles.

Plum and Pham Each advisor was assigned a jeep, a driver, and a bodyguard. Plum, my bodyguard, was a Montagnard (French for mountain people). Long before the Vietnamese, the Montagnards settled in what is now Vietnam and later were driven into the mountains by the Vietnamese. The Montagnards are an ancient people, older than Amen. They are the aboriginal people of Vietnam, unrelated to the Vietnamese, and represent about 8 percent of the population. They have marked physical differences depending on the ethnic group to which they belong, of which there are fifty. Physical stature, hair texture, skin color, and clothes identify the tribe. Each tribe has its own language, all of which derive from two linguistic groups. The languages, which are not related to the Vietnamese language, were considered by advisors to be somewhat easier to learn than Vietnamese because they have no differing tones. The Vietnamese looked down on the Montagnards and often referred to them as *moi,* meaning savage or barbarian.

Plum was thirty-three years of age, five feet tall, helpful, and loyal. Sometimes he was behind me, sometimes in front, but always he stayed close to me. His loyalty was due partly to training, partly to culture, and partly to self-preservation:

He would be treated badly if I was hurt. Plum was the only Montagnard with the battalion and the only Montagnard I ever met. He came from a tribe located six hundred miles away near the Laos border and had been in the army since the age of sixteen. His spoken Vietnamese was good, but he could not read or write it. This was not surprising, because his Montagnard language was never reduced to writing. In a strange way I identified with this man, who was living in a culture not his own and fighting someone else's war.

In addition to his backpack, Plum carried a Thompson .45-caliber submachine gun, which weighed just under ten pounds and was thirty-three inches in length. He also carried three twenty-round ammunition magazines. He was more cautious than I, always whispering to me to stay back: "Lieutenant, stop, don't go, don't go." He became excited during shoot-ups. After firefights he would run to the dead Viet Cong and shoot them again. He either thought this was prudent procedure or showed he was protecting me, or maybe it was the custom of his tribe. The other soldiers thought it was funny. Captain Beng smiled and the day went on.

Although Plum was loyal to me, his loyalty had its limits. His sense of survival was well developed. If I wanted to go in harm's way, he would warn me away; if I insisted on going, he would not follow. This affected my behavior, because I knew he would be beaten if he did not follow me. But my mission came first, and I would work my way to the sound of the gun without him.

Pham, my driver, was a Vietnamese. He was always annoyed with me because I drove the jeep and made him sit in the back. Plum, whom Pham considered his inferior because he was *moi,* sat in front next to me. I wanted the shooter up front. I was also assigned a translator, who spoke Vietnamese and French but, strangely, not English. He was reassigned, at my request, after a week. There was no replacement.

Four

IN THE FIELD

*One eye-witness is worth more than ten
who tell what they have heard.*
— PLAUTUS

Affectionate Reunions To seek out and destroy the enemy is an army's mission. The army finds the foe by analyzing information obtained through intelligence-gathering activities. In 1963 the ARVN conducted battalion-size operations to locate and kill the Viet Cong. These operations were always characterized by poor planning and slow execution and were often compromised by communist agents.

Combat operations were planned far in advance by ARVN division and regimental officers, each of whom had U.S. advisors of corresponding rank. The plans specified objectives, tactics, logistics, and air support. The province chief had the power to approve or disapprove ARVN operations in his province. There was no love lost between the province chief and the ARVN commanders. They both reported directly to President Diem and were rivals for his support. At best the province chief was lazy and indifferent; at worst he deliberately undermined the ARVN.

Briefings before an operation were conducted by Captain Beng. After an operation was approved by the province chief, Beng received written orders, maps, and a briefing from his superiors. The orders provided instructions, information, and guidance needed to plan, prepare for, and accomplish the mission. Upon Beng's return to the battalion, the officers would assemble around a table where the operational map was laid out. The orders were delivered by Beng in rapid-fire, staccato bursts while he jabbed at the map with his finger. The orders seemed to be clear, concise, and to the point. Beng gave an estimate of the enemy strength, answered questions, and pointed on the map to canals, roads, and other places that I assumed were assembly points, objectives, and pickup points. A typical briefing was over in twenty minutes, and usually the battalion was on the move within an hour. I followed what was said as best I could, but most often I learned only my code name, the radio frequency, the name of the city nearest to where the operation was to take place, and how (for example, via helicopter, boat, or truck) we were to get to the point of departure (where the walking started). I was never completely sure whether I understood the battalion's objective or mission. Early on, that concerned me a great deal, but I quickly learned that my uncertainty was not a handicap. I was just an advisor, and every operation was similar.

An operation could last as little as one day or as long as five days. Operations were daylong hikes down jungle paths and through canals, rice paddies, and villages, interrupted by enemy fire, booby traps, and long, unexplained delays. Our route and objective were supposed to be secret. However, if we were in the field for more than a couple of days, the soldiers' women would, without fail, meet us along the line of march. Joyous and affectionate reunions would ensue. If the wives and girlfriends knew where we would be, I was sure that the Viet Cong knew as well.

Although there were numerous operations, Viet Cong contact was disproportionately small compared with the effort and cost involved. It was commonly believed that the South Vietnamese government and the ARVN were riddled with Viet Cong spies. Villagers would say that the Viet Cong left an hour ago because they knew that soldiers were coming. It is possible that operations were planned for and conducted in areas where the ARVN knew that the Viet Cong were not present. It is possible that the operations were compromised intentionally so that the Viet Cong would leave the area before we arrived. Advisors came to believe both of these things.

Siesta Time There were various kinds of infantry operations. A sweep consisted of the battalion moving forward with the intent of flushing the Viet Cong out of their hiding places or drawing them into battle. Search and destroy involved encircling an area and gradually reducing the circumference of the circle. In hammer and anvil, in theory at least a tactically sound plan for routing out guerrilla forces, an ARVN unit was placed in a blocking position (the anvil) along a canal or tree line while another ARVN unit (the hammer) moved toward the blocking force, chasing (one hoped) the Viet Cong with the intent of crushing them against the anvil. The distances covered depended on the number of canals to cross and the scheduled duration of the operation. Spotter planes flew overhead to call down artillery on Viet Cong escaping to the sides. These operations, in actual practice, proved cumbersome, inefficient, and ineffective. Some days there was no Viet Cong contact, other days only sniper fire. We always moved slowly, which made it easy for the Viet Cong to escape. Any farmer who ran from us was shot, and the battalion score for dead Viet Cong was increased by one. Farmers who stayed were either harshly questioned by the soldiers or sent to the province chief for interrogation, or both.

It was obvious to me and other field advisors that these types of operations were of little value in defeating the Viet Cong. In spite of the name given to an operation by the Vietnamese, advisors joked that the words "search and avoid" were a better description of what was happening. Given the small numbers and dispersion of the Viet Cong, it would have been more effective if the ARVN had sent out platoon-size units, each on a separate mission, half the battalion at night and half during the day. That way, relentless pressure would have been maintained on the Viet Cong. It would have disrupted, confused, and disorganized them. Given the ineffectiveness and political and military mind-set of the ARVN, this did not happen.

The formation a unit took when it was in the field was tailored to the kind of operation it was performing. Sweeps were most productive when three rows of soldiers, each row separated by fifty to seventy-five yards, moved through rice paddies along the same axis. Upon reaching a tree line alongside a canal, soldiers were required to spread out, make contact with the adjacent company, and search each side of the canal. It was a slow but effective way to search a given area. But this formation was not Captain Beng's preferred formation, because it did not allow the battalion enough time to cover the day's required distance and also take the traditional midday siesta. Beng often moved the battalion in a single line, without searching canal banks, when our mission was to sweep an area. Imagine four hundred soldiers walking one behind the other over paddy dikes and canal bridges. It is not hard to understand why this type of formation encountered few Viet Cong to its front and only the occasional sniper fire from the flanks. But, incredibly, even in the middle of the war, the battalion usually took a siesta.

During siestas and other breaks in an operation, some soldiers slept, foraged, or wrote poetry while others amused themselves by flirting (and more) with the local women. I never saw any women forced to have sex. It wasn't necessary. Supply exceeded demand. Prices were low. Time has many uses.

The Point An "aspirant" held an ARVN rank between the highest sergeant and a second lieutenant. Such men aspired to become officers. They were young, right out of officers' school. If they proved themselves, eventually they were promoted to second lieutenant. My battalion had seven aspirants, each of whom took turns walking with the point squad on operations. They had no experience, but the point was where they were expected to prove themselves. On most operations, that was where casualties happened. There were plenty of replacement aspirants.

At the front of each formation was the point squad: an aspirant and six to ten soldiers. They were the ones who would trigger Viet Cong ambushes before the main body of the battalion reached the killing zone. The point squad was supposed to locate foot traps and disarm mines. Their position was a dangerous one and, to my mind, the only place where the ARVN acted like soldiers. They were alert and quick. They fired first and investigated what had startled them afterward. That was how they stayed alive.

It was frustrating and humiliating to stay with Captain Beng during an operation. He either ignored me or mumbled something incomprehensible when I commented. So I did not stay with him. I became a rifleman and went forward to where I could influence what was happening. When I arrived at the point, the aspirant would radio to Captain Beng and he would tell me to get back. I would mumble to the aspirant in English. The operation would continue. When time or a skirmish acted to reduce my level of frustration, I would return to the headquarters company. Captain Beng and I would exchange glares, then smiles, and the cycle would eventually repeat itself.

I should not have been at the point. It complicated the captain's job. I endangered myself, Plum, and the point squad. It was foolish. But I was not a bump on a log; I had to do something. Anyway, I wanted to mix in with the Cong. And I did. Generally, the point was the most dangerous location. The second-most dangerous place on an operation was anywhere near the soldier who carried the 3.5-inch rocket launcher. This shoulder-fired weapon was a fifty-inch-long metal tube that fired an explosive-filled rocket. It was most effective against fortifications and vehicles. A second soldier carried the rockets and served as the loader. In order to avoid wounding friendly soldiers, this weapon had to be used with utmost care. The loader's tap on the head of the soldier aiming the launcher signaled that the weapon was loaded and no friendly soldiers were in the back-blast area. When the weapon was fired, metal bits and other debris were propelled sixty feet backward in a thirty-degree arc.

Captain Beng kept the 3.5-inch rocket launcher in the rear with him so he could direct its use and lessen the possibility of losing it to the Viet Cong. He would authorize its use if the request was sufficiently urgent to convince him that it was really needed. The two-man team, amidst vocal encouragement from the soldiers they passed, would scamper up the trail, one carrying the rocket launcher and the other lugging a bag of rockets. The soldiers they encountered did not know where the firing position would be, but they all knew they could be wounded by the back blast so they sought protection. Shooting at the enemy stopped as battalion soldiers sought safer positions. When the launcher team arrived where it was needed, often conflicting orders or just general confusion caused the team to point the weapon one way, then another way. Each change in direction changed the location of the back-blast area and caused soldiers to rush to a safer place. As a result, there was no covering fire for the soldier who had to expose himself to fire the rocket on target. At times the excitement and fear were so great that the rocket was fired before everyone was out of the back-blast area and before a worthy target was selected. Early in my tour I was nearly wounded by just such an incident. A soldier close to me received a deep facial gash. I felt the heat and the blast but was unhurt. I do not know how it was possible that ARVN soldiers could have been so wacky and inept, but I witnessed those things and they were both.

Good Hygiene Leeches are bloodsucking worms indigenous to the rice paddies and waterways of Vietnam. They float in the water and bury their head in the skin of mammals. The leeches inject an anesthetic at the site of attachment, so the host feels no pain and is unaware of the worm's presence. Gorging on blood, it slowly grows from a tiny, dot-size organism to a thumb-size, pulsating entity. Days later when satiated, it falls off. Most times the host suffers no adverse affect, only a small red mark where the head was attached. But pulling the bloodsucker from the skin prematurely (before it is full) causes a painful, bloody tear and probable infection.

Leeches were a constant hazard for ARVN soldiers and advisors. We were frequently immersed in delta water, so every part of the body was accessible. Pants tucked into boots provided some protection, but when the water was above the waist the leeches flowed with the water through the shirt and around the body. Self-inspection was the only sure way to find the parasite, but man is not constructed to see every part of his body. Help is required. A common sight during a break on an operation was a soldier with his pants down being inspected by one of his mates. If a leech was found, the inspecting soldier carefully applied a burning cigarette or match to make the worm retract its head from the skin and drop to the ground. At first I wondered about this spectacle but quickly understood that what I was witnessing was not some perverse, sadomasochistic practice but simply good hygiene.

Leech infestation was a more serious problem for the Viet Cong, who frequently hid for long periods submerged in canals and village ponds to avoid capture. Loose-fitting pajamas and bootless feet allowed the worms easy access to the skin. That the Viet Cong were able to keep submerged while feeling with their hands for the growing parasite was a testament to their stoicism and self-discipline. The bodies of dead or captured Viet Cong were often covered with these bloated worms. The Viet Cong were a tough and self-sacrificing enemy.

Noise Discipline Maintaining silence on operations was difficult for small units and even more so for a battalion. Silence was especially important at night, but darkness made falls and stumbles inevitable. Noise betrayed a unit's presence and either invited ambush or gave the Viet Cong time to hide. The ARVN was notorious for its poor noise discipline. Day or night the ARVN troops were smoking, talking, clanging, rattling, and crying out. When my battalion was on an operation, either day or night, it sounded like a halftime ceremony at a college football game. Better to let the Viet Cong know that the battalion was coming so they could leave the area than for anyone to get hurt.

Like all tropical countries, Vietnam has a wide variety of insects: big, small, flying, crawling, and biting. The canals and riverbanks were lush with dense jungle vegetation, which provided cover for the Viet Cong. From time to time as the soldiers brushed against the bushes, tiny red ants would fall onto their necks and down their shirts. These were fire ants, which have a bite that feels like a cigarette burn. When this happened, no matter what the situation (be it under fire, on the march, or sitting in ambush), soldiers stopped what they were doing to get rid of the ants. They jumped from foot to foot and place to place, slapped their necks and backs, and pulled off their shirts. The burning lasted about thirty seconds, although it left no visible sign or aftereffect. Those ants stung, I know. These episodes added to the noisy presence of the ARVN unit and, together with the normal noise of high-spirited soldiers on the move, made stealth difficult to achieve. I never witnessed the enemy reveal his presence because of fire ants, another testimony to his hardened self-discipline.

Why the Viet Cong did not ambush more often, when they

were always there, was a mystery. They were like a slow-motion tango, those walks in the sun, and the noise and general goofiness just added to the nerve-wracking aspect of what appeared to be an uneventful day. My concern, and the concern of other field advisors, was that our fellow soldiers were going to get us killed.

What Is Happening? I was the only American on most of the operations. About half the time I did not know what was happening or why. The rapid verbal exchanges between the officers and soldiers, both face to face and over the radio, were lost on me, and it was distracting and disruptive for them to take the time to explain to me what was happening during an engagement or a maneuver. My questions were numerous: "Where are we going? What formation are we in? Why are four hundred battalion soldiers walking in a line one behind the other? Why aren't we where we're supposed to be? Where is the canal that the map shows is supposed to be on our left? What are we trying to avoid and why? Why have we stopped? Are we taking a siesta? Are the Viet Cong stopping also? When do we go forward? Who is shooting up ahead? What are we doing? Why aren't we moving? What is happening?" Frustrated and unable to get answers or information, I would move forward to find answers. I did not always get them, but I always tried to make an impact on what was happening.

Sometimes I would find dead or wounded ARVN or dead, wounded, or captured Viet Cong. More frequently there was no discernible reason to explain the stop and no answer to my questions; it was a mystery. I came to believe that many times Captain Beng did what he could to avoid the Viet Cong and kept me in the dark. In many situations the reason we stopped was that one or two Viet Cong with rifles held up the whole battalion while artillery was called in. Of course, before the artillery began, the Viet Cong had moved to different positions along our line of march, and the sequence of events would be repeated during the day.

Field Dressing A soldier's job is to fight the enemy. A sick or wounded soldier is not in fighting condition. The U.S. Army maintains that disease causes more casualties during wartime than do wounds and injuries. Training in the prevention of communicable diseases and in first aid has a high priority. All soldiers are trained in the basic principles of hygiene, sanitation, and first aid. Basic first-aid training includes learning the three lifesaving steps: Stop the bleeding, protect the wound, and prevent shock. The idea is to save lives and return sick or wounded soldiers to the fight as soon as possible. In fact, most U.S. casualties return to their units to fight again because of immediate first aid and prompt medical care due to the availability of helicopter evacuation. Soldiers are taught to examine the casualty before administering first aid in order to determine the number and severity of wounds.

Every soldier carried field dressings—bandages on his belt for use in the field. The bandages had an obvious practical value and a subtle psychological value: an unspoken promise of immediate medical care if wounded. I had only a few hours of first-aid training and was surprised at how capable I was at bandaging the wounded. Wounded soldiers are generally easy to medicate and bandage, because often they are in shock from the trauma and loss of blood.

A claymore is a three-inch-high by eight-inch-long explosive device that sits on three metal legs. It contains one and a half pounds of plastic explosive connected to a hundred feet of wire. The claymore was designed for ambushes and as a defensive weapon to break up enemy attacks. Several are deployed in front of the perimeter at different distances and facing in different directions, the wires of each traveling back to the soldier's hole. Under combat conditions it is a worrisome task for a soldier to keep track of which elec-

tronic firing device in his hole sets off which claymore.
When a soldier clamps the firing device, six hundred steel
pellets explode in a sixty-degree arc and cut down anyone
within fifty yards. Painted on the convex side of the mine
as a reminder and warning are the words, "Face Towards
Enemy." Because the ARVN soldiers could not read English,
many were unsure about the correct placement. They were
scared and frequently sought me out for reassurance that
they had placed the business end of the claymore away from
themselves. Starting in 1962 the United States supplied the
ARVN with these explosive devices. It was a continuous,
terrible tragedy that in ambushes the Viet Cong used the
claymores they bought on the black market with deadly efficiency.

In January the battalion point squad was ambushed as it
crossed a canal. Two soldiers were killed and five wounded.
The Viet Cong quickly left the field. I bandaged one of the
wounded soldiers, who had claymore pellets embedded in
his chest. It was a sucking chest wound; air was being sucked
into the chest cavity. This kind of wound is particularly dangerous because air does not leave the chest cavity during
expiration but builds up pressure, which eventually causes
the collapse of both lungs. A soldier's life depends upon how
fast the wound is made airtight. I applied the field dressing
quickly, and the sucking stopped and the lung began to function. I was about to give the soldier an injection of morphine
when I saw that his brains were seeping out of a small hole
in his forehead. I had forgotten to check for other wounds. If
I had, I would not have bandaged his chest wound. I would
have cared for some other wounded soldier who was more
likely to survive.

No Epiphany On February 8, 1963, while three truckloads of battalion soldiers were traveling in convoy from Bac
Lieu to Soc Trang, we were ambushed. The ambush was trig-
gered by the electronic detonation of a claymore mine under

a truck carrying twenty soldiers. The jeep I was driving was directly in front of the truck that was blown up.

The truck hit by the claymore overturned and fell on its side into the canal that ran parallel to the road. I did not know where the Viet Cong were shooting from until Plum pointed to a nearby tree line. I helped organize the defense and got the soldiers to return fire. This was difficult because the soldiers, upon taking cover, would not expose themselves. When they did return fire, they raised their rifles above their protective cover, without exposing their head or shoulders, and returned fire in the general direction of the Viet Cong. They did not look or aim; they just shot.

The Viet Cong let my jeep pass, then blew the claymore under the truck behind me, probably because a truck full of soldiers was a bigger and more rewarding target than a jeep carrying three soldiers. Thereafter, when traveling on the roads I always made it a point to drive immediately in front of a truck loaded with soldiers. Everyone had his own survival techniques.

No soldiers were helping the wounded in the canal. I went into the canal and, amidst the sound of bullets striking the truck, pulled the wounded to the canal bank, from where they were hauled onto the road by their buddies. Eventually the Viet Cong broke contact, but not before destroying another truck and wounding more soldiers.

Field dressings and tourniquets were applied, and the wounded were taken to a nearby airfield to await a cargo plane, which was conveniently available, to fly them to Saigon for medical care. Morphine injections were given to those in pain. Standard instructions included a warning not to give morphine to a casualty with a head wound. Morphine hides signs or symptoms that doctors in the rear should see in order to know how to treat the wounded soldier. Everyone knew the rule, but soldiers in great pain got morphine even if they had head wounds. You couldn't refuse. The empty syringe was pinned to the soldier's shirt to put the doctors in the rear on notice.

One of the soldiers took the force of the claymore blast and had numerous gaping wounds. The wounds were left unbandaged because it was clear that he would die soon. He was carried in a poncho onto the plane and placed on the floor. The other wounded soldiers and I sat against the plane's walls. The plane had no seats, partitions, or noise insulation. The clothes of the soldier wounded by the claymore had been blown away; he was nude. After a few minutes of flying time, I looked up and saw the wounded soldiers staring at the dying soldier on the poncho. He had an erection. Minutes later he died; it was not necessary to check his pulse. I remember thinking at the time, what does this mean? What does it say about life and man's nature? Is it about the need to procreate before death? Don't desert plants blossom and seed before dying? No epiphany occurred. Of course, now, being older and wiser, I think this is the way to go. I have since learned that the area of the brain that controls sexual arousal was probably stimulated by pressure from the man's head wounds.

When the plane landed, the soldiers, living and dead, were placed in ambulances. A doctor, an American major, thinking that my blood-soaked uniform was evidence of a wound, insisted that I get in the ambulance. I refused. He let me go when I undressed on the airfield so he could see for himself that I was not wounded. I took a taxi into Saigon, stopping along the way to buy slacks and a shirt. I went out that night. Saigon and its treats beckoned. Looking back, I wonder about my need, not to mention ability, to go on the town after such a day. The local hotel where I stayed had my uniform cleaned, pressed, and ready the next morning. I returned to my battalion a day later.

There was a war going on. Dead and wounded soldiers and civilians were common. That is what happens. On a conscious level I was not bothered by the sight of the dead and wounded or my involvement in it all. The only exception for me was the torturing of prisoners. That bothered me and still does. Both the ARVN and the Viet Cong did it. I never got used to it. I should have distanced myself from it. For a long time the totality of these experiences operated in my mind beyond my awareness. The violence and brutality of those times were part of a peculiar and disturbing dream I had for many years.

Government Forts Small government forts manned by up to ten soldiers from the civil guard or self-defense corps and their families were scattered throughout the countryside. They guarded bridges, roads, and government buildings. These soldiers were not well equipped or trained. Their living conditions were poor, the pay was low, and the danger was great. Some of the civil guard and many of the self-defense corps were Viet Cong, Viet Cong sympathizers, opportunists, or just survivors. The self-defense corps was especially susceptible to Viet Cong propaganda. It was not unusual for a fort to be overrun. The forts, made of mud and wood posts or of concrete, were surrounded by a mud wall; beyond that, barbed wire and sharpened bamboo sticks were embedded in the ground. At night the Viet Cong would call into the fort and tell the soldiers to join them, or they would attack and kill them and their families. It is not surprising that some soldiers (with their weapons) deserted or surrendered without resisting. What is surprising is that all of them did not give up without a fight. Graham Greene devotes a telling chapter in *The Quiet American* to the terror experienced by the soldiers assigned to these forts.

Terror The Viet Cong used terrorism to control those segments of the population who did not support them. Government officials, strategic hamlet chiefs, village chiefs, schoolteachers, merchants, and villagers were kidnapped and murdered. The victim was usually tortured slowly, then killed. Who killed him, how he died, and why was made known by the Viet Cong throughout the area. The use of terror was effective. Frequently the Viet Cong would kill an uncooperative village chief, and his successor too, if he did not cooperate. The third man who took over the job would be either sympathetic to the Viet Cong or so petrified that he would do what they wanted. This was a sure way for the Viet Cong to take control of a village. The effectiveness of this technique should not be doubted.

The people were terrified of the South Vietnamese government as well. Numerous government security agencies appeared to operate at will and independently from one another. Pity the poor person who came under their scrutiny and control.

On the night of April 26, 1963, a civil guard fort three miles from Chau Doc was attacked. When we arrived to help, the fort was burning and the officer and the sergeant were lying wounded on the ground. The thirteen other civil guard soldiers had shot them and deserted to the Viet Cong. Accounts of this and similar incidents circulated in the villages and undermined the resolve of the men defending nearby forts.

Three days later, at a nearby fort manned by self-defense corps soldiers, two wives left the fort to collect firewood. Some time later, two more wives and a soldier went looking for the first pair. By dark, none had returned. That night the Viet Cong surrounded the fort and threatened to kill the four wives unless the soldiers agreed to join the Viet Cong. The soldiers agreed, except for one soldier and his wife who said that they were Catholics and could not fight for the Viet Cong because the Viet Cong were communists. The Catholic soldier was overpowered and the fort burned. When we arrived, we found that the Viet Cong had tortured and killed his wife, then set the soldier free to tell the tale.

Body Count The success of an operation was measured

by the Viet Cong body count. Everyone, man or woman, young or old, killed by the ARVN during an operation was considered a Viet Cong, even those found without weapons or incriminating documents. The body count would be radioed to division headquarters and the bodies would be flown there for verification. Incredibly, the need to promptly verify the body count and move that number up the chain of command resulted, on occasion, in helicopters transporting dead Cong before evacuating ARVN wounded. Division, after verification, would inform Saigon. Of course each commander increased the body count number as it made its way up the line, because the larger the number, the more successful the commander appeared. South Vietnamese commanders were neither the first nor last to embellish the effectiveness of their combat troops.

Victuals Napoleon said that an army marches on its stomach. The U.S. Army believes this and makes a great effort to ensure that its soldiers receive sufficient nutritious food. The purchase of food and its cooking and serving are highly regulated. What to serve, when to serve it, and which menu to follow are decided by senior officers advised by trained nutritionists. Inspections to ensure proper food preparation, sanitation, and care of equipment are frequent. Good cooks are respected and pampered by their fellow soldiers. The army has mess halls in its camps and mess trucks for serving hot food in the field. A soldier can eat all he wants; most of the time there are no limits. Three meals a day are available in camp. In combat situations the U.S. Army tries to get at least one hot meal a day to every GI. All of this requires a large and costly commitment of men and resources. For every U.S. soldier in combat, at least seven noncombat soldiers are needed to supply and support him. Some of those are responsible for the combat soldier's food.

The ARVN did not feed its soldiers. It had no mess halls, nutritionists, or food inspectors. No victuals were provided.

The ARVN did not have the resources to do it the U.S. Army way. Instead, every soldier received a food allowance with his monthly pay. The extra money was for use by the soldier to buy rations at the local market. He bought what he wanted when he wanted it and cooked it the way he wanted. Five or six soldiers would pool their food and cook it over a single fire. Although some soldiers did not eat properly because they gambled their money away or spent it on girls, the allowance system worked. The local merchants liked it and the soldiers liked it. It worked well unless, as sometimes happened, the soldiers were not paid on time. When this happened they were not easy to control. They took what food they needed from the merchants and peasants. A hungry man also has no limits.

But the food allowance system did not work well on an operation. It added to the general chaos, because while the soldiers were looking for the Viet Cong, they were also foraging. On an operation, the soldiers brought with them rice tied in socks, which they carried in their packs, together with a pot or bowl. A meal in the field consisted of rice and whatever else could be found. Often they chased chickens in the villages and waded into ponds and canals to catch ducks. They placed the live poultry in their backpacks with the heads free to look around. The squawking added to the carnival atmosphere of the battalion on the move. Fruit and vegetables were collected where found. Although soldiers were supposed to pay for the food, and frequently, after one-sided negotiations, they did, often they did not. When this happened, the villagers watched, sullen and resigned, sometimes complaining but most times not. The officers did not interfere; foraging was necessary and allowed. At the end of the day the food was cooked and shared. Purloined chicken tastes just like purchased chicken. If the villagers were not paid, or not paid a fair amount, it helped the Viet Cong; it was another reason for the villagers to detest and fear the ARVN.

The Viet Cong were feared by the people too. The Cong murdered and beat those who did not support them. The Viet Cong lived off the land. They foraged for food too, but they did it in a way that did not totally alienate the villagers. Either they paid with money that was extracted as a tax from a nearby village, or their food was provided after lengthy propaganda lectures. In some villages, the people freely gave food to the Viet Cong. If they did not, the Viet Cong forced compliance and just took what they wanted. They did not go hungry.

The ARVN was the national army. Its soldiers came from all over South Vietnam. Its units constantly moved from place to place and had no relationship with the villagers they encountered every day. It was pure chance for a soldier to be from the village through which he walked. Sometimes the ARVN behaved badly. On the other hand, soldiers of the civil guard and the self-defense corps were recruited from and served in their home districts. Consequently they treated the people better and were in turn better liked than the ARVN. So too were the Viet Cong. They were local people. They knew the villagers and were known by them.

A Fortunate Lapse Some operations had air support; some did not. Propeller planes strafed and bombed when requested by advisors. Until my arrival in Vietnam I had never talked a plane onto a target. I had no experience and do not remember ever having received instructions on how to call in an air strike in support of ground troops. I learned by trial and error.

Directing a pilot to a target was no easy matter, especially amidst rifle fire, soldiers running this way and that, and the general confusion associated with enemy contact. To do my job, I needed to see where the Viet Cong were shooting from and I needed the protection of a paddy dike or canal bank.

My radio antenna marked my route and drew enemy fire as I ran and stumbled forward. Generally, by the time I found a protected place with an unobstructed view of the target, I was winded, my equipment was strewn behind me, and Plum was nowhere to be seen.

Directing a pilot to a target was not an exact science. Bombs on target were more likely if the communication between the pilot and me was clear, concise, and unambiguous. The instructions I radioed to the pilot had to take into consideration my location, the location of the target, and the direction the plane was flying. A reference point on the ground was necessary for accuracy; sometimes a smoke grenade would serve that purpose. Other times, the pilot and I would talk back and forth until we agreed on a land feature, from which directions to the target were given. But our perspectives were not the same; my view was horizontal, his was vertical, and every rice paddy, canal, and tree line looked the same from hundreds of feet in the air. Radio transmissions were not static free, and understanding the pilot's words was made difficult by Captain Beng and passing soldiers who shouted their advice in urgent, staccato voices. Misunderstandings occurred, and pilots and I made mistakes. Even though the pilots were highly trained professionals who checked and rechecked the target location with me, bombs did not always land on, or near, the right place. But always each impact, whether or not on target, was followed by cheers from the soldiers. And when the ordnance landed where I wanted it to, often the results were unintended. At times the bombs I directed to a target killed and wounded civilians. When the noise of combat stopped, cries of pain and grief soon followed. Often the result of my effort was a mixture of thatch, mud, vegetation, and body parts.

The first pilot I directed to a target knew right away that he was dealing with a green lieutenant. In response to my request, "Can you bomb and strafe the tree line on my left," he said, "Hi, ole buddy. Y'all need some heat down there? I'm here to help you. Remember now, when you tell me where to go, the directions have to be from where I am or from something we can both see. Don't give me directions from where you are. I don't know where you are or which way you're facing. Y'all understand?" With great patience he taught me how to direct a pilot to a target near friendly troops.

Although of psychological value to the ARVN, the use of air support in 1963 was of little military value and served only to entertain the troops, stop the battalion, and delay our pursuit of the enemy. And because errant air strikes often caused civilian casualties or damage to their property, they served to alienate the very people whom ARVN was charged with recruiting to its side.

In order to direct air support, I had to know the correct radio frequency and code name. The frequency and code name changed on each day of an operation. My diary lists radio frequencies and my code names, my favorite being Delta Fox: There you go, Martin Dockery, the Delta Fox. Others I remember were Crap Shooter and Finnan Haddie. I would receive this information from Captain Beng, who received it during his briefing from the 21st Division Headquarters. Because the Viet Cong had ARVN agents, I was always concerned that this information would be compromised and the Viet Cong would succeed in directing our air support on us.

One day I made a serious mistake that probably saved lives. Captain Beng asked me to have the planes bomb a large group of Viet Cong whom he had spotted in a distant rice paddy. I could see them with his binoculars: about thirty black pajama–clad armed men. I set the correct radio frequency and pushed the talk button, but then my memory failed me. I could not remember my code name. Breaking all the rules, I used my name in the clear. "This is Lieutenant Dockery on the ground. I see a large group of VC in a field. I want you to light them up." The pilot was both suspicious and angry that I had not used my designated code name. He had to be sure I was not a Viet Cong trying to trick him into bombing the ARVN. After answering a series of questions such as "Who does Mickey Mantle play for?" and "What's a Dodger?" I convinced him of my bona fides. It was reminiscent of dialogue from a bad World War II movie. While I was directing him to the exposed Viet Cong, another American voice came on the radio, gave his code name, and said, with emotion, "This is Bluebird Two. Please do not bomb my men." Black pajamas were also the uniform of the district civil guard, and Bluebird Two was their advisor. They were on the same operation as my battalion. I believe that if I had not forgotten my code name, the pilot would have quickly bombed those troops before their American advisor got on the radio and announced his presence with the misidentified Viet Cong. Apparently, the pilot never reported the dumb lieutenant who forgot his code name, because I was not reprimanded.

Some air strikes produced ludicrous results. Once, I called in air strikes on a resistance point; the Cong were shooting at us from a village. The battalion moved forward after the bombing and discovered two dead water buffalo, whereupon the operation stopped so that the buffalo could be butchered and the meat distributed to the soldiers. Of course, the Viet Cong did not wait around. The government was supposed to compensate the farmers for the dead animals, but I am sure that even if they did it was too little and too long after the event to be of help to the farmers.

Riverboat Operations The thousands of delta waterways provided a means for efficient and reliable transportation. The South Vietnamese Navy used U.S. World War II landing boats for transporting ARVN soldiers. Riverboat operations were usually conducted at night. They were always dangerous, even if there was no Viet Cong contact. The canals, rivers, and tributaries were of various widths and depths, and at night they were ominous and silent. Large overhanging tree limbs on both sides restricted navigability. The night smelled of engine smoke, and there was the roaring from the boats crashing into the banks, backing up, engines gunning, sloughing around, and the yells of frightened but determined men. It was scary as we moved through the dark night on those old, noisy rust buckets. The battalion would load onto the landing craft at night and be taken on a two- or three-hour ride through the canals to the landing site. Cannon fire from the boats would rake the site. The landing ramps would go down and the troops would charge onto the muddy, slippery bank and conduct a sweep looking for Viet Cong. Of course, it was never that simple. Assuming we had landed in the right place, which was difficult to know, we still had to orient ourselves by shining flashlights on maps to know which way to go. None of this was easy, and we got it wrong sometimes. Often we did not know where we had landed and could not locate our objective. The village we were to search could not be found. Something always went wrong on riverboat operations: inaccurate maps, unclear orders, lost boats, broken ramps, broken engines, bridge or boat collisions, groundings, and men overboard. Even if we made no Viet Cong contact, soldiers would be injured or drowned.

Prisoners Late one night as we motored down a canal in an old French-built cargo boat commandeered for our transport, we happened upon three sampans, two men in each. We fired on them because they refused to stop. Two were wounded and two killed. The living and dead were taken aboard. Rifles and ammunition were found on the sampans. I was proud of my people; they had done everything right. However, what I watched unfold was not right. Captain Beng wanted information, he said. The two uninjured Viet Cong were blindfolded, stripped, and lowered seriatim by their arms into the boat engine. They raised their legs in the hope of avoiding the moving parts of the engine, but without success. They could only raise their legs so far. Then screams and blood. They both gave information, but I never learned whether it was of any value or what Captain Beng did with it. The men were not killed. Their feet were bandaged. I watched all this and did nothing. They were the enemy. When you're merely an observer, it's fascinating. It's exciting and terrifying. You want to see how it ends. But at some point I became part of the scene, and my presence influenced and encouraged the players and validated the outcome.

A Pain in the Neck We loaded late one afternoon for my initial riverboat operation. The first thing the soldiers did was to find a place to nap. They stretched out wherever they felt safest, Captain Beng and the officers included. The boat crew and I were the only ones standing. After I learned it would be a four-hour boat ride before disembarking, I went searching for a place to rest. Stem to stern, the boat was a carpet of soldiers. Surprisingly, amidships, to the right rear of a mounted .50-caliber machine gun, I found an open space large enough for me to stretch out. With my head resting on my pack, I looked up and saw a piece of equipment attached to the bulkhead. Printed on it were the words, "Made in White Plains, New York," my hometown. Memories followed.

A .50-caliber shell is six inches long with a half-inch diameter. It consists of a bullet atop a casing packed with gunpowder. The bullet is propelled out of the barrel by expanding gas when the firing pin ignites the gunpowder. The spent shell casing is automatically ejected from the chamber so the next shell can be fired. As with most guns, the spent shell is ejected to the right rear.

At some point in the night, we were fired on from the canal bank. The .50 caliber near me returned a long burst of fire. The spent red-hot shells rained down on me. I was burned on my face and neck before getting to safety. The reason why the space I had chosen for my nap was not occupied when I got to it was that everyone knew it was the footprint of the machine-gun ejection pattern. That is, everyone but me. I was not sure whom I should be mad at, the soldiers for not telling me or myself for not knowing any better. Bad show, Lieutenant.

Helicopters Helicopters were a significant asset. They provided mobility to the infantry. They were used to take troops into battle, evacuate the wounded, and, importantly, maintain contact with advisors, who were scattered the length and breadth of the country. The U.S.-flown command and control Huey and H-21 troop carrier (banana) helicopters carried a crew chief, who "helped" the Vietnamese soldiers exit the aircraft quickly, tossed resupply bundles, and returned ground fire when the chopper came under attack. Choppers had a door machine gun mounted on a swivel bar that could be moved aside to allow troop entrance and exit. Each crew member had a rifle as well.

Choppers made a thumping sound that carried long distances over the flat delta terrain. Once your ear was attuned to the helicopter's rotor thud, the "whoop, whoop, whoop," you could hear the aircraft coming long before it was visible. It was a point of pride for a soldier to be the first to call out that a chopper was coming.

Several times a month a chopper would bring me my mail, the Sunday *New York Times* that my mother sent me, and toilet paper (oh so precious) that the U.S. Army provided. The choppers were supposed to come every week, but that did not happen, either because they could not locate my unit or because there was a higher priority. In December I complained to my parents: "It never rains, it always pours. Seventeen days ago a helicopter brought me mail and some goodies. Since then I haven't seen or heard from any Americans."

The *Times* was bulky. It came wrapped in plastic, generally three weeks after its date. Once, I got three at once. The pilot complained that he had become a newspaper delivery boy. I read the paper front to back and every word including advertisements. The newspapers were not burned when I was finished with them. They were recycled, kind of. I was the only one with toilet paper out there. Until the *Times* became available, everyone else used leaves and grass and whatever. Of course, the content of the newspaper had nothing to do with its ultimate use.

One September morning just weeks after I had arrived in Vietnam, I boarded a helicopter that was taking battalion soldiers to a landing zone near Can Tho. It was always difficult to be heard over the penetrating noise of a helicopter, so I was surprised to hear someone clearly address me by my first name. The pilot, Bert Sandvoss, and I had graduated in 1956 from Archbishop Stepinac High School. We visited briefly and promised to keep in touch.

It was a hot landing zone, and the choppers came in at tree level with protective fire provided by the door gunners. I watched for movement in the tree line but did not see where the Viet Cong fire was coming from. Bert dropped us in the middle of a flooded rice paddy and flew off for another load of soldiers. We had not seen each other since graduation, nor have we seen each other again since that September morning.

Another sudden contact with a distant home life occurred on April 20 when a helicopter pilot, upon seeing my name stitched to my uniform blouse, asked if I was related to Michael Dockery. Michael, a first cousin, and the pilot were classmates at Niagara University.

A Night Medevac Late one afternoon during the monsoon rain, the Viet Cong dug in at a tree line and from forty yards took the battalion under fire as we crossed a rice paddy. Based on the number of firing positions and the width of their position, I guessed that there were about twenty-five

Viet Cong with two machine guns. They had been in front of us all day, shooting soldiers in the point squad, then fading away. They had picked the time and the place. It was raining, it would be dark soon, and we would not have air support.

The soldiers in the battalion were walking on the paddy dikes in three parallel columns about forty yards apart. The men were, as always, strung out, smoking, holding hands, babbling to one another or chewing sugarcane, and not alert to the danger when the shooting started. The lead soldiers took cover alongside the dikes. So did I. Some soldiers returned fire. After a few minutes our machine guns began to fire and we lobbed mortars at the tree line. Captain Beng followed the textbook solution by ordering elements of the battalion forward through a tree line on the right side of the field, a flanking movement. Nothing happened. No one moved. The prone soldiers ignored Captain Beng as he walked upright amidst them, threatening to shoot them if they did not move forward. Confusion reigned. Incoming fire forced Beng to the ground. The soldiers' return fire was ineffective, because they did not look when they fired their rifles. But I had scrambled to a good position behind a dike, and my return fire was on target. I knew that my fire was effective because I attracted immediate counterfire.

All of this happened in a space of twenty minutes, I guess. But honestly I did not know then how long that action, or any action, took. It could have been much longer or much shorter. Combat feels compressed, distant, and vague. Fear and the noise and smell of other frightened men and their weapons distort one's sense of time and reality. A soldier's instinct for survival is not distorted, but soldiers must overcome this instinct in order to accomplish their mission.

Teamwork is necessary to achieve success in battle. By shooting their rifles without looking, the ARVN soldiers escaped being wounded, but shooting without looking lessened their chances of hitting the Viet Cong. In combat a unit must bring its fire to bear on the enemy. Even if the enemy is not hit, a hail of bullets will most likely prevent accurate return fire or cause the enemy to move. The Viet Cong fire was aimed, concentrated, and effective. The Viet Cong suppressed their individual survival instinct for the good of their units, and the units were frequently successful. The ARVN, on the other hand, frequently acted as individuals in combat and not for the good of the battalion. Although ARVN soldiers were more numerous and better equipped than the Viet Cong, they often suffered higher losses. In battle, as in life, one must aim at a target in order to be successful.

Soon it was dark, and the soldiers left the field and established a defensive line. We lost contact with the Viet Cong, although occasional sniper fire evidenced their presence. What I noticed about this firefight and other combat was that although I was active and intense, later I remembered very little. I could remember what I did but not my words or thoughts.

Vietnamese chopper pilots were asked to evacuate the dead and wounded, but they refused to come because of the dark, the rain, and possible Viet Cong fire. At Captain Beng's request and using the ARVN radio net, I called the American helicopter unit in Saigon and requested a medical evacuation. I told the pilots that there were Viet Cong near the landing zone and informed them of the torrential rains. Within an hour, using a radio beacon as a guide, two choppers landed in the dark and rain, loaded twelve wounded and four dead, and lifted off for Saigon. I knew that some of the wounded would not live through the night. Before the aircraft departed, I spoke briefly with the pilots. They were calm and professional. One of them asked, "Are you the only American with these ARVN?" The other said, "We can get you out of here. Ride back to Saigon with us." It was a tempting invitation, but I could not accept it under those circumstances. As in most situations, pride won over discretion. Those

American pilots were courageous and dedicated. They faced danger to do a job that the Vietnamese pilots should have done themselves.

A Solo Exit On some operations, soldiers would be ferried by choppers to a landing zone near suspected Viet Cong locations. The beautiful view below of the serene and timeless rice paddies and canals lined with verdant jungle growth was soon forgotten as the fragile helicopter dropped swiftly toward the earth. Each chopper carried ten to twelve soldiers. Three or four choppers would land at the same time, so if the Viet Cong were shooting they would disperse their fire on multiple targets and not concentrate on a single chopper.

On those operations, everyone was scared: the pilots, the soldiers, and I. Believe me, I was scared. We were exposed to enemy fire and knew we were in extreme danger. There was nowhere to hide. We all feared the bullet below; its vertical trajectory terrorized. With hope, soldiers sat on their steel helmets and pilots sat on thick metal plates. I learned that fear has a dry, metallic taste. Sometimes we were fired on as we approached the landing zone. We heard the echo—a wrenching, screeching sound—as bullets gored the chopper's metal skin. No one had to tell me what caused the sharp reports and the aircraft to shudder; it was ground fire hitting the helicopter. Choppers that had previously been in hot landing zones were easy to identify; they had masking tape covering bullet holes to keep out the rain.

Fear is a powerful emotion; one acts without thinking. It is sudden, brief, natural, and instinctive. At times it can numb the mind, paralyze the body, and cause one to act in strange and unusual ways. For me the worst fear was that others would find out that I was afraid. That particular fear and my training motivated and directed me to act in the correct way, most of the time.

I was expected to inspect the men's equipment, to encourage them, and to show bravado. Sudden plunges and rises and unexpected changes in the chopper's attitude made the floor slope and sway wildly, and constantly challenged one's ability to stand without lurching and stumbling about. The door was always open, and there was no safety line. Kerosene fumes, the rolling and shuddering, and the earsplitting noise of the engine affected us all. Many times one soldier would get sick, then another would follow suit. Vomit odor filled the space. I learned to walk on the puke-covered floor, knees bent, hands grasping convenient metal or flesh. I pretended to inspect, encourage, and act the brave part as I walked by the seated soldiers and shouted *giet cong* (kill the communists) and other words of encouragement, which none of them could hear. Some soldiers nodded, acknowledging my effort. Others, those with wide eyes and vacant stares, did not know where they were, or why, or even who they were; they were terror struck.

Usually the choppers did not actually land; they hovered just above the ground while the troops jumped out. Everyone was supposed to exit quickly to reduce exposure to themselves and the choppers, which were vulnerable while virtually motionless. One time, pumping adrenaline, I exited first and, while firing my weapon, started toward the tree line from which the Viet Cong were shooting. That was standard procedure for a squad on line but not for a lone officer, I am embarrassed to say. I looked over my shoulder and discovered that the soldiers had not left the chopper. I was in the wrong place, out front and alone. Fear and excitement caused me to act contrary to all my training. I ran back to the helicopter and hectored them out. Sometimes we yell at others to mask our mistake. I had to contend with incoming fire and terrified soldiers. Eventually I got them to return fire and move toward the Cong, but not before taking casualties. When we got to the tree line, the Viet Cong were gone. This activity did not conceal the stupidity of my solo exit, but it helped me feel somewhat less silly. It seems foolish now, but then, even under those extreme conditions, I was worried about looking silly and about the soldiers knowing that I was afraid. After that experience I always waited for some of the soldiers to exit before I did, so I would not end up alone in the paddy. I figured that the rest of the squad was more likely to jump out if some of their mates had already gone, not necessarily because the American had jumped.

Paddy Water On operations I wore a radio on my back so I could talk with American pilots and direct air strikes. The radio (PRC-10) weighed about ten pounds; its tall whip antenna was a marker for an officer and attracted fire.

From the air, a helicopter pilot could not tell the depth of paddy water. Landing a chopper in a flooded rice paddy was dangerous. So the pilot would hover just above the water and the soldiers would jump out. Once when I jumped, the added weight of the radio and my inability to find firm footing caused me to lose my balance and go under. The taste and smell of the feculent paddy water and muck were not pleasant; rice paddies were fertilized with human and animal waste.

Ap Bac These things that happened, and my reactions to them, were also experienced by other advisors, my friend Mike Blackwell included. We learned the same things. The few differences were minor and were accounted for by our personalities and those of our counterparts. At the battle of Ap Bac, Mike also experienced in a real way the practical difficulties of being an advisor in a little understood and alien cultural environment, and he experienced the bungling ineptitude and political motivations of Vietnamese commanders.

In January 1963, near Ap Bac, a small village in the delta forty miles southwest of Saigon, about 350 Viet Cong engaged a much larger government force. The government soldiers were from the ARVN 7th Infantry Division and the district self-defense corps, and their firepower was far superior to that of the Viet Cong. The Viet Cong conducted themselves well, and the government forces performed miserably.

The senior U.S. advisor on the scene was so appalled by the ineptitude of the South Vietnamese officers that he wanted to take command away from the Vietnamese officers and have the American advisors lead the soldiers. The Vietnamese refused. They would have none of that. They were more worried about their superiors, military and political, and the crazy Americans than about the Viet Cong. At the end of the daylong battle, sixty-one government soldiers were dead and a hundred were wounded. Five helicopters were downed and two American crew members were dead. Mike and his battalion were at Ap Bac; the American captain who was the leader of Mike's advisor team died there.

Ap Bac demonstrated to senior American officials that the Viet Cong were exceptional fighters even against government troops reinforced by U.S. helicopters. The outcome at Ap Bac reflected what field advisors in the delta knew: Militarily the Viet Cong were formidable. A lengthier description of what happened and of why it went wrong for the South Vietnamese military is provided by Neil Sheehan in *A Bright Shining Lie: John Paul Vann and America in Vietnam.*

The following afternoon I was alone at the Can Tho airfield hoping to hitch a ride to Saigon. A jeep drove up and dropped off an American colonel whose name I recognized as the senior American advisor to the ARVN 21st Infantry Division. He was my big boss. I introduced myself and told him I was assigned to the 2d Battalion, which was guarding a cement plant under construction in Kien-Giang Province. He said, "Yes, I know there is an advisor at the cement plant" and "Nice to meet you." He told me about Ap Bac and noted that it was not "our" division that had been mauled. He called the battle a debacle and said the South Vietnamese government was blaming it on the American advisors, a calumny that would permanently weaken our working relationship with the ARVN. He was going to Saigon to be briefed about the battle. I took this to mean, to get the U.S. story straight. At his invitation, I traveled to Saigon that afternoon on his plane. He was upset by the outcome at Ap Bac and the loss of American lives. I made an effort to engage him in conversation; on the basis of my personal experience, I described how difficult it was to get Vietnamese officers to accept an advisor's advice. I was arguing that Ap Bac was the fault of the Vietnamese and not the advisors. He did not pick up on this but instead asked about my family and career plans. We continued talking past each other for a while, until I realized that he was not going to discuss Ap Bac anymore. Rank has its privileges. I turned to other subjects.

The Missing Guards Although helicopters were a huge advantage to the ARVN, they caused burdensome supply and logistic problems. A high level of maintenance was necessary to keep them reliable, and they were not always available due to the downtime for maintenance. Maintenance occurred in Saigon where the choppers were based. Their fuel capacity allowed them to fly round-trip to anywhere in the delta, but they had to be refueled if involved in an operation. The fuel was a kerosene called JP4; it was transported in fifty-five-gallon metal drums by truck from Saigon several days before an operation start date. The drums were then stored under guard until needed. All this activity was supposedly conducted in great secrecy, but in reality nothing the ARVN did escaped the watchful eyes of Viet Cong agents.

The battalion moved to Long Xuyen for a series of operations, one of which was to be by helicopter. Two Vietnamese officers and I stayed in a house with a large yard but no wall. Twelve soldiers lived in the yard as security. Returning one evening after a daylong walk in the sun with the battalion, I discovered a hundred fifty-five-gallon kerosene-filled drums stacked in the yard. They contained helicopter fuel for use the following morning. It was difficult getting to sleep that night knowing what would happen to me if the Viet Cong blew the JP4. At 4 A.M. I left my bed and went into the yard. It was dark and quiet, and the guards were gone. Their tents and hammocks were empty. I was armed; I walked the yard, seeing nothing. Flickering shadows and noise in the underbrush made me nervous. I awoke the Vietnamese officers, and we stayed in the yard until 7 A.M., when trucks took the drums to the choppers. The missing soldiers returned soon thereafter and explained that they had slept farther away because they were afraid that the Viet Cong might blow up the fuel. Reasonable, but what about me and the other officers? The soldiers were reprimanded for abandoning their posts but were not disciplined as far as I knew. There is no way I can ever know, but I suspect that the Viet Cong were going to blow the JP4 early that morning and the soldiers had been warned away. Perhaps my 4 A.M. inspection of the stacked fuel drums scared the Viet Cong away and prevented them from blowing up the fuel, as well as me and most of Long Xuyen. Then again, one well-aimed mortar round would have done the trick.

The Frenchman When I arrived at the airfield that morning, my troops were seated on the ground in rows ready to go. Nearby, in similar rows, were about two hundred other soldiers without identifying unit patches on their uniforms and apparently without officers. As I approached them, a tall, thin man in dark pants and a long-sleeved shirt walked toward me from a group standing to the rear of the seated soldiers. He was a Frenchman and told me in Vietnamese that the soldiers were his and they were going on the operation. He did not understand me when I requested more information. Captain Beng told me to stop asking questions; there would not be any answers. I thought that the Frenchman was CIA or a French army officer on special assignment to the South Vietnamese government. Although I did not know who he was or what he was about, the pilots were expecting him. The Frenchman and his soldiers were dropped away from mine at a different landing zone and apparently with a different objective. Although extreme, this is an example of the puzzling situations that occurred on a daily basis. Most times, cultural barriers were the reasons for my confusion. At other times, information was kept from me intentionally. My frustration was perceptible.

A Wooden Pillow Everyone became drenched on operations during the monsoons. If it was dark and we did not know the size and location of the Viet Cong unit we were chasing, we would stay in the waterlogged rice paddies until morning. We slept against the paddy dikes, our legs in the water up to our knees. If the battalion was not in contact with the Viet Cong, we would bivouac in the nearest villages. The villagers did not like this, because they had to share their huts and food with the soldiers. One time, Captain Beng and I shared the village chief's wooden platform bed (no mattress), which had a carved wooden pillow. The chief and his family were out of luck that night. They had to find another place to sleep. The water buffalo, the farmer's most valuable asset, was sheltered at night in the house and was disturbed by our presence. It snorted, pawed, and pulled at its tether all night long.

The water buffalo is a measure of a farmer's wealth and status. It does the heavy work. Unfortunately for the animal and the farmer, the beast has a poor cooling system—it does not sweat—so it must spend the middle of the day in mud and water. At times villagers could be seen running back and forth carrying water to throw on a prostrate buffalo that was worked too long in the midday sun.

Village Searches Every delta village looked the same. As we entered them, defiance and apprehension were evident in the eyes of the peasants. They remembered the outcome of prior searches. They were fearful and spoke only when spoken to. Eventually their curiosity got the better of them and someone would ask about the tall Westerner in their village. They were curious about my height, skin color, and hairy arms, but most of all they were curious about my status. The questions were always similar: "Is he a Frenchman? Is he in charge? Why is he here?" They were surprised to learn that I was an American. Even when told that I spoke Vietnamese and could understand them, they never spoke to me directly. It was always through the soldiers.

In the course of an operation, the battalion walked through numerous villages, each of which was searched, house by house, for weapons and Viet Cong. The walls, roof, dirt floors, and paddocks were probed. Pigsties and cooking braziers were disturbed. Storage containers for rice and water were overturned. Grenades were thrown into the canal to surface submerged Viet Cong breathing through reeds. The canal bank was examined for entryways to underground rooms. The men and women who had not fled were interrogated. At times, weapons or Viet Cong documents were found, with adverse consequences for the village and villagers. The wells were blown. Houses were set on fire, but not before everyone moved far enough away or found protection from the exploding ammunition, which might have been hidden in the thatch. Those who had been living in the houses were tied up and sent to the province chief for interrogation. Those found hiding weapons were lucky if they survived the soldiers' reprisals.

Most of the time, nothing was found and no information was obtained. Sometimes the villages were empty. Frequently, children and the old were the only people present, and they disingenuously (perhaps) explained that the bunkers and bomb shelters in the village were to protect people from the ARVN. The women would say that the men were in the fields. Many men hid from us to avoid interrogation or being drafted. For the same reasons, I believe they must have hidden from the Viet Cong when they could. If we found able-bodied people, they were sent back to the province headquarters for questioning. Some returned on their own; some, I am sure, did not. Needless to say, none of this endeared us to the people.

It was believed that in the evening the Viet Cong would visit each village we had passed through to find out what we had been told, to discipline, and to propagandize. The Viet Cong impressed many of the young people. Regardless of their allegiance, the peasants were in a difficult position. The majority of villagers just wanted to be left alone. They all wanted to be out of the line of fire. Many moved to the cities, which is one of the reasons why Saigon has quadrupled in size since 1963.

Fire Contagion   Fire contagion is a term sometimes used today to describe a situation where all the police who respond to a call fire multiple rounds at a dangerous or presumed dangerous person when one or two shots from one or two cops would seem to have been enough to stop the person. There have been situations where as many as ten cops fired hundreds of rounds at one unarmed man. Once one cop shoots, the others shoot also. The reason for this phenomenon is not fully understood. Fear, solidarity, tension, and training are partial explanations. Maybe it has to do with sharing the responsibility—safety in numbers. Maybe it is instinct. The cops are often severely criticized, and there are public calls for discipline. But I understand their reaction and do not think they should be punished.

Soldiers react the same way. I never saw just one soldier shoot at a possible Viet Cong or in the direction of presumed danger. All that was needed was for one soldier to start shooting, then all those around him would shoot in the same direction. They did not need to see a target, because they all felt in danger. I found that I was no different.

We were operating in an area known to be sympathetic to the Viet Cong. Sniper fire was directed at the battalion during the day, and three soldiers were wounded by booby traps. It was the middle of the afternoon and we were walking through the third abandoned village of the day. We saw no adults or children, although we passed tethered water buffalo, and chickens and pigs scurried about. Cooking fires were hot. The rhythm of the village had been interrupted by us. All of us were tense and alert and felt danger. A clanging noise came from a house off the path to my right. One soldier fired, then six or seven of us fired hundreds of rounds.

The rifle shots from the first soldier were contagious. He must have seen something that caused him to shoot. We shot up the thatch house. Afterward, a young woman and a tiny newborn were found dead on the dirt floor. We had killed them. Maybe she had knocked something over that made the noise. Probably the woman had been unable to leave with the rest of the villagers because she had given birth only hours earlier. The battalion left the bodies in the house and continued the operation, but not before Captain Beng's bodyguard "found" Viet Cong documents in the house. In a frenzy the soldiers torched the village and shot the animals. We all knew what had happened, but in some strange, perverse way this destructive action cleansed us and justified the deaths. We hadn't planned to shoot up the house or kill the woman and her baby. Those things happened. No one was at fault. Collective action weighs less heavily, if at all, on one's conscience. I was more annoyed than troubled or sad. I did not, and do not, feel any guilt. But I did recall the Jesuit question, "Martin, what have you done?"

No *Chieu Hoi* In an attempt to undermine the Viet Cong by encouraging individuals to return to the South Vietnamese side of the civil war, the government distributed leaflets offering amnesty to any Viet Cong who surrendered, told all he knew about the Viet Cong, and had not committed a war crime. This Open Arms program, or *Chieu Hoi,* was highly touted as a great success, with exaggerated claims of hundreds or thousands (take your pick) of Viet Cong surrendering every week or month (take your pick). My sense was that there was some success. Viet Cong did surrender, and Viet Cong who were found by their comrades to have a *Chieu Hoi* leaflet were no longer trusted. A Viet Cong who presented a *Chieu Hoi* leaflet to authorities in a province or district capital was granted amnesty. However, it did not work in the field. A *Chieu Hoi* leaflet was not honored by the ARVN, perhaps wisely, after an exchange of fire or from a sniper hiding in a grass-covered hole. I saw Viet Cong, some wounded, who were shot trying to surrender while grasping their leaflets and shouting, *"Chieu Hoi, Chieu Hoi."* There was no *Chieu Hoi* for them, not then under those circumstances.

Life Is Cheap I have heard many Americans say that life is cheap "over there." Over there generally means some third-world country. Implicit in what is said is that those people are less civilized than we and less moved by the loss of life; therefore, we are superior. This idea is not accurate anywhere. There were dead and wounded, combatants and civilians, on both sides, but I did not see anything that indicated that the Vietnamese cared less about human life than Americans did. Soldiers cried and civilians cried, if that is the test. Americans are good at killing. Remember our Civil War and all the wars that followed, up to and including Vietnam. Every twenty years we seem to go to war. Men kill men for many reasons. It is fair to say that under the right circumstances, and depending on what is at stake, life is cheap for all of us.

I was not involved in any daylong, pitched battles. What I did see were brief, chaotic, and confusing firefights and ambushes, few lasting more than fifteen minutes. On occasion a Viet Cong company gave battle in the afternoon, and the engagement lasted until darkness. In such cases, the Viet Cong were always dug in and well prepared. My unit would stop and laboriously prepare and ponderously execute a plan of attack, which always seemed to allow the Viet Cong a way to escape. When the battalion was ready, the Viet Cong would melt away. I came to expect but not understand the ARVN's slow response time and lack of aggressiveness. I suspected it was related to a hope that the Viet Cong would just go away. But hope is a risky strategy. Sad to say, in the long run it did not work. It rarely does.

After a skirmish, the ARVN wounded were cared for. Viet Cong bodies and prisoners were proudly displayed. There was no quarter given. The ARVN soldiers tortured and killed prisoners, men and women, wounded or not. The first time I witnessed it, I did nothing. I watched but did not interfere. Today I don't know why. All my education and training failed me. My intervention on other occasions did not prevent the torture and killing, only delayed it. If I stayed with the prisoners, they might not be hurt, but when I left they would be cut, stabbed, and mutilated.

When the Viet Cong killed and tortured captured soldiers, they also killed the soldiers' families when they could. Several months before I arrived, the Viet Cong captured three battalion wives who were outside the camp gathering firewood. They tortured and mutilated them. The following morning their bodies were floated on rafts down the canal into the camp. Captain Beng repeated this story to me every time I complained about prisoners being tortured.

The battalion was on the final day of a three-day operation in the vicinity of Long Xuyen. Booby traps, falls, and heatstroke took their toll, but except for occasional sniper fire there was no enemy contact. Three days of searing sun, choking dust, and enduring thirst sapped the soldiers' stamina. They walked quietly, stooped and with heads down. No yelling back and forth. It was just another endless hike with heavy loads through jungle and rice paddies. Captain Beng and I were with the headquarters company in the rear of the line of march. Near noon, the point stumbled upon armed

men cooking rice in a clearing. It was unusual for the Viet
Cong to be caught in the open. Both groups were surprised.
Following a scramble for cover and a chaotic exchange of
gunfire, the enemy fled. One was captured. He had a face
wound, not serious but bloody. He could walk. A Viet Cong
was dead and three ARVN were severely wounded. When we
arrived at the scene, the young aspirant in charge of the point
squad was shouting and waving his pistol in the captive's
face. The aspirant was agitated and aggressive and threatening to shoot the prisoner. Captain Beng shouted, "The
province chief wants the prisoner. Don't shoot him." It was a
direct, lawful order from the aspirant's commanding officer.
Under protest the aspirant holstered his weapon. The prisoner was to be interrogated at the province headquarters and
imprisoned unless he invoked *Chieu Hoi*. Encouraging prisoners to embrace *Chieu Hoi* was official government policy.
If the prisoner was contrite and agreed to inform on and fight
against his former comrades, he would not be jailed. Otherwise, confinement for years under dreadful conditions
awaited him.

We were walking in the middle of the lead company to a
nearby field where helicopters would evacuate the casualties
and the prisoner. The wounded ARVN were in the rear with
the headquarters company. Their buddies from the shot-up
point squad struggled to carry the wounded on makeshift
poncho stretchers. The prisoner was one step in front of me
on the trail. My proximity would protect him, I was sure. His
arms at the elbows and his hands at the wrists were tied behind him.

Suddenly a deafening blast close by stunned me. Something hit my face and arms as I stumbled forward. Regain-
ing my balance, I instinctively turned, weapon at the ready,
toward the noise. Soldiers, some grinning, were bunched up
behind me. Standing among them was the aspirant with a
.45-caliber pistol in his hand. He had shot the prisoner by

reaching around my right shoulder. The head exploded, and blood and bits of gore splattered me. Most everything above the ears was gone. I angrily explained what happened to Captain Beng and in the strongest terms condemned the aspirant. Beng disarmed the aspirant, who was then sent under guard by helicopter to the division headquarters. The headless Viet Cong together with his dead comrade and the wounded ARVN were loaded on the chopper as well.

Days later I reported the execution to my superior. He said he would take it up with the division commander and the province chief, but there wasn't much we could do about it. "We are only advisors," he said. Later Beng told me that the aspirant was forgiven by the division commander and the province chief because he was young and had killed the prisoner after a battle in which three of his men were gravely wounded. The aspirant did not return to the battalion. Instead, he was sent back to aspirant school for retraining and reassignment. Beng told me that the aspirant would never be promoted. I was dumbfounded and appalled, because I had expected him to be severely punished.

Violence and brutality were blatant and wanton on both sides. The Viet Cong shot ARVN soldiers whom they captured. They had no prisons. It was a dirty civil war. The foe was ruthless and vicious. The wives and children of ARVN soldiers were targets and were killed when found unprotected. Rules of war were uncertain at best under those circumstances. Officially the South Vietnamese government subscribed to the international rules of war, which among other things specifically prohibited the killing of prisoners. In reality, on the ground there were no rules; therefore, there was no meaningful punishment. The aspirant was transferred so that the twin embarrassments of public insubordination and prisoner execution in front of an advisor would be forgotten. Today I am not sure how the aspirant should have been punished.

It took a couple of days before the ringing in my right ear stopped, but the memory of the personal affront and the horror of the moment remained for years. That was the only time I saw an ARVN soldier disciplined for mistreating prisoners. It is no wonder that the aspirant was sent back to school. He disobeyed a direct order from Captain Beng, disappointed the province chief, and executed the prisoner in front of me. Most likely his punishment resulted from the insubordination, not the execution.

The U.S. Army takes the rules of war seriously. Mistreatment of prisoners is not tolerated. If the aspirant had been in the U.S. Army, he would have been court-martialed, and at the least imprisoned or possibly executed for murder. There were credible witnesses and clear, unimpeachable evidence of his crime. But make no mistake about it, the U.S. Army protects its soldiers who do what they shouldn't do during combat-induced stress. Some awful things just happen. Not every misdeed is reported up the chain of command, and not every misdeed that is reported is acted upon. Circumstances are considered. Allowances are made. There is no sheriff there. That's the way it should be. We would all go to jail if we were held accountable for our every misdeed and every pain we caused others.

Political and military leaders are more culpable than soldiers because they have the time to explore moral issues before committing their subordinates to a course of action. The leaders draw fine distinctions to justify tactics and strategies that lead to victory. It is understood that artillery landing in a village will kill and wound civilians. Pilots, with impunity, expect civilians to die when they bomb railroad yards and factories in cities. They call it collateral damage and say that civilians are not the intended target. Many times distinctions of convenience are relied on to justify acts that would otherwise be recognized as immoral and thus condemned. Mostly it is the leaders on the losing side who are held accountable.

Interrogations Advisors received a three-hour course on interrogation techniques at Fort Bragg. The purpose of the course was to teach methods of gaining information from a prisoner by breaking his will to resist. The lectures were preceded by obligatory statements dealing with prisoners' rights under the Geneva Convention and U.S. law. Interrogation was presented as a planned, rational, and controlled exercise. One would have thought that it was a patient search for knowledge, like epistemology. The course was academic and sterile. It did not account for a prisoner's resistance or for sadistic instincts. Today I still remember the sequence of steps we were instructed to follow during interrogations: capture, disarm, restrain, search, isolate, strip, blindfold, deny succor, instill fear, create uncertainty, interrogate, exploit inconsistencies, and interrogate further. We were told that just as night follows day, useful information from the prisoner would follow from these steps.

The reality was that the search for information was almost always a pretext for revenge and reprisal and sometimes sadistic pleasure. Often no pretext was needed or pretended. Prisoners were taken after an engagement during which the soldiers' friends were killed or wounded. Emotions were inflamed and the soldiers were on the boil. Their ears were ringing from the sounds of battle, and fear and the astringent smell of gunpowder were in the air. Their mouths were dry. Adrenaline mixed with survivors' guilt. The immediate aftermath of an engagement was like a place between a dream and reality, a place best passed by, a place one should not visit. The interrogations that followed were not quests for information but merely excuses to test the laws of physics against the rules of anatomy. I can see it all now. No one there was innocent. No one. These experiences were mine as well as theirs. I could have, should have, done more to stop what happened.

Although I did not know it then, I left my innocence in

those places. I never recovered it. One doesn't. I learned things about man. Most people possess a latent sadism. Under certain circumstances we are all capable of terrible deeds. That is one of the imperfections of mankind. These situations include total control and power over another person; feelings of anger, fear, and loss; and being beyond the reach of civilizing restraints. These things coincide in combat situations where young men who are given arms and instructions to kill are expected to follow written rules of war. And most times they do. But soldiers in all armies are capable of barbaric acts, Americans included. This should not surprise anyone. It is natural. It resides in our hearts. It is part of the human condition, and clergymen, statesmen, and poets cannot explain it or cure it.

Hunker Down Artillery is an area weapon, and the killing zone is a function of shell size and type. Shells that explode on impact are effective against fortifications. Troops in the open are targeted with shells set to explode above them, sending shrapnel straight down. It takes skill to use artillery in support of infantry, skill that can be acquired only through constant training. Proper maintenance of artillery pieces is equally important. Artillery can be effective when used by competent soldiers, but even professional soldiers in modern, well-trained armies make mistakes. When the shells land in the wrong area, the wrong people get killed.

Usually artillerymen cannot see the target, so they must know precisely where they are, and the map coordinates of the objective. In the U.S. Army in 1963, a forward observer selected a target and communicated it to the fire direction center. Highly trained enlisted men then calculated necessary commands to be sent to the guns. Upon receipt there, settings would be placed and the mission fired. The forward observer would then adjust the fall of shot to coincide with the target and keep on firing adjustment rounds until the target could be engaged in a mode called fire for effect. Then an

entire battery or a battalion, or several battalions, could engage the target. If a mistake was made about the location of
the guns, or the azimuth or distance to the target, the calcu-
lations for the fire mission would be wrong and the shells
would land somewhere other than intended.

It was unlikely that the first shell would land on target anyway, but its impact point was used as a reference from which
the forward observer radioed distance and direction adjustments to the target. The artillerymen, in turn, applied a mathematical formula to determine adjustments in elevation,
direction, and amount of propellant. Eventually, after more
radioed adjustments, the shells would creep onto the target.

Proficiency in mathematics and map reading, a high level
of training, and adherence to a regularly scheduled maintenance protocol are prerequisites for the effective use of artillery. The ARVN lacked these attributes. It trained little and
maintained its equipment even less. Few officers or enlisted
men had the requisite mathematical competence. Effective
use of artillery was further limited by the lack of useful
maps. Available maps were inaccurate, not reliable at all.
Captain Beng, to his credit, was good with a map, but many
times he could not locate exactly where we were. Nor could
I. At times we guessed.

In theory the ARVN had artillery support. Every district
headquarters had two 105mm howitzers, each pointing in a
different direction. Many of my battalion's operations were
conducted within cannon range. But requesting artillery fire
was complicated, because the request had to go to regiment,
then over to province, then down to district. All this by radio.
When a "worthy" target presented itself, the map coordinates
were radioed by a battalion officer for approval. If the various commands approved, Captain Beng would put on his
helmet and everyone in the battalion would hunker down,
tensely awaiting the arrival of the first shell. No one knew
where it would land. Shells were liable to land anywhere.

Sometimes they exploded behind us, or in front, or three rice paddies to our left, where they sought a human harvest. At times we heard the cannon fire but did not hear the shell land. At other times we heard the round explode but did not know where it had landed. So many things could go wrong. And often they did. Artillery fell on soldiers, peasants, villages, water buffalo, and perhaps Viet Cong. Incompetence ruled the day.

In 1963 artillery was an inappropriate weapon used by poorly trained soldiers against small Viet Cong groups. It was dangerous, ineffective, and counterproductive because it alienated the peasants, whom the South Vietnamese government needed on their side in order to win.

Booby Traps Booby traps cause confusion, delay, and injuries. They lower morale. A well-designed and properly installed booby trap is extremely dangerous. It springs suddenly upon an unwary victim and strikes before he has time to recognize the danger. The care and transportation of a soldier wounded by a booby trap diverts resources from the fight against the enemy. The Viet Cong employed such traps on delta trails and paths. The foot of an unwary soldier would trip a wire two inches high stretched across a path, triggering an explosive device. Another kind of booby trap was the *punji* trap, a grass-covered pit dug under a path. The covering would collapse under the weight of a soldier, who would fall into the pit and land on sharpened bamboo sticks. Other traps were electronically exploded; some were activated by the pressure of a soldier's foot stepping on the trigger device.

The soldiers walked single file looking for the Viet Cong. I always walked in the footsteps of the soldier in front of me, eyes down to locate my next step, then quickly up to scan the front and sides. If he did not step in a booby trap, neither would I. The Viet Cong, who most likely were from the villages connected by the path, would set booby traps and occasionally fire from concealed locations. Villagers hid from the ARVN with good reason. Soldiers would make people from the last village walk at the front of the column as they moved between villages. Who better to know where the booby traps, mines, and ambushes were? Who better to step on the mines or in the booby traps?

As the drama unfolded, everyone played his part. The commandeered villagers followed by the soldiers of the point squad would move quickly until they came to a spot on the path that they tried to step over or around. The soldiers watched closely and would not let them detour. Hesitancy and fear betrayed the villagers' secret. In desperation one of them would say, "I see a trap over there by the tree." A soldier would say, "How can you see it if I can't? Did you set the trap? Were you going to let us walk down this path and get injured? Why didn't you warn us in the village?" The villager would be beaten or pushed into the trap, depending on the anger and memories of the soldiers.

Sometimes the civilians who were forced to walk at the point did not know where the booby traps were placed. They were unaware of the locations, but they knew the danger. When the inevitable occurred and the civilian was injured, the ARVN bandaged their wounds and they were treated with kindness and respect. Their wounds were proof that they were not Viet Cong.

It was a good strategy for the ARVN because it reduced their casualties. The villagers would not sacrifice themselves. No matter which side the villagers were on or how much they knew, the drama always ended badly for them. The ARVN was violating the international rules of war by using civilians as shields. But these civilians were considered combatants by the ARVN because, in most cases, they knew the location of the traps. In many villages the civilians voluntarily cooperated with the Viet Cong, setting traps, providing information, and carrying supplies. Guerrilla wars do not fit neatly into the framework of international law. I never attempted to interfere in these situations. It seemed harsh, but just. I was learning that there is not always a bright line between right and wrong.

High Water During the rainy season the rains soaked us and masked the noise of the battalion on the move. They also made for dangerous situations. On a rain-drenched afternoon during the monsoon, the lead company stopped. I went forward to see what the problem was and found that there was no bridge in sight and the soldiers were afraid to cross a twenty-foot-wide canal because of the water height. All my persuasion and exhortations could not get them to plunge in and cross to the other side.

To shame them I entered the water and began walking to the far bank. After several steps the canal bottom suddenly sloped downward and I was over my head with my rifle raised out of the water. I was weighted down with boots, backpack, radio, field dressings, rifle, ammo, and canteen. My lungs demanded oxygen; I needed to breathe. I was in trouble and started to panic. Fortunately, after six or seven steps the canal bottom sloped up and my head broke the water. The men had been right about the water height. Not only did I nearly drown because of my arrogance, I was now in Viet Cong country and separated from my men by high water. I wondered, as I stumbled up the far bank, whether the Viet Cong knew I was there, alone. Were they watching? Was I in their sights? Captain Beng arrived at the canal within minutes after my crossing. He appeared agitated. After some anxious minutes someone produced a rope, and I fashioned a help line to assist the battalion across the canal. Of course the Viet Cong did not wait around. I felt bad because I was America's representative and had made a fool of myself. It was not the first time, nor would it be the last. But I did get the battalion across the canal, and we did continue the chase.

After-Action Reports The U.S. Army is a large institution with all the bureaucratic trappings of governmental and commercial entities. In order to memorialize, record, and evaluate, written reports are required to be prepared on almost every activity; they are forwarded up the chain of command for review (presumably) and filing (for sure). Advisors were required to promptly prepare and file written descriptions of combat operations with the regimental U.S. advisor. Analysis of after-action reports by qualified intelligence personnel provided useful information about the enemy and his tactics.

I was aware of this requirement; immediately after my first operation and while still in the field, I wrote my report in longhand on pages from a yellow pad. I had never written one before and did not have a form to follow, but I gave it a lot of thought and was satisfied when days later I sent it off with a chopper pilot to the regimental advisor. My transmittal note requested after-action forms and asked whether the attached report was satisfactory and if not, how I should change it to make it better. I never received a response.

After considering the difficulty of writing reports in the field, of not knowing exactly what was supposed to go into a report and the uncertainty of delivery, I decided to prepare and file reports only upon request. If someone asked for an after-action report, I would file one. The aftermath of my decision was telling: Not only did I never receive comment on the report I filed, I received no forms; no inquiry was ever made as to why I was not filing reports; and no one ever requested that I file a report. Several possible explanations occurred to me: My first report was never delivered; there were no forms; my first report could not be improved upon; no one cared whether or not I filed reports; battalion advisors were exempt from filing reports; no one else filed reports; no one knew I was in the field; no one knew I was in Vietnam. To be fair, the regimental advisor probably didn't expect me to file reports because he knew of my isolation and the attendant difficulty of writing and delivering field reports. Anyway, I never filed another report, was never criticized for not doing so, and never knew why I was not criticized or, indeed, whether reports were required. And wisely I did not ask.

Lost in Translation In addition to Viet Cong booby traps, there were, not surprisingly, cultural and language booby traps everywhere. Misunderstandings were frequent and were as likely to be the result of cultural differences as of mere language difficulties.

Although I had an assigned driver, I insisted on driving my jeep. Most Vietnamese officers drove their jeeps, their drivers beside them. A male thing, control. One morning the battalion was moving by truck convoy. As we went through a village, a chicken and nine chicks crossed in front of my jeep. My jeep ran over the chicken. I stopped, ignoring Pham and Plum, who insisted that I continue with the convoy. Within minutes at least fifty men, women, and children had gathered to lend support to the grieving chicken owner, an old village woman. Pham and Plum nervously faced the crowd with their weapons at the ready. The old woman wanted compensation for the dead chicken and for the nine chicks, which she said were sure to die without the hen. After some one-sided negotiation, I quickly paid for the dead chicken, too much I am sure. And she got the carcass and the chicks.

At the officers' dinner that day, Captain Beng criticized me for putting myself and the others at risk by stopping in a dangerous place. Of course he was right, but I had tried to do the right thing, "win the hearts and minds of the people." Wanting to explain the circumstances, I told him in my best Vietnamese that I had killed a chicken. Everyone at the table became silent, then quickly all burst into laughter. Captain Beng looked at me; he repeated what I said and asked if this were so. I answered yes. More laughter followed. After much teasing, which continued for my remaining months at the battalion, the officers in turn and with glee told me that I had used a Vietnamese colloquialism meaning, "I have a dead cock." They employed ribald pantomime to make sure I understood. Some humor is universal. I am confident that during my time with the battalion, I made many other linguistic and cultural mistakes that they did not tell me about.

This particular anecdote and my experience as an advisor are fitting allegories for America's disastrous Vietnam involvement. In a sense these stories both paralleled and illustrated the U.S. dilemma in Vietnam. Our motives in Vietnam were well intentioned, and our actions were performed to the best of our ability, but we ended up the fool because we didn't know what we were doing. We did not understand what was going on in Vietnam. We were in a foreign land among people of a different culture and mind-set. It was not possible to translate our objectives and strategies into actions taken by the Vietnamese. The information sent across the cultural divide was not the information received. There was a disconnect. One thing was said and another thing was heard. One thing was meant and another thing was understood. The truth is, no one knew the truth. Meaning, intent, and truth were lost in translation.

Five

THE CEMENT PLANT

I watch, and am as a sparrow alone upon the house top.
—Psalms 102:7

The Cement Plant Life for an advisor, especially an advisor in a remote area, was often mundane and boring. Days would pass without any combat or attack or any remarkable events occurring, except that everything was remarkable in this existence. Total immersion in a rural, undeveloped Asian culture and environment under wartime conditions and near total separation from other Americans or things familiar created a twenty-four-hour-a-day surrealistic existence where nothing that happened could be considered unusual, although life itself became essentially unusual to the point of being bizarre. I was a stranger there, and it amazes me to this day how quickly I came to accept matter-of-factly the most remarkable occurrences without thinking of them as such and without real surprise.

The battalion was stationed at several places during my tour of duty, and from these places it conducted operations throughout a broad area of the delta. For five months, beginning in October 1962, we were stationed at a cement plant that was being built by a French company. Four French engineers supervised the peasant laborers. They shouted in French to the Vietnamese foremen, who did their bidding. Although I could not understand what the engineers said to the Vietnamese, the demeanor of the engineers conveyed contempt.

The cement plant was located eighteen miles south of the

Left: Chau Doc, Vietnam, 1963. I lost forty pounds in eight months.

Above: Paratrooper training, Fort Benning, Ga., 1961. After completing infantry officers training all officers went to specialized schools. Combat branch officers usually became paratrooper or ranger qualified, sometimes both.

Left: Army of the Republic of Vietnam (ARVN) soldiers were fully equipped for battle when they went to the field. Their equipment came from the United States and included steel helmets, M-1 rifles, automatic weapons, and mortars.

Hamlets and villages encountered, either on a sweep or as an objective, were searched thoroughly by government troops. Usually only old people, women, and children would be present when government soldiers arrived. Viet Cong would hide submerged in the canals. They breathed through hollow reeds.

Village men hid from the government because they were in a no-win situation. Some were Viet Cong; some were only villagers. The Viet Cong told them to hide from the government and reveal nothing.

Right: Men and older boys of fighting age, if found by the soldiers, would be taken prisoner, interrogated on the spot, sometimes tortured for information, and then escorted back to district headquarters for further interrogation. If soldiers found anything incriminating, they would burn down their house.

Below: Prisoners would be transported to district headquarters for interrogation. If released after questioning, they had to make their own way back home— sometimes an arduous journey. This treatment was fodder for Viet Cong propaganda, and was counterproductive to winning the hearts and minds of the people.

U.S. ARMY PHOTOGRAPH

Men hiding in the fields were occasionally captured by government forces sweeping the area. Even if they hid in their own rice paddy because they feared the ARVN and were discovered, they were presumed to be Viet Cong.

A Viet Cong with hands tied behind his back being taken to district headquarters by three soldiers. The likelihood of the prisoner surviving the trip was not high.

Captured Viet Cong, left, and their weapons on display. At this stage of the war the Viet Cong had a mixture of French, Japanese, American, Chinese, and homemade weapons.

The severity of the interrogations at the district headquarters depended largely on the attitude of district officials. The South Vietnamese government offered a *Chieu Hoi* program, which was an amnesty program for Viet Cong who would renounce the communists, give information, and turn over weapons.

Civil guard outposts were ramshackle and primitive with weak defenses. As many as ten soldiers and their families would be crammed inside at night. They were easy prey for the Viet Cong.

Tiny forts and outposts were at the outskirts of every town and dotted the rural landscape. In district towns the forts were generally more substantial and reinforced with defensive systems including moats, barbed wire, and mines.

Right: Crossings of waterways too deep to wade across were especially laborious for government troops. Sampans were rounded up and commandeered from local sources, and troops, with general confusion, would cross, a few at a time, and wait at the bank for the rest of the unit. "Hot pursuit" was the stated tactic, but it rarely happened.

Below: Muddy roads, flooded rice paddies, and swollen canals and rivers repeatedly slowed the forward movement of government forces, while the Viet Cong used these phenomena as avenues of escape. The element of surprise was always on the side of the guerrillas.

Above: Search and destroy operations were the primary tactic in the war against an elusive guerilla enemy force. Often derided by advisors as "search and avoid" because of their ponderous, halting, and seemingly purposeless meanderings, these operations were often frustrated by ineffectual leadership.

Left: Self-defense corps "citizen soldiers" were not as well equipped as the ARVN and wore an assortment of uniforms. Sometimes they looked much like the guerillas they were chasing.

Right: Helicopters could insert troops quickly into suspected Viet Cong–controlled areas and catch the enemy by surprise. Often the paddy water was high, there was confusion and floundering around, and movement toward the tree line objective was slow.

Below: Regardless of ideology civilians caught in the middle of a war are always the main victims. Transport of wounded to a medical facility was difficult and dangerous. Often the only recourse in the flooded delta was to attempt the perilous journey by sampan.

Self-defense corps soldier on patrol in Gulf of Siam. These citizen soldiers searched fishing and cargo boats in coastal waters looking for Viet Cong.

ARVN on the Mekong River at the beginning of a riverboat operation. Hours later and miles away they would land in the dark, hopelessly disorganized, amidst much noise and confusion, on the slippery bank of a minor waterway.

My cement plant hooch was located in a row of huts, which included officer living quarters, an operations/briefing room, and an eating room for battalion officers. The entrance to the hut is to the right of the thatch-enclosed shower stall.

Pham (left), my driver, and Plum, my Montagnard bodyguard, posing at the cement plant. During the rainy season several inches of water covered the ground.

This bridge collapsed under the weight of an armored personnel carrier (APC). APCs supplied to the Vietnamese by the United States were fearsome attack weapons when racing across open rice paddies in the dry season. During monsoon season when the canals flooded they were much less effective. This photograph says a lot about the futility of an army equipped with modern weapons fighting a peasant guerilla force in an undeveloped country.

APCs could swim across canals and rivers but they encountered problems trying to climb the oozing, muddy banks out of the water. Vietnamese troops were suspicious of them and absolutely refused to ride inside when the APCs were in the water.

The cement plant village was typical of poor rural villages in the delta. Stores and houses were of pole and thatch construction with dirt floors. Thin front poles held an awning roof that could be lowered at night or during a monsoon rain.

I am in front of a restaurant at the cement plant. The girl was never without the child. She said he was her son, but he was probably her brother.

Right: The "parade ground" at the cement plant. Between operations the battalion rested. There was no training. There were no inspections by Captain Beng and no parades. Soldiers wandered around visiting family and friends.

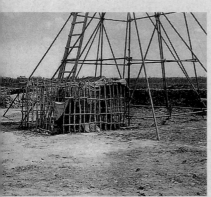

The battalion jail was small and primitive. For security, the "tiger cage" was located next to the watchtower. Prisoners were unprotected from the elements. Punishment for soldiers was nonjudicial and the length of incarceration was at Captain Beng's discretion.

Volleyball was one of the few diversions available at the cement plant. Pham is at left, looking at the camera. I am front, center. On the right is a battalion soldier of Cambodian heritage, dark-skinned and taller than the Vietnamese.

Top: The battalion officers are enjoying a barbecue on an island in the Gulf of Siam. I am on the far left. Captain Beng, who is squatting at the far right, took a chance by taking his officers and staff on a three-day unauthorized holiday to one of the offshore islands.

Middle: The moat and punji sticks were part of a strategic hamlet's defensive perimeter. The Viet Cong often constructed camouflaged "manhole" booby traps with sticks pointed up and down in the hole. A person who stepped in one, especially while running, could impale his leg as it went in, and tear it again as he reflexively pulled it out.

Bottom: An ARVN guard and I in front of a safe house in Bac Lieu. We had had an unpleasant encounter with "ugly Americans" the evening before this photograph was taken.

My friend Kim Anh and I at the Caravelle Hotel dining room, Saigon, 1963. The gray summer suit, white shirt, and tie traveled at the bottom of a duffel bag from New York to Vietnam and back again.

U.S. ARMY PHOTOGRAPH

Tranquil scene, Vietnam, 1963. Boats like these were used for fishing and for cargo hauling. Thousands operated close to shore along Vietnam's 575-mile coastline. Weapons and other supplies were hidden on some of these boats for delivery to the Viet Cong.

city of Ha Tien, at the far point of the delta in Kien-Giang Province. It was on the Gulf of Siam near the Cambodian border. It was at the back of beyond. The area was remote, rural, poor, and swampy. There was no running water. A generator that powered the battalion radio also provided electricity for several lightbulbs in the officers' quarters. Our mission was to guard the construction site and conduct operations as needed. One company remained to guard the cement plant and the soldiers' families while the rest of the battalion went on operations throughout the delta.

A small village lined the road in front of the cement plant. It provided housing and support for the construction workers. Except for the French engineers' house, every structure was made of bamboo and thatch. My hut of bamboo and thatch shared common thatch walls with neighboring huts occupied by the battalion officers. The entryway to my room had no door, only a piece of cloth for privacy. The room was six feet wide by twelve feet long; it held two canvas army cots. A single lightbulb attached to a frayed cord hung over my cot, which was under a dark green mosquito net hanging from the six-and-a-half-foot-high ceiling. The privy was thirty yards beyond the perimeter, a three-foot-high dirt wall. The low ceiling and the lack of a window or an opening directly to the outside made my room dark even in the middle of the day. An opening in a side wall led to an eight- by twenty- by six-and-a-half-foot room with a large table that was used for map work, briefings, and the officers' meals. The map room had an opening directly to the street.

At night, rats scurried across the floor and in the walls and, yes, from time to time they visited me on my cot. A kick would send them to the floor. They lived in the dirt wall that encircled the camp. Numerous openings in the wall were connected by a maze of tunnels, which contained nesting chambers. The rats hurried about day and night foraging at will throughout the camp. From time to time when they became too numerous, Captain Beng would direct soldiers to pour gasoline down the rat holes. Beng would light the gasoline, and flames and smoke would travel the tunnels and shoot out the holes. Some smoldering rats would escape, squealing as they raced to the swamp beyond the wall.

I could not relax in my room. As I lay on my back with my pistol at my side, it was difficult to sleep. I was sure the Viet Cong knew where I slept and knew that there were no doors and no guards. And I did not fully trust the ARVN. Paranoid? I don't think so. Realistic concern? Definitely. Many times I thought, What am I doing in this place? Of course, the answer was that I had volunteered.

One night I awoke to whispering near my cot. It was pitch black. The mosquito net separated me from two or possibly three people. I grasped my pistol and waited in fear. I don't know why I didn't shoot them. They whispered again and left. Were they Viet Cong? Thieves? Soldiers bringing me a girl? Did the thunderous thumping of my heart tip them off that I was awake? After relating this episode to Captain Beng the next morning, he posted a night guard at the entrance to my hut for the rest of our stay at the cement plant. Thereafter, I still did not sleep much. Although I had to worry only about the guard, I was like a nest on the ground, vulnerable.

When not on an operation, I followed a routine at the cement plant that included patrolling and sitting in ambush, the locations of which rarely changed. That way the Viet Cong would not be surprised and no one would get hurt. I read books (there was an informal circulation library for advisors; helicopter crew chiefs distributed used paperbacks), wrote letters, listened to Captain Beng's battery-powered radio, played volleyball, attended sick call for the villagers with the ARVN medic, visited the construction site, and endured inspections by politicians and senior ARVN officers. Several times I was invited by the district chief and the province chief for an evening meal. These were social events, gatherings of the local notables. In spite of my junior rank, inevitably I was seated next to or near the most senior person at the table. My host was conscious of my patron.

In October 1962 I heard about the Cuban missile crisis on the radio from an English language program broadcast from China. The radio account was a little different from the one I read in the *New York Times* weeks later. The Chinese broadcast was about U.S. imperialist aggression against Cuba, a communist brother. The imperialist pirates were interfering with international trade and preventing medical supplies from reaching Cuba. The *Times* described a U.S. naval blockade of Soviet missile ships that was necessary to protect Miami, Atlanta, and Washington, D.C., from nuclear attack.

My stay at the cement plant coincided with the rainy season. Except in the huts, which were built on raised dirt platforms, water was two to four inches deep for almost three months. It was truly awful for everyone. Going to the privy was an adventure. The only breaks from the monotony of the rains were Viet Cong activities and battalion operations.

The Viet Cong never directly attacked the cement plant. There were rumors that the French company paid them tribute to stay away. More likely they were not strong enough to overrun five hundred ARVN soldiers. But at night they shot into the camp and ambushed the listening posts and night patrols. Because they could not attack the cement plant, they attacked the nearby civil guard forts at night and ambushed the battalion forces sent in relief. In addition, they planted mines on the road servicing the cement plant, not every night but frequently enough that road travel was risky. It was safer to travel in the afternoon, because morning traffic was more likely to detonate mines laid the previous night. The ambushes and mines were successful in killing and wounding soldiers and civilians. It was not actually necessary to mine a road in order to stop traffic. Often the Viet Cong would dig a hole or shallow trench in, or leave a pile of dirt on, the road. Vehicles would stop until someone approached these possible mine sites and determined whether or not they were harmless. It was a dangerous job. Although not deadly, these fake mines were psychologically demoralizing and undermined the government almost as effectively as real mines.

Government employees in the village were Viet Cong targets. In January I attended the funeral of the local schoolteacher who had defied their order to close the school. They horribly murdered him in his home and left his body at the school. No new teacher came. The school stayed closed.

Girl Du Jour Vietnamese girls are like American girls: some pretty, some lovely, some smart, some personable, but all difficult. The foreign land, their features, and the circumstances made them exotic. The big difference between American girls and Vietnamese girls was that the Vietnamese girls were available morning, noon, and night. Sex did not seem to be a question of morality or commitment. The Vietnamese were casual about sex.

Captain Beng took it upon himself, either as my protector from nonvetted femmes fatales or as my tormentor, to present me with a constant stream of girls. Not every night, but frequently, both in the field on operations or at the cement plant, he would bring girls to me for my pleasure. I was never sure whether he was just a good host or was testing me. I never knew, but I did not accept these *filles de joie*. There was something untoward, something unprofessional, something compromising about his generosity. I was the representative of the United States of America and I was not going to compromise my position. Happily, there were other girls in other situations where these strictures did not apply.

Marry the Wives The cement plant was important to South Vietnam because of the cement it would produce and as proof that the government could protect a foreigner's investment from being destroyed by the Viet Cong. If the Viet

Cong destroyed the partially completed plant, it would be a devastating blow to the South Vietnamese government and a great victory for the Viet Cong. The importance of the cement plant was evidenced by my battalion's mission and by the frequent inspections by high-ranking politicians and officers. Captain Beng's job as plant protector and my job as his advisor were subject to scrutiny during these inspections. I had little to lose, but for Captain Beng these inspections were as dangerous as field operations. A negative report by any of the senior people would cause him serious problems. My diary records that entourages led by the head of the South Vietnamese CIA, the South Vietnamese vice president, and a U.S. general visited on separate days in December. Three inspections were made in January by high-ranking persons, including the South Vietnamese general in charge of the Psychological Warfare Department and his American advisor. When they left they gave the oh-so-helpful advice that the soldiers should marry their "wives."

On the one occasion that the division U.S. advisor came to inspect, I told the U.S. colonel how difficult it was to get Captain Beng to accept any of my advice. The advisor said he understood the problem because little of his advice was accepted by the Vietnamese officer he was advising.

Another Man's Wife The cement plant road was lined with small dirt-floor huts. Although people lived in the huts, the front rooms of some were used as shops, where food and small items were sold. Many evenings I stood on the bridge in front of my hut to watch the sun set on the Gulf of Siam. The canal was straight and the sun seemed to travel down it and disappear into the Gulf, with golden red rays bouncing off the placid water. Most evenings I would change into my black pajamas, the native dress, and walk the road to have a beer. For the first few weeks crowds followed and gawked, but after a while, although noticed, I was left alone. I was always on edge, but it wasn't possible for me to spend night after night holed up in my hut sitting on a canvas cot. The officers spent the evening with their families. I was on my own.

The Vietnamese beer I remember was called *ba muoi ba,* which means thirty-three. The number appeared prominently on the label. The beer was brewed near Saigon and sold throughout the country. *Ba muoi ba* was awful, but it was wet and had a kick. The beer tasted of formaldehyde; it was rumored that the chemical was used to disinfect the bottles and as a preservative.

The evening quiet was often interrupted by the sounds of gunfire and mortars from nearby posts under attack or from hot ambush sites. Artillery rumble carried far in the dark, still delta night, and artillery flashes danced low on the flat horizon. These nocturnal displays of noise and light did not disrupt the evenings.

One night while walking back to my hut, I became involved in a discussion with two men. The topic must have been interesting, because we continued the discussion in one of the houses along the road. Word spread quickly that the American officer was in Huong's house, because within ten minutes the room was full of people. My host sent out for a beer; then, when someone said that Americans like ice in their beer, ice was sent for. Everyone in the room was standing except for me and the two men. The three of us were seated at a small wooden table, which held my beer bottle and a glass of ice. I realized that I had gotten myself into what might be a dangerous situation. I did not know these people. No soldiers were in the room. It was unnerving to feel so vulnerable.

If I left before finishing the beer, Huong would lose face in front of his neighbors. They spoke with one another about me while they watched me finish the beer. I understood them to say: "How old is he? Is he married? Does he like it here? Is he lonely? Does he want a woman?" Eventually Huong called to his wife in the back room, and the crowd parted to let her slight, lovely figure reach the table. Huong spoke; his words were clear and crude. There was no mistaking what he meant. He offered me his wife for the night. I could have her in the back room or I could take her back to my hut. During advisor training at Fort Bragg, I was told that the Vietnamese sexual mores were different from ours, but I never could have imagined this kind of situation. Now I had to deal with a big "face" problem: how to refuse Huong's kind offer without insulting him and his wife in front of all his neighbors. I told him and everyone else in the room, and they most definitely listened with interest, that I was a Catholic and it was against my religion to sleep with another man's wife. I saw disappointment on the wife's face, or maybe it was relief. My explanation was acceptable. I shook hands all around and hurried back to my hut.

The Security Agents Spies, agents, and informers were utilized by the South Vietnamese government and the Viet Cong. Cyclo drivers, bar girls, soldiers, farmers, government bureaucrats, schoolchildren, and teachers were employed by one side or the other to observe and report. The various government security forces were responsible for uncovering Viet Cong agents. Most government departments had security personnel, some uniformed but most in civilian clothes. The civilian security agencies were feared, and justly so. They were armed and brutal. They took people at random off the street, or so it seemed. They intimidated and tortured. The Viet Cong did the same thing. It was a difficult life for the people of Vietnam.

One morning at the cement plant, two black Citroen sedans with military escort drove up the road. Four middle-aged Vietnamese men wearing sunglasses, black trousers, and long-sleeved white shirts commandeered Captain Beng's hooch for two days. Captain Beng's house was the biggest in the village except for the Frenchmen's. It was free-standing, off the road, and near the fortification that housed the battalion radio. His house was more secure and more comfortable than other hooches; no fool he. For two days the government agents questioned the battalion officers, including Captain Beng, and the noncommissioned officers, each man separately. In the evenings they kept to themselves. They had brought a young peasant girl with them to pass the time. They slept and ate in Beng's house, guarded by their military escort. Watching the officers enter the house I wondered, of course, what was going on and whether they wanted to question me. Was I next? In fact, they showed no interest in me and, to my surprise, left without meeting me. I was surprised because all government people of whatever rank or status, whether out of courtesy, curiosity, or self-interest, made a point of introducing themselves to me, the American advisor. It was a mark of their independence and power that they ignored me.

Maybe the security agents were trying to get the officers to inform on one another, or maybe they were gathering information about me. Perhaps the Frenchmen in charge of construction at the cement plant were the subjects of an investigation. Whatever it was all about, I never knew. No one would tell me. The agents left on the morning of the third day, apparently satisfied. None of those questioned was marked or taken away.

The United States also had people roaming the countryside with armed escorts on confidential missions. One afternoon a message came to me from the division advisor in Can Tho, sent through ARVN radio in Vietnamese and delivered in person by Captain Beng. He told me that I had received a message saying that American security officials were coming in the morning. That was the message I got, nothing more, nothing less.

Two trucks arrived. One carried Vietnamese soldiers and the other held radio equipment, supplies, and three American civilians. The civilians placed pole- and pie-shaped antennas around the truck, started a generator, and spent three days and nights adjusting radio dials and listening with earphones. They told me, with straight faces, that they were "testing." No further explanation was given. Maybe they were testing to see whether our agents in North Vietnam or China were still alive.

They brought their food with them in an ice chest. I joined them each evening for chicken and hamburger barbecues. We talked about Vietnamese politics, the Viet Cong, my situation, and ARVN ineptness, but not about their mission.

Discipline The U.S. Uniform Code of Military Justice (UCMJ) is given to all officers and is available to all enlisted men. It sets forth the rules that govern all aspects of military justice. Procedures and rules applicable to the charge, the investigation, the trial, the sentence, the appeal, and the punishment are clearly stated and are adhered to throughout the military. The purpose of the UCMJ is to list crimes and infractions, ensure the uniform administration of military justice, and protect the fundamental rights of U.S. soldiers.

The ARVN had something similar: a book setting forth the law and rules of justice applicable to all soldiers. However, ARVN officers did not use it. They had their own version of military justice. Captain Beng was prosecutor, judge, and jury. Infractions were dealt with immediately and harshly. There were no hearings, deliberations, or appeals. Disobedience, insubordination, and not responding fast enough to orders were punished on the spot with a stern reproach, preceded or followed by a beating or a threat of one. Beatings were administered by Beng's bodyguard, with Beng joining in on occasion. The beatings were not intended to injure, but to hurt and humiliate. They were executed with an open hand, fist, or stick.

The bodyguard was thirty-eight years old with no family. He was tall and thin with a fierce, wide-eyed look. He had the ability to become enraged in a matter of seconds. I

thought the man was either a talented actor or totally deranged. He was with Beng every waking hour. His duties included supervision of the night guard at Beng's house and
acting as keeper of the jail. The soldiers feared him. He never
acknowledged my presence. He looked right through me.

Serious offenses such as thievery, rank insubordination, or
injuring another soldier in a fight were punished by jail time.
The jail was a four- by four- by four-foot cage made of bamboo poles placed two inches apart and laced together with
hemp strips. It was referred to as a "tiger cage." It was not
possible to stand up inside it. There was no protection from
sun or rain. It was located directly under a fifty-foot bamboo
lookout tower, which was manned by two soldiers twenty-
four hours a day. The moon provided good illumination most
nights, but on moonless nights the guards could not see
whether anyone was approaching the cage or the perimeter.

Punishment by confinement in the cage lasted up to five
days, but the soldier did not know how long his punishment
would last. I do not think Captain Beng knew either. It all depended on how he felt on any given day. It was uncommon to
have more than one person in the cage at a time, but at times
there were. Inmates were given water three times a day and
rice once a day. Once in the cage, the soldier was not let out
for any reason. Part of the soldier's punishment was to live in
his own filth. Beng's deranged bodyguard was in charge of
this sinister place. He taunted the inmates, poking them with
sticks. At night he could be heard threatening and insulting
the inmates. When Captain Beng decided that the punishment was over, family or friends came to take away the released soldier, who usually was unable to walk on his own.
That is the way it was—brutal. I would not have been surprised if Beng or his bodyguard was shot by one of their
own.

The Wild West Late one night, the district headquarters
ten miles distant from the cement plant was attacked. We

could hear shooting and explosions. The district chief radioed for help, and Captain Beng quickly organized a company-size relief force. The trucks and jeeps, including mine with me at the wheel and Plum and Pham on board, went barreling down the moonlit road, aware of the possibility of and fearful of an ambush. After an uneventful but hair-raising ride, we drove through the stockade gate, which was quickly closed behind us. After some consultation, it was decided to charge out the back gate in the direction of the attack, confront the Viet Cong, and kill them.

The gate was opened and about twenty soldiers charged into the darkness shooting their weapons. I was with them and found myself running on the joists of a bridge that the Viet Cong had tried to destroy but had succeeded only in blowing off the wooden cross planks. There was no return fire; the Viet Cong had left. The bridge would be repaired in the morning. We had tea with the post commander, then returned without incident to our camp. These great "victories" happened often and were headlines. Later, Captain Beng, directly, and Plum, obliquely, criticized me for joining in the charge out the gate. Captain Beng would have been criticized if I had been wounded, and Plum had to follow me, thus endangering himself.

Chopstick Proficient Breakfast in the delta was always noodle soup and hot peppers. The evening meal was a rice dish with fish, poultry, or pork. I ate both meals at a local restaurant.

I knew how to use chopsticks, but I was not proficient. The Vietnamese control chopsticks the way a point guard dribbles a basketball. They are so skilled that the sticks appear to be extensions of their fingers. Except during operations, the battalion officers shared a midday meal. Each officer had a rice bowl, a glass, chopsticks, and a deep porcelain spoon for soup. Rice, fish, poultry, pork, goat, vegetables, and *nuoc mam,* a fish sauce, were placed in the center of the table. On occasion, meat that I could not accurately identify was served. It was often probably rat, bat, or dog, all of which were sold in the markets. The poultry and pork were chopped up with a machete into bite-size pieces. Everyone helped himself. One selected what one wanted from the common dishes, held it briefly over the rice bowl, then ate it. The bowl was held below the lips, and rice was shoveled into the mouth with the chopsticks. One's chopsticks moved from the common serving dish to the rice bowl or directly to the mouth, then back to the common dish. It was a communal meal; the food as well as the germs were shared. It was a hygienist's nightmare. Several sets of chopsticks would vie for the choice bites. At times three sets of chopsticks would be rooting around in the same common bowl. The most skilled, those with the fastest sticks, would get the most and best food. Dueling chopsticks, so to speak. It was no place for a novice.

Fifteen minutes into my first meal with the battalion officers, I managed to get some rice and some vegetables, but not without dropping sticks and food. Captain Beng noticed my ineptness and announced that I was not getting enough food and should be helped. At every meal for the next couple of weeks, individual officers would, at their whim, place choice morsels in my rice bowl. I had to endure this humiliation until I became chopstick proficient. Much later I learned that the Vietnamese consider the practice of placing food in another's rice bowl an acceptable and courteous act.

No meal is complete without *nuoc mam,* which is made by tightly packing fish and brine in vats for several months. The mixture ferments and decomposes and in time produces a clear amber-brown sauce that is rich in proteins, vitamins, and minerals. The *nuoc mam* vats are tapped and the nutritious fish sauce is bottled for sale. Second-run, lower-quality *nuoc mam* is made by adding water to the vat after the original tap runs dry. What remains in the vat, the *mam,* is extracted for sale. The Vietnamese claim that their teeth are good because of the high calcium content of *nuoc mam*.

The meals were prepared by the cook, who was a soldier, and were served by the cook's wife. If the dishes were dirty or the meal was unsatisfactory, the cook would be beaten in turn by the officers, my protestations notwithstanding. Once a week the officers gave the cook money to buy food. His wife would collect the cash from each officer except me. One week I insisted on paying her. I did not want the Vietnamese officers paying for my meals any longer. It did not seem fair. When Captain Beng learned that food money had been collected from me, he beat the cook in front of me, the officers, and the cook's wife. He may have been merely disciplining the cook, or the wife, but more likely he was teaching me a lesson.

The Icemen The delta is at ten degrees north latitude; it is tropical and always hot. Beer, soda, and water were available with every meal. A glass with ice was placed next to each eating bowl. One of the early mysteries for me was where the ice came from. There was no refrigeration in the villages or at the cement plant, yet even the smallest, most remote village had ice available for drinks.

There was a curfew in the delta, and peasants were supposed to be in their homes after dark. Anyone afoot after curfew was presumed to be a Viet Cong and subject to being shot. Early one morning, while it was still dark, the ice mystery was solved for me when three flat-bottom sampans that were being poled through the water by thin men entered our ambush site alongside a canal. I was sure they were Cong, but as I released the safety on my weapon Plum put his hand on my arm and whispered, "Don't shoot. They are not VC." The soldiers were not surprised by this sampan convoy. The men came to the canal bank when hailed. Under a thatch cover on the bottom of each sampan was a large, rectangular piece of ice. I learned that the ice moved this way early every morning from the ice factories in the cities through the maze of canals to most delta villages. The cement plant ice came from the city of Ha Tien, which was eighteen miles distant. The icemen were lucky; no contraband was found on their person or under the ice. They were let go to continue with the ice delivery.

The Mistress Families made their way from camp to camp following their men, living together when they could. There were no barracks or family quarters for the battalion; soldiers and their loved ones found shelter where they could. At the cement plant, wives and children lived with the soldiers in grass shacks, caves, dugouts, and makeshift shelters under trucks. Most slept off the ground on hammocks or anywhere that gave them protection from the sun and rain. It was an unhealthy and demeaning way to raise a family. The families of officers lived in the cities to avoid the danger of traveling with the battalion and the primitive conditions.

Captain Beng's wife and family lived in Saigon. His mistress, a woman of indeterminate age, lived with him wherever the battalion was located. She was fond of makeup, high heels, and brightly colored clothes, in the field no less. One afternoon a message arrived by ARVN radio that the captain's wife was fifteen minutes away. She and their two young children were coming to the cement plant for a two-day visit. In haste the mistress made a noisy, theatrical departure from the captain's quarters with her belongings under her arms. Beng's bodyguard, in full voice, supervised her reluctant move. The wife returned to Saigon after two days and the mistress returned immediately. That night there was a commotion at the captain's quarters. He had been stabbed in the stomach by his mistress because he gave his wife her radio. I called in a helicopter to take him to Saigon for medical care and explained to the dispatcher that the captain had been wounded in a domestic incident. Captain Beng returned six weeks later, but without his mistress. She was in jail. His only comment to me about the incident was that the mistress was more dangerous than the Viet Cong, Viet Minh, Japanese, and French combined, because none of them had ever wounded him.

Monkey Man The Vietnamese are a handsome people who seem to always smile. They are polite and quick to help. The Vietnamese knowingly say, "Vietnam is a country of smiles with a thousand meanings." The people are small, thin, and muscular with oval eyes. They have a head of thick black hair but little body hair. By comparison, Caucasians have a lot of body hair. Complete strangers would run their hands over my face and arms, amazed by the bristle on my face and hair on my forearms. They felt it and commented to one another.

At the end of each day, the soldiers bathed in the canal at the cement plant. After the first couple of days of not washing, I overcame my modesty and washed in the canal. I looked up to see about fifty villagers watching me. One little boy was pointing at me and saying, *"Con khi, con khi,"* which I knew meant monkey. Captain Beng heard about the incident and had a thatch-enclosed shower built for me, just like his. The cook was responsible for keeping water in the tank, which was heated by the sun. Gravity did the rest. Knowing that a hot shower was available at the end of an operation helped me through those long, sweltering days.

The Privy The perimeter of the battalion compound was marked by a three-foot-high dirt wall. It was a defensive feature that provided shooting positions for ARVN soldiers in the event of a Viet Cong attack. Thirty yards beyond the perimeter, removed from the food preparation and living areas, sat the headquarters company outhouse. Like every other structure at the cement plant, the privy was made of bamboo poles and thatch. It had half sides for modesty and a roof for protection from the elements. The floor was fashioned from poles lashed together. Spaces between the poles allowed for a view below. The privy rested on a two-foot-high dirt foundation over a four- by four- by four-foot hole.

Day and night, rainy season and dry, people waited their turn. Those who could or would not wait found a place to their liking somewhere between the perimeter wall and the outhouse. There was no seat as with western toilets, just a hole cut in the bamboo floor. One did not sit, but instead squatted over the hole with feet on the poles while struggling to maintain balance. Balance was never so important. Finding a safe place for the feet was difficult, evidenced by the mistakes and carelessness of previous users. Swarms of flies rudely disturbed one's efforts. No water was available for hand washing. My old newspapers became toilet paper.

It was the tropics. It was warm and the outhouse was open to the air. Through the spaces in the bamboo flooring, the pit could be seen bubbling: nature at work. Wisps of stinking vapors wafted from below. My nose was a-twitching. I could hear the hissing and popping of the process as well as see the rats that had tunneled through the dirt foundation. Thousands of maggots were decomposing the organic matter. The pit throbbed from their efforts. Amidst the burping waste, leaves, grass, and bits of *The New York Times* appeared, disappeared, and reappeared again.

Every month a new hole was dug twenty feet away, and soldiers moved the privy to its new location using built-in carrying poles. The old hole was left uncovered for a week to get the job done, then filled in with dirt. Although environmentally correct, none of this was hygienic. Rats, flies, and dirty hands regularly traveled round-trip from the privy to the living and cooking areas. An advisor's role was to encourage improved sanitation. Given the situation, the only practical suggestion would have been to move the privy farther from the perimeter wall. I did not give that advice to Captain Beng. The sanitation instructors at Fort Bragg would have given Captain Beng and me a failing grade, but I think they would have understood the real-life situation: It was dangerous to move the outhouse farther outside the perimeter.

The "exposed" position, the balancing, the overstimulated senses, the rats below, and the danger of a Viet Cong strike made for anxious and fitful excursions to the privy, especially at night. I knew that the Viet Cong were out there and so did the soldiers. We carried our weapons on these trips, but to my amazement the Cong never attacked. Maybe it was because a downwind approach to the privy was the only concealed route available to them.

Coca-Cola By the early 1960s, American consumer goods had penetrated every part of the world. Even so I was surprised to find soap, toothpaste, shaving cream, cigarettes, film, and other products of American companies for sale in the villages. That most ubiquitous of American products, Coca-Cola, was available in the tiniest of hamlets, even in the most remote areas of the delta. Coca-Cola was sold in the traditional thick, pale green bottles with a vaguely feminine shape.

The peasants recycled everything. Empty containers had value, and Coke bottles had many uses other than just drink containers. Gasoline for motorbikes and motorized cyclos was sold by the Coke bottle measure. No caps, just cloth rags as stoppers. Men played a gambling game in which the spin of the bottle played a part. Fishermen used the bottles as weights to keep their nets down. Broken Coke bottles were embedded atop the walls surrounding the homes of the wealthy. Very egalitarian, those bottles.

It seemed that all Vietnamese men smoked cigarettes, certainly all ARVN soldiers. Mostly it was in the usual fashion, with cigarette pressed between fingers to lips. Other times the men inhaled through a hollow-fisted hand, with the cigarette held between pinky and adjacent finger. Bamboo was crafted to create ingenious smoking devices and was added to Coca-Cola bottles to make water pipes. The bottle was repeatedly tapped at the "bustline" with a pointed stone. Eventually, glass chip by glass chip, a hole was forced through to the interior and a bamboo tube was inserted down to the bottom of the bottle. A cigarette or loose tobacco was wedged in the exterior end of the bamboo, then about two inches of water was placed in the bottle. When the soldier lit the tobacco and inhaled through the top of the bottle, the smoke drawn into his lungs had been cooled by having passed through the water in the bottle. The rankness of Vietnamese tobacco justified all that effort.

I didn't spend much time with the Frenchmen who managed the construction of the cement plant. They were older, in their forties, and we didn't have a common language or background. They did not speak Vietnamese or English, and I did not speak French. I had one dinner with them at their concrete and stone house, the only such structure for miles around. Servants prepared the meal and placed food, beer, and soft drinks at the table, which was set with knives, forks, spoons, cloth napkins, and matching dishes. A touch of home. So civilized. We toasted Kennedy and de Gaulle and tried to make ourselves understood. As the meal was ending, three peasant women arrived and were seated away from the table on chairs against the wall. They were working girls rented by the Frenchmen for the evening. The women spoke among themselves about the food left on the table and the hairy men. They giggled. One of the Frenchmen became angry because he couldn't understand the women and shouted at them to shut up. *"Fermez les bouches,"* he said, and they did for a while. But when they resumed talking and laughing, he rushed at one of the women, pulled off her black pajama pants, and sodomized her with a Coke bottle. She was compliant but far from happy. She and her family needed the money. Two of the Frenchmen thought it was funny; the third objected, as did I. I never imagined the possibility of such depravity. The evening was over for me. I left. The women remained. The ability to bear humiliation is in direct proportion to one's needs and status. One result of colonialism is the humiliation of the subjected, and eventually the degradation of the colonists.

A Three-Day Pass Captain Beng did not speak English, but on occasion he surprised me with an English expression. At one officers' meal he rattled his chopsticks for silence, looked at me, and in perfect English said "three-day pass." In the U.S. Army this means a three-day excused absence. He told those at the table that we were going to an island in the Gulf of Siam for a three-day vacation. He looked at me and said "beach." He must have consulted a Vietnamese-English dictionary to impress me; it was flattering.

The Gulf of Siam was a five-minute truck ride from the cement plant. Thirty soldiers, the battalion officers, wives, and children were loaded onto three fishing boats. We motored four miles into the Gulf to a small island, at one time an active coconut plantation. The French had abandoned it, leaving the coconut trees, a main house, and a long, single-story beach cottage with rooms facing a beautiful sandy beach.

We ate rice, bananas, coconuts, and fish. Several times Captain Beng took the officers "fishing." The boat was maneuvered over a reef and he dropped concussion grenades into the water. Thirty to forty fish of different sizes, shapes, and colors floated to the surface, belly up. He did not let anyone else do it. He was the fisherman; he was in charge. The fish were barbecued on the beach in banana leaves; the children played their games, and the soldiers played soccer. It was a great and memorable time.

In the afternoon of the second day, there was heavy radio traffic between Captain Beng and the lieutenant left in charge of the four hundred–plus soldiers back at the cement plant. The regimental commander was looking for Beng, and the loyal lieutenant was shielding his captain. He told the commander that Beng was looking for Viet Cong near the Gulf of Siam. I learned that the good Captain Beng had separated his officers from their men and taken the battalion leadership on vacation to an island four miles out to sea without getting permission from and without telling his superiors. It was his battalion and he had decided to take a three-day pass. A Viet Cong attack at the cement plant under those circumstances would have been disastrous. Either he had great faith and trust in the battalion's noncommissioned officers left at the cement plant, or he did not think an attack was possible, or he just threw caution to the winds for three days at the beach. He would certainly have been relieved of his command and probably court-martialed had he been in the U.S. Army. He was running with scissors, and I was his advisor. The return trip was uneventful. If he suffered any repercussions, I was not aware of them.

The Errant Cleric The South Vietnamese government had to contend with armed religious groups such as the Cao Dai as well as with the Viet Cong, thus making their pursuit of the Viet Cong more difficult. Caodaism is sometimes referred to as the Triple Religion, because its tenets incorporate parts of the teachings of Confucianism, Buddhism, and Taoism. It calls itself the Third Alliance Between God and Man and has adopted the Catholic hierarchy; it has priests, cardinals, and a pope.

One morning Pham and Plum came running to me, saying that we were going on an operation. We jumped in the jeep, and at the rally point found Captain Beng and three trucks loaded with armed troops. "What's happening? Where are we going and why?" I asked. Captain Beng replied rapidly, either because he was in a hurry or perhaps because I was bothering him and he wanted to make it difficult for me to understand, in which case he succeeded. Immediately, he sped away. We followed him down dusty roads and through small towns. Plum, always alert, sat beside me. Pham, as usual, was resentful that he, the Vietnamese, had to sit in the back while Plum, the *moi*, sat in the front. During the fifteen-mile ride, I tried to make sense of Captain Beng's response to my plea for information. He had said, "We are going to get a bad priest, a bad Cao Dai priest." I had come to fight the Viet Cong, not shoot up the Triple Religion. I wondered what the bad priest had done. Why were we going to get him? Was there going to be a shoot-out? I could see the headlines back home, "Lieutenant Dockery killed by priest" or, worse, "Lieutenant Dockery given medal for killing priest."

The province chief and his soldiers were waiting for us in a town along the way. Five minutes later, the combined force of a hundred soldiers stopped on the main road in front of a Cao Dai temple. The soldiers deployed. The province chief and Captain Beng were met by the priest in front of the temple. No Cao Dai soldiers were in sight, but people were converging on the temple from all directions. The priest was calm and composed, even conciliatory. The ARVN officers postured, lectured, and harangued in deep, angry voices. The crowd now outnumbered the soldiers, but no weapons were visible in the crowd.

I learned that earlier that day, the Cao Dai priest and his followers directly challenged the South Vietnamese government by making each vehicle that used the road in front of the temple pay a toll. Armed Cao Dai soldiers had collected tolls and given the money to the priest. The province chief wanted to take the priest for "questioning," but the priest said he was Cao Dai and his people would not let him go. "Besides," he said, "the money is for charity, not for guns." I noted that he did not say that he would not go, which would have been a direct challenge to the province chief. The stand-off ended with the province chief, somewhat mollified, telling the priest not to do it again. The priest was silent. He promised nothing. We drove off at the same breakneck speed that had brought us there. The province chief saved many lives that day because the Cao Dai crowd was not going to let him take away the priest without a fight.

Diplomacy While South Vietnam was fighting the Viet Cong, it also had to placate and subdue the Buddhists, Cao Dai, and Hoa Hao. In addition, South Vietnam's borders with Laos, North Vietnam, and Cambodia had to be defended. The mountainous border with North Vietnam, separated by the Ben Hai River at the seventeenth parallel and known as the DMZ (Demilitarized Zone), was fortified, and crack military units opposed one another. Laos was not a concern. It was weak politically, economically, and militarily. It had no territorial claims on Vietnam. Not so Cambodia, the land of the Khmer people and magnificent Angkor Wat and other ancient religious centers.

Cambodians and Vietnamese have a long-standing and intense dislike for one another based on several hundred years of intermittent warfare and territorial claims. Over time Vietnam was successful in acquiring disputed territory in the delta and incorporating it into Vietnam.

The Cambodian army was a ragtag collection of men and boys who were called soldiers. It was much smaller than the ARVN and, in terms of equipment, training, and leadership, much inferior. Cambodian troops could not win in a battle with the ARVN, nor could they defend against the Viet Cong and North Vietnamese soldiers who used the Cambodian side of the border as a sanctuary.

Although the ARVN was the superior army, Diem's strategy was to avoid conflict with Cambodia while trying to defeat the Viet Cong. The border was nineteen miles northwest of the cement plant and, except at designated crossing points, was not marked or fortified. Frequently we conducted operations within that nineteen-mile zone in order to interdict Viet Cong supplies coming into Vietnam from the most southern terminus of the Ho Chi Minh Trail. Equally important, the battalion sought to prevent the Viet Cong from crossing into

Cambodia to recuperate and resupply after attacks in the delta. The ARVN and advisors were strictly forbidden from violating the border. A Cambodian response was unlikely, but an ARVN operation in Cambodia would have created an unwanted international incident. The Viet Cong knew that the ARVN would not cross the border and planned their attacks and escape routes accordingly.

Captain Beng was not allowed to take the battalion within three hundred yards of the border. If during an operation we approached the border, he frequently checked our position on the map and even consulted with me and his officers to see whether we agreed with him. Amidst much talking, guessing, and pointing, we always came to a consensus. But given the fact that the border was unmarked and the uncertainty of knowing exactly where the battalion was located when it was on the move and when everything around looked the same, none of us was ever sure.

One morning a hundred soldiers left the cement plant by truck. We were going to the frontier post on the only road within miles connecting the countries. Captain Beng told me there was a problem with the Cambodians. An incident had occurred at the frontier and we were being sent to deal with it. Shots had been fired and people killed. The incident concerned Cambodian complicity in smuggled goods, unpaid custom duties, and, I later learned, the province chief's surcharge. It was a matter of sovereignty and corruption and, I later learned, the province chief's unpaid surcharge.

The frontier post, located just east of Ha Tien, was fortified and barricaded on both sides. A road barrier would be moved when each side was satisfied with the paperwork and payments required to allow the crossings of people and goods. As we approached the border, I saw Cambodian soldiers in defensive positions, guns visible from fortifications, and an ancient French armored car fifty yards to their rear. Bodies lay close together on either side of the open barrier.

They had not been moved. The situation was grim. I was sure there would be more shooting.

The trucks stopped a hundred yards from the barrier, and the Vietnamese soldiers moved to positions facing the Cambodians. Under the Cambodians' watchful eyes, our machine guns and mortars were trained on them. We far outnumbered and outgunned them and they knew it. A truce was hastily arranged, and Captain Beng and his Cambodian counterpart met near the bodies. They postured, accused, discussed, and negotiated. Captain Beng came back to the ARVN position to confer by radio with the province chief, who thought the Cambodians would be more agreeable if the American advisor showed himself to them. Although this was not part of my job description, I broke cover and walked from place to place. Afterward Captain Beng returned to the border and threatened an attack if the custom duties and surcharge were not immediately paid. I had been sent to Vietnam to help the South Vietnamese government protect itself from communism, not help the province chief collect a bribe. Although initially my mission blinded me to this reality, over time it became obvious that many senior Vietnamese, government and military, were using Americans to further their own interests. I came to understand from this and other experiences that Americans did not understand what was happening in that society.

Eventually money was paid by the Cambodians, blame was allocated, and bodies were recovered. The Vietnamese soldiers got on the trucks and drove away. Except for the initial shots, none was fired by either side that day. The ARVN displayed its force and that was enough. Intimidation, diplomacy, and self-preservation prevailed. If only it had been that easy with the Viet Cong. The incident would, however, be stored in the collective memory of those involved and serve to reinforce the mutual animosity and justify retribution in the future.

Six

DELTA LIFE

*I say that all society is founded on the death of men.
Certainly the romance of the past is.*
—OLIVER WENDELL HOLMES

The Delta Tibet is the headwater of the 2,800-mile-long Mekong River, which flows through China, Myanmar, Thailand, Laos, Cambodia, and Vietnam. The Vietnamese call it *Cuu Long,* the River of Nine Dragons, because of the maze of tributaries, which flow through the delta into the South China Sea. The delta, which covers 16,000 square miles, was created by the Mekong over countless eons by deposits of fertile alluvium.

The Vietnamese in the south refer to the Mekong Delta as the heart of Vietnam. The delta is flat, fertile, and crisscrossed by hundreds of interconnected rivers, streams, and canals. Roads join the cities and major towns. Isolated villages and hamlets sit astride the canals and frequently are connected by footpaths and single log bridges. The houses are made of bamboo and thatch, with dirt floors and no plumbing or electricity. Outhouses are built over the canals. One can see fish reaching above the water line to catch the falling feces. Water buffalo are kept in the house or in an attached paddock. Vegetables are grown on a frame of bamboo suspended over the canals. Fishing nets are placed over the canals on a frame attached to a support pole, balanced so the net drops into the water when a person steps onto the pole. After a short time, the person steps off the pole, the net rises

119

out of the water, and the fish are removed from the net. The waters teem with fish; no hooks or bait are necessary.

Rice Rice and its cultivation are central elements of Vietnamese life. Rice as a life-giving force is a recurring theme in Vietnamese literature and the arts. The discovery thousands of years ago of how to cultivate rice successfully allowed for the development and growth of the Vietnamese people and their culture. The two are intertwined. In the Vietnamese language, *an* means eat and *com* means rice. From ancient times, *an com* meant food or evening meal.

The Mekong Delta is one of the major rice bowls of Asia. The peasants work the land, which is lush, fertile, and productive. Rice farming is labor intensive. There are no machines. The farmer and his family, aided by a water buffalo, work long hours to produce two rice crops annually. The production cycle of rice sets the rhythm of life. In 1963, and for many years before, absentee landlords owned the land. The rice farmers were tenants. The landlords were said to be mostly ethnic Chinese and French. A portion of every rice harvest went to them.

The delta landscape is stunningly beautiful and serene. Dikes and vegetation-lined canals that stretch for miles separate large, rectangular rice paddies. Peasants, side by side, bent at the waist in rolled-up pants and wearing conical hats, cultivate the rice. Dry or rainy season, early morning to early evening, year-round they toil, they and the water buffalo. The backbreaking work of a rice farmer, unchanged for millennia, goes on in war and peace. Farmers were always in danger of being caught in a cross fire and from random artillery, mines, booby traps, and being arbitrarily conscripted into one or the other of the opposing forces.

Early rice is sown in June and July and harvested in November and December. The second rice crop is sown during August and September and harvested in February and March. Rice cultivation in the delta has several steps. The seeds are planted close together in a flooded nursery and after reaching six inches are separated and replanted one by one, four inches apart in a flooded field. The water provides support and nourishment to the rice plant. The water is moved from canal to paddy and from field to field, as needed, by bucket or by the use of gravity, dikes, and ancient ingenious hand- and foot-powered devices.

After the harvest the farmer threshes the rice from the plant, dries it, packs it into sacks, and transports it to the middleman, who pays the farmer what he says is the market value. Until 1975 ethnic Chinese merchants controlled the rice trade and were resented by the Vietnamese farmers, who believed that the price paid for the rice was less than market value. Given human nature and the control the merchants had, they probably did not pay a fair price for the rice. Over time this resentment turned into seething bitterness and indignation and explained in part why the Vietnamese treated the ethnic Chinese so harshly after 1975.

It was a bad sign when the battalion had to cross a rice field in which there were no water buffalo or laboring peasants. It was unusual, and the likelihood of taking fire as we crossed was higher than if the paddy was being worked. The peasants knew where the Viet Cong were and they didn't want to get caught in the line of fire, so they hid when the Viet Cong and ARVN were near each other. When a firefight began as we crossed a paddy being farmed, the farmer would try to lead the water buffalo to safety by grabbing the tether attached to the metal ring in the water buffalo's nose. At times the beast, crazed by the noise of guns, would break free of the farmer and run this way and that in the field, amidst the bullets, the farmer in pursuit of his prized and most valuable possession. Most times there was no harm to the beast or the farmer. The takeoff and flight of the parasite-eating birds that feasted on the backs of the buffalo added to the fantastic aspect of this tableau.

In the delta, because of the low, flat land and frequent flooding, the dead are buried above ground in concrete or clay vaults placed atop earthen mounds. Many of the burial vaults are located in the rice paddies. Some burial sites are elaborate with multiple coffins in good repair and tended to by the family members even though the coffins hold the remains of ancestors long gone. Some burial sites are neglected, with tropical vines covering the vaults and the crumbling concrete unrepaired. Pieces of paper upon which prayers have been written are attached to the vaults and flutter in the breeze. As the battalion walked past the burial vaults with weapons in hand and danger near, not surprisingly my thoughts focused on dying and death. But only in a metaphysical sense. Not my death. Just the concept. I was twenty-three.

Financial Advice Being alone in a foreign country and culture, under stressful conditions, affects one's sense of security and well-being. Advisors reacted to these circumstances in different ways. While driving through a village I had not previously visited, I saw a jeep parked in front of a typical local restaurant with a dirt floor and a roof and sides of thatch. Thinking the parked jeep might be a sign of good food, I went in. I found an American, Captain Smith, sitting there alone. He was the district advisor, and I was in his district. He was a big fellow, a black man with a prominent Adam's apple, and quite gregarious. He had not spoken with an American in six weeks and wanted to talk. He asked me to join him for lunch. He had a lot to say, on many subjects. He talked about the frustration of dealing with his Vietnamese counterpart. I was informed about his current financial position and his plans for retirement, which would be in two years and during which he would be financially secure because he had invested in mutual funds. He advised me to put money in mutual funds because that would reduce risk. His retirement dream was to raise horses and muck out stalls. He told me about his three children and his prior assignments. He talked and talked and talked. Captain Smith also explained that the local people had never seen a black man and they insisted on pinching and touching his skin. That, and the staring, he found unnerving. He had been alone with the Vietnamese for too long and was anxious and ready to return home. I did not know whether he was a financial wizard, but I was sure he was a good man who just wanted to get out of there. It was time for him to leave Vietnam and return to the United States.

Wet and Dry Seasons There is no cold season in the delta. It is always hot, but there are extremes of heat and humidity. There is a monsoon season and a dry season. Schoolbooks provide descriptions of monsoons, and I had read about and studied them. I knew about monsoons in theory, but nothing prepared me for the May to November Vietnam monsoon of 1963.

The monsoon begins by raining once or twice a week for two to three weeks. Gradually the rains increase to every day and finally to all day and night of every day. In the middle of the monsoon, it rains nearly nonstop for three weeks; then, over the course of eight weeks, it gradually stops. The soil can absorb only so much water. The canals and rivers can drain only so much water. The houses are built on dirt platforms or stilts and thus are dry inside, but outdoors the water and mud are ankle deep. Military operations were conducted during the rains. I was never really dry or clean during the monsoon season. I was alternately wet, steamed when the sun broke through, dripping with sweat from walking through rice paddies and on canal banks, and drenched again when the rains began anew. I developed rashes, sores, and skin infections. Small scratches, which became open sores, healed slowly and were a constant irritant.

In hot, humid climates, fungal infections of the skin are common. Excessive sweating and frequent immersion in canal and paddy water caused softening of the skin. Areas such as the groin, armpit, and feet are ideally suited for the growth of the tiny, plantlike germs that caused this condition. I suffered from a groin fungal infection the entire time I was with the battalion. It would clear up when I was dry but come right back when I was wet. It was chronic; nothing would cure it, and it was painful. Everyone welcomed the end of the monsoon season.

Just as the monsoon season sets the rhythm for part of the year, so too does the dry season for the other part. The dry season (November to May) begins at the end of the monsoon season. Gradually the rains fade away and the waters subside. There is no rain for four months. The rice paddies dry up and the relentless sun bakes the land. As the battalion walked mile after mile through the delta provinces in the dry season, each step kicked up dust, the aggregate of which hovered around and slightly above the battalion as it moved to its objective. Some of the dust rested in the throats of the soldiers; the remainder hung above the battalion, where it served the enemy by marking our location. Despite the protection offered by a wide-brimmed bush hat, my face was sunburned and my lips were dry and cracked. My fatigues, wet with sweat and dirty with dust, stuck to my body. I drank water to clear the dust from my mouth, quench my thirst, and replenish the water lost through sweat. Soldiers toppled from the heat. Clammy skin and vomiting signaled heatstroke. Everyone welcomed the end of the dry season.

A Smell Not Too Good The monsoon rains affected everyone adversely, not only Americans to whom the monsoons were a new experience, but also the Vietnamese. Even though the monsoons came yearly and were necessary for the rice crop, ARVN soldiers and villagers tolerated them no better than Americans. The rains affected all aspects of life. Everything was soaked and mildewed. Mrs. Hien's well-written and credible explanation of why she had a problem returning fresh, clean uniforms to the American officers at Can Tho is an example of how the rainy season made daily life difficult. Note also Mrs. Hien's shrewd comeback in the fifth paragraph.

THE MRS. HIEN LAUNDRY   Can Tho 26 June 1963
(For U.S. Mil. Pers. Only)

Dear Sirs:

We have the honour of writing you this letter to expose you of the following:

First, we would like to explain to you about: "sometime laundry had a smell not too good." That was something that grieved us not a little. As you know it is rainy season at the present time in Vietnam and all fatigue suits as well as white shirts must be starched while there is no sun, sometime one week, two weeks or more, so it is very difficult to get away from a "smell not too good" in the fatigue suits, etc. . . . and you don't know how much trouble and pain we have in this dirty season. However, we hope you will understand that we always try to do our best to give good service and we only wait for your good wishes that are your understanding and satisfaction.

You are Guests of our Country and we respect very much and we are very happy to serve you with all our enthusiasm but unluckily if sometime we commit a mistake, that was not our intention, we sincerely beg your pardon, please don't be angry with us but please let us know, so we can correct it, we will be very grateful for your generosity. We also promise to make progress every day to please you, our very amiable and respectable Customers.

As many times we have informed you that our Laundry men don't speak English, so a note is necessary to be sent (with your dirty laundry) when there is something that concerns the laundry service, it will surely be done.

We would also like to ask you to pay your laundry bills no later than the 2nd of each month, so that we can pay our Helpers (15 men) on the 1st. Many months before, our Helpers got pay too late, on the 6th or the 7th, therefore, as they said, they have found a lot of problems in their living.

Please receive here our best regard.

Thank you very much. May God Bless you.

Truly Yours:
Mrs. HIEN

Potable Water Miletus, a Greek philosopher, was thinking of survival when he said, "The first of things is water." Water requirements of the human body vary with air temperature and amount of exercise. At high temperatures, evaporation of sweat is the only means of cooling the body, and large amounts of water are lost. This water must be replaced in order to maintain one's level of activity and health. If water deprivation occurs, in a relatively short time the body temperature will rise and heat exhaustion will occur. When water is lost through perspiration, vital body salt is also lost. I took salt tablets when I was on an operation, but finding safe drinking water was not always possible.

Safe drinking water is a given in the United States. In Vietnam, potable water was almost never available because of poor sanitary conditions. Except for the cities there was no indoor plumbing, and treatment facilities for city water was either nonexistent or primitive. Canals were used as toilets and to wash in. The paddies were fetid because they were fertilized with human and animal waste. Few villages in the delta had wells, because they were at or below sea level; in the small number of villages that had wells, the water during the dry seasons was brackish. In the rainy season, the standing water quickly became contaminated, teeming with disease-bearing organisms.

The villagers obtained fresh water by collecting rainwater in large clay pots placed under the roofline of their houses. The four-foot-high, bulbous-shaped pots had lids of wood through which a collecting pipe entered from the roof. Although not appreciated by the villagers, I and every soldier in the battalion filled our canteens with fresh water from the clay pots whenever possible. Otherwise, I filled my canteen from whatever water was available and, for the first month, added purification tablets that made the water safe to drink, although it left a chemical aftertaste. I soon ran out of tablets and was unable to get an immediate resupply. When I realized that the battalion cook used unsterilized water from the canal with which to cook and wash dishes and his hands, and the water used to make ice served with the beer at every meal was untreated, I stopped worrying about the purification tablets. The canteen water tasted a lot better without them. To drink four quarts of water a day when on an operation was not unusual. It was necessary. Salt tablets and plenty of water were needed to prevent the nausea, blurred vision, and dry, clammy skin associated with heat prostration.

The water was always warm and suspect. When available, coconut milk was a welcome alternative. A soldier would either shoot coconuts out of a tree or scamper up a tree and knock them to the ground. Another soldier, skillfully using a machete, would crack open the coconut. Even under the noonday sun on the hottest day in the middle of the dry season, the milk of the coconut was cooler than the ambient temperature. However, almost everything is someone's property, and the villagers watched sullenly as their coconuts were taken.

Poverty The countryside was lush and the soil was rich. The high temperature and plentiful water allowed a year-round growing season. Poultry and pigs were in abundance, and fruit and vegetables were plentiful. Vietnam was the rice bowl of Asia. Neither substantial housing nor closets of clothing were required. It seemed like a paradise. How could anyone want for anything?

There were some very wealthy people in Vietnam. They lived in beautiful homes well tended by servants, their children were educated at the best universities, and the families traveled abroad. They owned land and were in commerce, the government, and the military. From time to time I saw men who exhibited their wealth in the traditional Chinese manner: being overweight or having long, untrimmed fingernails that curled under in grotesque circles. These men were obviously rich, because such a person would not be overweight or have long, unbroken nails if he had to do physical work.

In spite of the productive land and mild climate, many of the Vietnamese, whether from the country or the city, lived in abject, unrelenting poverty. Saigon and the other cities swarmed with crowds of unattended children who were orphaned or abandoned. They were beggars and thieves and relentless in their efforts.

The rice farmers and others in the countryside were tied to the land by their poverty. They had to feed their families and pay the landlords as well. The people worked hard; everyone labored, children and the aged too, often at tedious, repetitious, strenuous, and dangerous jobs. They worked for their next meal; there were no savings to fall back on. The reasons for this poverty were many, some unique to Vietnam and some not: absentee landlords and tenant farmers; a hundred years of colonial rule, and payment to France for the privilege; no mechanization and no industrialization; and forty years of war.

Beggars, rock breakers, wood gatherers, cyclo drivers, and other poor peasants were eager for alternatives. The poverty made it easier for the Viet Cong to advance their cause. The Viet Cong and their promises were an alternative to poverty.

The Rock Breakers Concrete was needed for the construction of the cement plant and other building projects. Stones were added to cement to make concrete, so the demand for stones supported a local industry of rock breakers. Families consisting of parents, children, and grandparents camped at granite outcroppings and broke big rocks into little rocks and little rocks into small stones. All day long they hit rocks with hammers until they had accumulated a small pile of stones in the desired size. After several days, when the piles were large enough, the stones were carried in cans balanced on a shoulder at either end of a bamboo pole to the nearest waterway for sale to a middleman, who would take the stones by sampan through the canals to the cement plant. If the stones were the right kind and size and the sale price was low enough, the owner of the sampan would buy them for resale to the builders of the cement plant. The rock breakers' ability to profit from their labor was at the mercy of the sampan owner, who held the high card in the price negotiations. The rock breakers purchased food for their children with the proceeds of the sales.

On operations, we encountered these poor souls who were making little rocks out of big ones. The rock breakers had meager accommodations, often only lean-tos covered with grass. There was no drinkable water, and no stores or schools nearby. These people were near the bottom of the social scale: above beggars but below cyclo drivers and wood gatherers. They lived without hope of improvement for their families and with little control over their daily lives or their future. They broke rocks for their food and struggled for their existence. They received no government protection or services and had no reason to support the government. They were too vulnerable to take sides against the Viet Cong.

The Wood Gatherers One of the memorable odors of

Vietnam is burning charcoal. Charcoal was the primary cooking fuel. Every house had a charcoal burner, a brazier generally big enough to hold two pots. The brazier was metal and rested, for safety, on three legs. Four legs wobbled if the legs or the surface were uneven. Vendors traveled the streets and pathways carrying hot coals in a brazier and food suspended at either end of a pole. The food was cooked to order on the spot for a customer. Assuming an average family of seven, one brazier per family, two hot meals per day, and a 1963 population of 18 million, there were probably 5 million cooking fires a day in South Vietnam. The odor of burning charcoal was everywhere. Curiously, given the wood and thatch building material and the millions of open charcoal fires every day, it was surprising how few house fires I saw.

Charcoal was an important component of the Vietnamese economy. In 1963, the manufacture, transportation, and sale of charcoal were second in importance only to commerce in rice. Mostly, charcoal production took place near wooded areas. Hot coals at the bottom of a rectangular pit were covered with green vegetation. Branches and small logs were placed on top, then covered with earth. Hours later, after the wood had been heated in the absence of oxygen, the earth was removed and the charcoal was ready for transportation by sampan to villages, remote and near. Baking had reduced the wood to the carbonaceous material known as charcoal.

Some charcoal-making facilities were substantial, ten or more pits per site. Some were just single pits in backyards. Whether large or small, the charcoal-making facilities needed wood. The wood gatherers worked in small crews. Every day men and women scoured the countryside, gathering, stacking, and carrying wood. It was carried high on the back, huge bundles tied to the shoulders and supported with a headband. The wood gatherers were paid by the bundle. Their job was physically demanding, dangerous, and low paying, and offered no opportunity for self-improvement.

On operations, we encountered the heavily burdened wood gatherers toting their loads from woodlands to the charcoal pits. They moved bent at the waist for balance. During the journey they stopped to rest standing upright, their loads leaning against trees or embankments. As we passed I wondered whether they had become Viet Cong yet. Even if they supported the government, fear of Viet Cong reprisal prevented them from providing useful information to the ARVN.

The Cyclo Drivers Cyclos were the most common form of transport in South Vietnamese cities. Although there were various kinds of vehicles, most cyclos were rickshaws consisting of a seat and three wheels, with the driver seated behind the passenger on a high bicycle seat. The passenger was protected from the elements by a canvas awning and sides. The driver pedaled people and cargo in all weather at all times for a negotiated fee of pennies per trip. It was a difficult job. The drivers labored long hours ferrying people to and fro. Many of the drivers did not own their cyclos but leased them by the day.

It was hard to judge the drivers' ages. They were all males with torn clothes, dirty feet in sandals, and lean, sinuous bodies. I used the cyclos in Saigon, but always with a feeling that I was somehow exploiting the drivers. I paid the negotiated price, but I was uncomfortable with the idea of a man of another race using his strength to haul me around so I could save my strength. It seemed wrong to this American.

Socially, driving a cyclo was considered one of the lowest jobs, suitable for only the poor and uneducated. It was believed by many that cyclo drivers were either Viet Cong or Viet Cong sympathizers.

Bamboo Rice cultivation requires strenuous labor. Not so bamboo. It grows wild the length and breadth of Vietnam, from the mountains in the north to the lowlands of the delta.

Stands of bamboo are found near every village and along every waterway in the delta.

Bamboo is classified as a grass, a woody grass. It grows in hollow sections separated by joints and, depending on the type of bamboo, can reach a height of forty feet and a circumference of eighteen inches.

Bamboo has many uses. The hollow sections are used as bowls and containers for food and water. Chopsticks are made from bamboo slivers. Young shoots are served as vegetables. Bamboo, when split, sharpened, fire hardened, and placed point up at the bottom of a grass-covered pit along a trail, wounded soldiers and civilians alike. Bamboo was also prepared this way as a defensive perimeter in six-foot-wide bands around government forts and strategic hamlets. Strong and able to support great weight, it is used to build houses, cages, privies, carts, and scaffolding for construction of multistory buildings.

Thickets of bamboo are difficult to traverse. The plants grow inches apart and provide perfect hiding places. Two feet into a bamboo stand makes one invisible from the path—a good ambush site. Wind causes bamboo to sway and make loud, cracking sounds. The first time I heard this noise, I mistook it for Viet Cong gunfire and threw myself to the ground, which was followed quickly by the laughter of all around me. Bamboo is resilient. Heavy wind and rain can knock a stand flat on the ground. Within days it rights itself and is as tall and straight as before.

It is not surprising that something so ubiquitous, useful, and resilient has come to symbolize virtuous qualities revered by the Vietnamese people. In the arts, bamboo represents strength, practicality, permanence, and resilience. The Vietnamese have endured thousands of years of successive conquests and in each case have thrown out the foreigners: the Chinese, French, Japanese, and Americans. The Vietnamese, like the bamboo that regains its height and strength after being knocked down, are strong and resilient.

The Market Every city and town had a meat and vegetable market. Refrigerated and packaged food was not available. Fresh food was harvested and sold daily. Dry season and wet season, the centrally located market was a gathering of farmers and middlemen at which vegetables, fruit, poultry, fish, and meat were sold at negotiated prices. The farmers arrived before dawn and set up their goods next to one another on tables or the ground. Generally small stalls of wood, grass, fabric, or tin were cobbled together, one next to the other and each individually constructed of its own materials and design.

The markets were a cultural shock. Some of the fruits and vegetables were unfamiliar to me. Live chickens, ducks, and pigeons were hung by their feet until selected by a customer. Then the fowl were butchered on the spot, plucked, cleaned, and wrapped in newspaper or large green leaves. Live fish and crustaceans were displayed in water-filled pots. They too were killed, gutted, and cleaned while the customer watched. Slabs of pork, beef, and goat lay uncovered on the tables. Rat, dog, and bat meat were also for sale.

Many of the vendors chewed betel nut, the seed of the betel palm fruit, and spat the juice on the ground. The nut, a mild narcotic, stains the teeth and lips a reddish black, making for interesting smiles. The Vietnamese claim that the dark stain is good for the teeth. I am not sure about that, but it looks ghoulish.

As the morning progressed at the market, the ground became slippery with saliva and the blood and entrails of butchered animals. Feathers, chicken and fish heads, scales, and intestines were underfoot. Great gobs of bloodred betel nut spittle were splattered about. Black flies covered the unprotected meat. Their hum and the shrill, singsong bargaining of the peasants filled the air. Rats appeared to feast on the garbage and were not disturbed. As the sun rose higher and the butchered remains accumulated, a stench filled the air. All the shopping was done by 1 P.M. and the vendors went back to their farms to work in the rice paddies. In the late afternoon, cleaners arrived to sweep up in preparation for the next morning. I did not have to go to the markets, but I knew that the food from the markets ended up in my bowl.

Another cultural difference, which I had to contend with and could not avoid, was the practice of people urinating wherever and whenever they wanted. At least in the cities, male and female would pee in the street. In the countryside they would not get off the path. One had to step around them, carefully, while they urinated. They never looked at anyone, and no one was supposed to look at them. They were modest, never exposing themselves. Because there were no bathrooms, the only alternative to the path was the flooded rice paddy. Because it wouldn't do to get Grandmother all muddy, the path became the toilet.

The Lieutenant Colonel Inspections and visits from senior U.S. officers stationed in Saigon were a disruption. On occasion, desk-bound officers with enough influence to get the use of a helicopter would land, hoping to go on an operation that, properly written up back in the comfort of their safe area, would reflect favorably on their careers. Late one morning a lieutenant colonel arrived by chopper and asked to go on an operation. I told him that none was scheduled that day. He insisted. I spoke to Captain Beng, who repeated that none was scheduled but he would check with his regimental commander. At 6 P.M., after the lieutenant colonel's request had, I'm sure, gone up the Vietnamese chain of command to Saigon and probably crossed over to the U.S. side and back, Captain Beng announced that there would be an operation that night. We all knew and resented the fact that the lieutenant colonel had made the battalion go on an operation for his benefit, to further his career.

The lieutenant colonel brought with him an automatic shotgun of which he was proud. It was his favorite. During the operation we received fire; we took cover squatting in the muck behind a paddy dike and returned the fire. The lieutenant colonel discharged his shotgun in the direction of the Viet Cong. The extraordinary barrel flash from the shotgun lit up our position and attracted more Viet Cong fire. I could feel the dike give as bullets struck the other side. The ARVN soldiers moved away because the lieutenant colonel was attracting enemy fire by pinpointing our position. He and his favorite shotgun endangered everyone. Mortar rounds landed behind us in the water. Water dampens the explosive effect of a mortar round, so the explosions were contained and no one was hurt. We were in the field most of the night and there were ARVN casualties. The officer's arrival caused Captain Beng considerable disruption, and he and I lost credibility because a senior U.S. officer did not know how to conduct himself in the field. I suspect, however, that the account of his actions that he reported to his superior was glowing and that his next efficiency report included a laudatory description of his leadership under fire.

Beer Can from Heaven Although the delta is flat, occasionally one sees a limestone extrusion several hundred feet tall. I called them improbable mountains. One morning, Captain Beng took me to see a shrine carved inside one of these mountains. He told me that the monk who cared for the shrine was crazy. That could have meant anything. The shrine consisted of three rooms, one on top of the other, connected by steps and tunnels, all chiseled out of the limestone. There were candles in the rooms and on the stairs. The monk, an elderly, bald man with a longish white beard, greeted us. As we entered the first room, he pointed at a wall and said he had killed and buried two Japanese soldiers there during the Japanese War, World War II. I wondered why he was telling me this story and whether it was a warning. The second room had an altar and a large Buddha, a statue too large to get in the door or up the stairs so it must have been made in the room. The monk said that the third and last room was the most important shrine of all. Upon entering the third room, he prostrated himself and prayed. On the altar was an empty beer can. The monk rose to explain that the can was holy because it came to earth from heaven on a rocket ship.

The Safe House Some things took a long time to accomplish and some never got done. Shortly after arriving at my battalion, I received a radio message telling me that in addition to my duties as an advisor, I was in charge of leasing, renovating, furnishing, and supplying a house in the city of Bac Lieu for use by transient Americans. It was to be a safe house for U.S. military and civilian use. At my earliest convenience I was to report to a Colonel Ted in Can Tho for details. Given the fact that there were plenty of officers in Can Tho with time on their hands and I was many miles away without radio communication of my own, I wondered about the priority of this project. Sitting across from Colonel Ted weeks later, I was informed that the army had been using the house in Bac Lieu for more than a year without a written lease because no one would identify the owner. Rent was paid monthly to a man who said he was the owner's agent. The agent would not name the owner of the house. Colonel Ted explained to me that the army had inherited the house from the CIA, that the situation was intolerable because using the house without a lease was against regulations, and that we were going to get to the bottom of it. He said "we."

The house did get renovated rather nicely, furnished adequately, and supplied generously. I acted as liaison, from afar, between and among the U.S. contracting officers in Saigon, Colonel Ted, and the Vietnamese contractors and suppliers. All this without a lease. No one ever found out who the owner was, but the agent kept collecting monthly rent. Was the owner the agent, the province chief, or the mayor, or was he a Vietnamese general or politician? Was the CIA the owner? Was the landlord a Viet Cong? Maybe the situation was not incomprehensible, and maybe Big Ted was just smart enough not to try too hard to figure it out.

I stayed at the house three times. It was located on a corner of the main street in the middle of the city. Houses abutted on each side; there was no yard. It was a three-bedroom town house with two bathrooms, a living room, and a dining room. It also had a delightful roof garden. Vietnamese soldiers on guard at the front door controlled guests allowed to spend the night, much to the anger of disappointed Americans who did not know the rules. No girls were allowed, because they might be Viet Cong. The first night I stayed there, a thirty-year-old American in civilian clothes appeared at the door and asked to spend the night. He was carrying a Swedish K machine gun. The civilian was CIA and was on his way back to the States. He did not want to talk about where he had been or what he had done. He wanted to talk about his problem. The Swedish submachine gun had been purchased from his predecessor for fifty dollars. It was not legal for him to take it home. I paid him fifty dollars for the gun and two cans of 9mm ammunition. Thereafter I felt a lot safer with my fully automatic Swedish K than I had with the army-issue semiautomatic M-2 carbine. I gave the gun to Captain Beng when I left the battalion.

The Ugly Americans Most Americans behaved themselves in Vietnam. They were courteous, civil, and sensitive, just like at home. But sometimes they were insulting and ugly, just like at home. During my last night at the safe house in Bac Lieu, the "ugly Americans" made an appearance. I heard shouting and raised voices. At the front door I found two middle-aged American men berating the guard, an ARVN private, in English. The Americans had brushed past the soldier and were encouraging two Vietnamese girls to do the same. The men had been partying and wanted to continue the party in the house. The soldier could not stop them; it was an American safe house. But he did stop the girls. I heard him tell the girls that he would shoot them if they tried to enter the house. That was his job. They believed him and would not come near the door.

I explained the house rule of no women to the Americans. They became belligerent. They said they were from the U.S. State Department and demanded entry for the four of them. Under most circumstances that would have been enough: The higher one's patrons, the higher one's privileges. But I did not want them in the house. They had insulted the guard and were an embarrassment to my country and me.

They postured and asked for my name and rank, and belittled me when I said I was a first lieutenant. I asked them for identification. They refused. I told them to "leave forthwith" and "depart the premises." The girls left with the Americans. As they departed they promised to report my behavior and crude language to my superiors. They did not, or if they did I never heard about it. I apologized to the soldier and thanked him. He said it was his job and thanked me for my help. These two guys were certainly "ugly Americans," but most of the Americans I came in contact with, military and civilian, acted as responsible representatives of the U.S. government.

Alcohol was not a problem in Vietnam, at least for the Vietnamese. However, it was not unusual to see Westerners making their way unsteadily through the streets of Saigon. I wrote home that, "When these people drink, which is infrequently, they do so temperately. Not at all like the Americans and the Frenchmen who drink to excess. The only public drunks are Westerners."

City Lights At times, advisors, no matter what their rank, did the wrong thing out of arrogance or sheer ignorance, or both. Their belief in their superiority and invincibility led to mistakes and embarrassing situations. Late one afternoon, a U.S. Air Force colonel arrived by jeep without escort at our base camp and insisted on a ride and escort down the coast to Rach Gia. Captain Beng said no, the roads were not safe at night, but he did arrange for two motorized sampans and ten soldiers to take the colonel by sea. I never found out where this character came from or who owned the jeep, which he gave to Captain Beng in exchange for the boat ride.

I went along out of a sense of concern for the colonel. It was dark when we got to the boats. The sampans had the eye of the Cao Dai religion painted on the bow. The colonel was pigheaded and insisted on operating the lead sampan. After half an hour, the soldiers discovered that the city lights the colonel thought he was headed for were the lights of a fishing fleet heading out into the Gulf of Siam. All ended well, though, and we arrived safely at Rach Gia, but late into the night.

Christmas Eve Mass Captain Beng, a Buddhist, sometimes amazed me by his thoughtfulness. On December 24, 1962, we were just concluding an operation somewhere in the delta. He asked me if I wanted to go to Christmas Eve Mass. "Yes," I said. He arranged for me and a dozen soldiers to take sampans down a nearby canal to the first road that crossed the canal. A truck was waiting there, and off we went for a half-hour drive followed by a fifteen-minute walk.

It was dark, and Mass had just begun when we arrived. The soldiers surrounded the bamboo and thatch church and I walked in. The people were all seated on the dirt floor. There was no electricity. The church was illuminated by candle lanterns made of paper. When the priest at the altar saw me standing at the rear, he asked me in French, "Why are you here?" When I explained in Vietnamese that I did not understand French but wanted to hear Mass, he sent a man outside who returned with a chair. The chair was placed at the front of the congregation. At the priest's insistence, I sat in the chair, my rifle on my knees. He asked me in front of the seated peasants if I wanted to confess my sins. I answered yes, but I didn't know the words; my Vietnamese was not good enough. What vexed my conscience? What didn't? He asked if I was sorry for my sins, and I said yes. Without further conversation, the priest gave me absolution.

I was able to follow the Mass because it was in Latin, but not the sermon, which contained many Vietnamese words I had not heard before. The songs were in Vietnamese. Sung as if by larks. A cappella. During the sermon, one of the lanterns caught fire. A man quickly appeared and placed a ladder against the bamboo rafters. He climbed up and extinguished the fire, and the Mass continued.

I was struck by the humility, piety, and dignity of my fellow worshippers. The Mass was moving for me. I asked God to help these people. I saw in them a basic, centered faith. They believed, period. No explanations seemed necessary. At that time, my faith needed explanations, reasons, and answers. Today, I do not need any.

Although the trip to the church was well planned and went like clockwork, no arrangements for the return trip had been made. We spent the night at the nearest village. It took most of the next day to locate the battalion. I often wonder whether I endangered this priest and his congregation by my visit.

Irish Nuns Somehow I became aware that Irish nuns were running an orphanage near our camp. Because my parents were born in Ireland, I wanted to visit these people. One morning I set off by truck with an escort of soldiers and a present for the nuns, a box of candy. The orphanage was one hour away, far off a dirt track. It consisted of a school and two houses. Children were playing near the school, but no nuns were in sight. I walked up to the largest house and was greeted at the door by two Vietnamese priests, one thin, almost skeletal, the other huge, obese. What followed was a fiasco. It may have been the only time I could not make myself understood, although I understood them. They insisted on talking to me in French, because the only Caucasians most Vietnamese had ever met were French. I did not know the Vietnamese words for "nun" or "holy lady" or "Irish lady." I said that the candy under my arm was for the Catholic *ba. Ba* means older woman.

Unfortunately it can also mean wife, depending on the context. My two-handed pantomime of a woman's anatomy did not help the situation. The big priest asked the nearest soldier what I wanted. The soldier answered that he did not know. The soldier was then told to tell me that they were Catholic priests and did not have wives. I realized that it was time to leave when the soldier explained to me in Vietnamese what the priest had told him in Vietnamese. It was frustrating for me but common for Vietnamese not to understand what I was saying until they were told by the people who were with me that I was talking Vietnamese. Then they would understand me. I presented the priests with the candy, but not before pointing at the school and the other house. I still wonder who got the candy. Perhaps there never were any nuns at the orphanage or they were away for the day. Maybe the children received the treat. On the other hand, the big priest looked as though he ate a lot of candy, and the thin priest looked as though he could use it.

Payday In order to limit the effect on the local economy of Americans spending dollars, an advisor received his pay in two parts: $100 U.S. in cash and the rest by check in dollars, which could be deposited by mail in a U.S. bank or cashed in Vietnam for piasters (also called *dong*), the local currency, at the official rate of 73 piasters to the dollar. (Today, after decades of failed communist policies and of U.S.-led economic sanctions, the exchange rate is about 16,000 piasters to the dollar.) The black-market rate, which in November 1962 was 92 piasters to the dollar, was available everywhere. My November 1962 letter home showed my cynicism about the South Vietnamese government's unwillingness to control the currency black market:

> This buying and selling of dollars doesn't harm the U.S. at all, but it is detrimental to the Vietnamese economy. The Vietnamese Government makes no effort to curb the black market because the government officials hoard the dollars. That's right, most of the Greenbacks filter back to several highly placed government officials. These people are making get-away kits in anticipation of a collapse of the present government.

At the beginning of the month, a pay officer flew from city to city to pay the advisors. They did not come to the cement plant where I was stationed and, except for one occasion when I was in Long Xuyen, I was not paid by the pay officer. My location was too remote or the battalion was in the field. Twice I received my pay envelope with my mail after signing a receipt brought by the helicopter pilot. Other times I collected back pay when I got to Saigon. It was forced savings. The Army Finance Corps was annoyed when I did not get paid on the first of the month because my checks piled up, causing paperwork for them.

On April 1, I was at a local restaurant in Long Xuyen with ten other advisors waiting for the pay plane. Two advisors were eating lunch; the rest of us were drinking coffee or beer. A Vietnamese businessman with a briefcase entered and sat at a nearby table. He ordered coffee. Shortly thereafter we heard the noise of the plane's engines. Those of us not eating quickly paid and rushed to our jeeps for the short drive to the airfield. The businessman finished his coffee, paid his bill, and left, leaving the briefcase on the floor next to his table. The two advisors who stayed to finish their meal were injured when the briefcase exploded. Of course it was stupid for advisors to gather in this same restaurant at the same time on the first of each month. The Viet Cong had probably been planning this operation for months.

A Bad Idea Is Hard to Kill In order to win the war, the government of South Vietnam initiated military action against the Viet Cong and took actions to win the support of the people. Military action consisted of operations against known and suspected Viet Cong units and efforts to close the borders. Identification cards, checkpoints, and curfews were used to control the population and restrict Viet Cong movement. Civic action programs were undertaken, including helping with the rice harvest; economic aid; building and maintaining bridges, canals, wells, and other infrastructure projects; free medical programs; and building strategic hamlets. Land reform, although never successfully implemented, was recognized as necessary to win the support of the peasants. Although the strategic hamlet program did not address corruption or land reform and caused inconvenience only to peasants, the South Vietnamese government viewed it as the single most important step in gaining the support of the people. This program consisted of moving the peasants, with or without their consent, into government-fortified, -built, and -defended villages. The government, to discourage return, burned the home villages, which were near the peasants' rice paddies and graves of their ancestors. Hamlet leaders were elected with the intention of introducing democracy. In June 1963, the government claimed that 33 percent of the population was in strategic hamlets and there were 2,560 completed hamlets, with an additional 1,800 planned. The word "completed" must not translate well from English to Vietnamese. I saw few functioning strategic hamlets, and those were showcases. Most of those I saw were under construction or, in some cases, already abandoned.

The objective of the strategic hamlets was to provide protection to the peasants from Viet Cong influence and to cut off the Viet Cong from their support bases, denying them food, supplies, intelligence, and recruits. Hamlets were fortified with barbed wire, moats, bamboo fences, spike traps, booby traps, and guard towers. Armed militia protected them.

The program was ill conceived and insensitive and exploited by corrupt officials. It ignored the old Vietnamese proverb that "the power of the emperor comes only to the bamboo hedge of the village." The program was gross interference by higher authorities in village affairs. It did not work. The people resented leaving their homes, and Viet Cong agents infiltrating the hamlet militia and the leadership used this resentment to undermine the government and the hamlets. Another reason the program was unpopular was because the traditional village council, the *ban hoi te,* the wisest men in the village, and the *huong chu,* the village chief, were replaced, at America's insistence, by secret ballot. Although the secret ballot is one of the primary tools of democracy, it was an alien and unwanted concept in the conservative villages of the delta. They had a system for choosing their leaders that had worked for a thousand years and did not want to change to a foreign system. Village elders knew best, not the young, uninformed, and inexperienced who might be elected village leaders by other young, uninformed, and inexperienced voters. Additionally, the farmers had to walk considerable distances to farm their fields, their ancestors were now dishonored by abandonment, their homes burned, and the people removed from familiar surroundings. From the peasants' point of view, Viet Cong control, lectures, and propaganda were replaced by government control, lectures, and propaganda. None of this worked, and inhabitants of the hamlets fled at the first opportunity and rebuilt their homes. This program, which was strongly promoted and paid for by the United States, was expensive in terms of effort, money, and, most importantly, loss of goodwill. Eventually it was abandoned.

The people did not trust the government and were suspicious of its incentives and policies. In February I wrote home about a government attempt to reduce meat consumption: "Today I found out that the government passed a law forbidding people to eat meat on Friday. There's no punishment allotted for an offender, but anyone caught selling meat on a Friday can be imprisoned. Remember at least 90% of the population isn't Catholic. I only hope the Buddhists have a forgiving nature when they control the government."

The South Vietnamese government introduced the ban on Friday meat consumption as a wartime measure to stretch the food supply. If the government had picked some other day of the week, it probably would have been accepted, but the Buddhists and those of other religions knew that the Catholics were prohibited under pain of sin from eating meat on Fridays. Non-Catholics thought they were being forced to adhere to a Catholic practice, so they refused to obey the ban. There was too much mistrust of Diem and his government of Catholics. The law was repealed. In retrospect it seemed like a reasonable government measure in wartime. If meat had been prohibited on a day other than a Friday, Catholics would have had two meatless days a week.

Propaganda Films Guerrilla wars are fought on many levels. The side the people are on eventually wins. The successful use of propaganda is a proven way to convince the people to join your side. The Viet Cong conveyed their message at compulsory village meetings where communist cadres "instructed" the people. The South Vietnamese government controlled the radio and press. The content was censored and the government message was printed and broadcast. Every city and town also broadcast government propaganda from strategically placed loudspeakers. From time to time throughout the day, the loudspeakers would blare patriotic songs and strident messages from government leaders. The government also had a program to reach villages and hamlets that had no electricity. The effort expended by the government to bring its message of good government to the rural populace was truly extraordinary and indicative of the importance attributed to it. I witnessed only two of these events and will always remember them, not for the ideological content or the "professional" production but for the theatrics and the childlike reaction of the villagers.

During the dry season the government sent propaganda units into the countryside. They showed films of government leaders explaining the overwhelming success of various programs that were of great benefit to the peasants. These units traveled by truck escorted by truckloads of soldiers. The trucks would arrive at a village unannounced in the late afternoon and set up a movie screen, projector, and generator. The Viet Cong would not have time to organize an attack because the screenings were not scheduled in advance.

The word was then sent to the nearby villages and hamlets that a government film would be shown at dark and everyone was invited. Most Vietnamese had never seen a movie but had heard of them. By dark hundreds of noisy, chattering men, women, and children were seated on the dirt in front of the screen. The generator was started and lights lit the area.

At the appointed time the lights were dimmed and the projector was started. The light from the projector lit the screen and bathed the area with a wide beam of bright light. To much excitement, heads and hands of those not yet seated appeared in silhouette on the screen. Insects of different sizes and shapes darted into the beam and cast their shadow onto the screen. Bats chased flying bugs. Dogs barked, ran, and fought.

The movie began with messages from President Diem and other government officials. On the screen, thin men in white shirts and black ties displayed captured Viet Cong, plump pigs, and new water pumps. After thirty minutes of government propaganda, cartoons were shown. In the middle of nowhere, somewhere in the Mekong Delta, I watched Donald Duck, Mickey Mouse, and the Road Runner with hundreds of rural Vietnamese. They were the same cartoons I had seen as a child. Adults and children laughed and jumped around, and insects crashed into the screen. The film broke from time to time but was always promptly repaired.

The second time I saw the propaganda units in action, cartoons were not shown. Instead, after the filmed speeches the projector was turned off and a ragged trio of black bears was put through their paces. Under lights they rode bicycles, wrestled, and did somersaults. I don't know whether the films were successful in spreading the government's message, but they were wonderful entertainment for the villagers and me.

Monkey Bridges Most of the Vietnamese soldiers came from the countryside and therefore instinctively understood things such as water buffalo, rice cultivation, fire ants, and how to cross monkey bridges, the single log bridges that spanned the canals. In the course of a day's pursuit of the Viet Cong, it was necessary to cross numerous canals, sometimes by wading but most often across one of these bridges. They were usually located near villages. The canals were of different widths and depths. The procedure was to wade across the shallow canals, keeping your weapon and other treasured items held high. Deep canals were bridged by bamboo poles lashed together with grass ropes. For canals that were deep and wide, poles were secured end to end. The bridges were high to allow for boat traffic. Bridges shorter than ten feet had no railings. Longer bridges had railings on one side secured to, but slanting away from, the bridge. These bridges, long or short, were ingenious, Rube Goldberg–like devices. They were chancy and intimidating and always a challenge. Often they were slippery. The Vietnamese in twos and threes, placing one foot in front of the other, scampered across with only occasional falls. Not so with me and other Americans; we were big, unsure, and awkward on these bridges. We all had problems, especially in the rain. When my turn came to cross, groups of soldiers would form on either bank to watch me inch my way across, slowly sliding one foot behind the other. For their safety, I suppose, no one joined me on the bridge. Success was greeted with congratulatory shouts from the assembled crowd. Unsuccessful crossings elicited laughter and enthusiastic retrieval efforts. Every advisor I spoke with had trouble crossing the monkey bridges.

A March letter conveys my irritation at the Vietnamese soldiers' sense of humor:

> When I first began work with the soldiers I thought
> they were making fun of me because of the constant
> laughter but I soon realized this mirth was part of the
> soldiers' personality. They find humor in almost any
> situation. I've seen them laugh and joke when the Viet
> Cong are shooting at them. They think it's funny if
> someone is wounded or dead—I'm not kidding, I've seen
> them. Perhaps the funniest thing that can happen is for an
> American to trip and fall or break through one of their
> little footbridges and fall in the water—great joke.

Included in the envelope with my March 7 letter was the following clipping from the English-language *Times of Vietnam,* which I offered to my parents as further evidence of the Vietnamese macabre sense of humor:

LIGHTER SIDE

Tipped about an opium-smoking den down on Le Truc Street here, police raided the house in the night of March

3 and caught two persons in the act of smoking hard. One of the two, a Chinese resident, was so frightened upon seeing the police that he fell into unconsciousness. He died on the way to the hospital.

Another police raid occurred in the same night. The target was a house in the Ba Chieu area. Arrested were 38 teenage girls and boys. They were holding a secret dancing party.

Mrs. Nguyen Thi He, 60, of Go Noi hamlet, An Nhon Tay village, had a fatal dream one night last week. Members of her family said they found her dead in bed after hearing her shout for help against "pirates attacking the house."

Le Truc Street was in Cho Lon, the Chinese section of Saigon. Although illegal, opium-smoking dens operated openly in Cho Lon. The police, in return for protection money, allowed them. Graham Greene, in *The Quiet American,* provides a good description of the bamboo pipe, the sweet smell of burning opium, and its effect on the smoker.

The Italian Legionnaire France had soldiers in Vietnam from 1860 to 1954, when the Viet Minh defeated them. The French sued for peace and withdrew their soldiers to Algeria (their next colonial defeat). From time to time, I heard stories of French soldiers who had deserted to the Viet Minh or were taken prisoner and never returned and were supposedly living in delta villages. Until April 1963 I discounted these reports because I had been in Vietnam seven months, walked the delta, and not encountered any former French soldiers.

On April 25 the battalion spent the night in a delta village, where Captain Beng and I had dinner with a large Italian man who kept brushing back the few remaining strands of hair on his head. He introduced himself as Michel and told us he had deserted from the French Foreign Legion in 1953 because he did not want to kill Vietnamese for the French. Michel showed me his French military papers, his passport, and the last letter from his mother; all were tattered and yellowed. He produced a gold-colored medal given to him by the Viet Minh for courage. Michel had not been back to Italy and had no plans to go because he said he had no money and was fearful of being imprisoned if he did return. His Vietnamese wife prepared and served the meal while their four children scampered about.

Michel operated a small store out of their house from which he sold gum, cigarettes, rice, soft drinks, tea, coffee, cakes, ice, flashlight batteries, pencils, and other small items. Somehow this was enough to provide for his family. Michel said he was happy, and he seemed happy. I wondered how it affected a man to leave his family, country, and culture forever and make his way in a completely different culture and environment. I also wondered about his allegiance. Would he report our conversation to the Viet Cong later that night? Had they instructed him to invite us to dinner? Was he gathering intelligence for them? It was unlikely that he was just dumb and happy and unaware that he was endangering himself and his family by socializing with us. But he did strike me as a hopeless romantic, a poor soul stuck in a trap of his own making. I do not believe the rumors about U.S. soldiers who deserted or were captured and stayed in Vietnam after 1975 because I am unaware of any credible proof. However, my encounter with the Italian legionnaire does mean it is possible.

Chinese Medicine Chinese and western medicine existed side by side in Vietnam. Pharmacies dispensed herbal remedies made from ground-up organic and inorganic ingredients, but they also carried penicillin, antibiotics, and other western pharmaceuticals, all without prescription. Row upon row of potion-filled jars lined the shelves. The shop owner would recommend a medicine depending upon the ailment described. The battalion officers patronized these shops and so did I. Although I don't think the Chinese medicines cured anything, I always felt better after following the shop owner's advice.

One popular remedy for pain and headaches was similar to acupuncture in that it provided relief, but no one knew why. The practitioner would swab the interior of small glass teacups with alcohol. The alcohol was then lit, and as the cup was placed upside down on the part of the body that hurt, the flame was extinguished. The vacuum that was created drew the skin into the cup. The inverted cups, usually twelve of them, were left on the skin for ten minutes with the skin sucked into the cups. In fact, although the pain disappeared at the conclusion of the treatment, you were left for days with twelve half-dollar-size red welts on your body.

Another traditional pain cure marked the skin for days with red bruises. The skin that covered the part of the body that hurt was grasped between thumb and forefinger and firmly squeezed for fifteen minutes. Relief for sore throats, headaches, sore muscles, and stomach pains was sought in this manner. Until someone told me what caused the red welts I saw every day on people's faces and bodies, I thought they were evidence of some tropical skin disease.

The Chinese Problem In 1963 the population of Vietnam was 88 percent Vietnamese, 2 percent Chinese, 2 percent Cambodian, and 8 percent Montagnard and others. Several thousand French and Indian businessmen lived in the cities. Chinese businessmen, merchants, and landlords lived in the cities and towns and in most villages. The Chinese owned shops, factories, and rice paddies. They were the middlemen in the rice trade and controlled the transportation and price of rice. The Chinese were successful businessmen, industrious and wealthy, but even though their families had been in Vietnam for hundreds of years, many never learned to speak Vietnamese properly. For these reasons they were resented by the Vietnamese.

China and Vietnam have been traditional enemies for thousands of years. On several occasions in the distant past, China conquered Vietnam. Once, China ruled Vietnam for nine hundred years before being driven out. However, during the Vietnam War the Chinese provided arms and equipment to the North Vietnamese and allowed the passage of Soviet aid. The North Vietnamese could not have won without Chinese support. After the war, distant memories of mistreatment and subrogation were recalled and old resentments revived. As a result, official government policy forced approximately 200,000 Chinese out of the country. Their lands and businesses were confiscated, and those who remained were heavily taxed. They might have been treated differently if in the past they had paid fair value for the rice and learned how to speak Vietnamese correctly. I wrote my parents: "The Chinese are very much disliked by the Vietnamese. There are about 400,000 Chinese in the country. Most of them live in Cho Lon—the Chinatown of Saigon. They are an industrious people. Most of them are merchants and promoters."

On Exhibit It was a continuous challenge to deal with a people whose language and culture I understood in a limited way. I failed to see problems and cursed my own stupidity. Likewise, I came to understand that I was a mystery to them, not only a cultural mystery but a physical curiosity. The following excerpt from an October 1962 letter to my parents reveals what I mean: "They will walk up to you, grab your hand, and follow you around. I've had as many as thirty walking with me. They will touch your clothes, feel your skin, pull the hair on your arms, touch your boots."

Their curiosity and the touching were unnerving. It is not acceptable in our culture, and I would not put up with it in the States. I was always on watch, not able to relax anywhere outside of Saigon. I stood out. At five feet eleven, I was six inches taller than the average Vietnamese man. I was a Westerner. I was a target. Their attention intensified my concern for my personal safety. They were all around me. I was concerned that these people who were staring at me and feeling my body were going to shoot or stab me. At such times, I felt less secure than if I had been on a combat operation. Plum, my bodyguard, was with me only when I was on an operation. I would have liked him with me at all times, but it was not possible. Off duty, I wore the black pajamas worn by the peasants, always with a pistol on my belt or in a shoulder holster, sometimes under and sometimes over my shirt. I never could decide which gave me a better chance while walking in the towns and villages: show the pistol to keep away the Viet Cong or conceal it to surprise them. I was in a war zone, with my hand grasping my concealed gun, surrounded by a native crowd, some of whom were the enemy. Everyone was in danger, all of us.

Isolation I experienced constant uncertainty and an acute sense of isolation when I was with my battalion. I was isolated from my cultural and psychological supports. Friends and familiar architecture, language, food, sanitation, music, manners, and people with similar educational backgrounds were missing. Except for the pursuit of the Viet Cong and the desire to survive, I had nothing in common with the officers and men of the battalion. I had no buddies. Many advisors were unable to continue under the effects of having to be constantly alert and isolated. We were all different. Either I had strong psychological underpinnings or had none to be unbalanced, because the isolation did not appear to affect me at all. I was content in my isolation. I enjoyed it and thrived on it. The pressure of being under constant stress and danger invigorated me and heightened every experience. However, it was a constant source of irritation to know that my government had left me out in the field alone and without support to do a job that someone felt was important. There were times when I wondered whether anyone knew I was out there.

Most of us go through life uncertain, isolated, and alone, and only a few care when we are gone. All are busy with their own lives. Even though culturally I was isolated and disconnected from the Vietnamese, I learned about them and their country. I came to understand them and myself. By osmosis I took in the meaning of our shared experiences and circumstances. It was not an intellectual exercise; it was a subtle and gradual absorption of ideas, concepts, and values. I learned by listening, observing, and questioning. I came to understand, like, and respect the Vietnamese and their accomplishments, values, and culture. Isolation was a catalyst for my personal growth. Introspection followed isolation.

Many times as I trudged through endless stretches of rice paddies or lay on my canvas cot, I wondered what these people thought of me and other advisors. I was a physical and intellectual curiosity to them. They may have thought that the American advisors were naive, incapable, arrogant, and stupid, but I do not think so. I think what bothered them most was that they could not figure out why America was in Vietnam, just as a lot of Americans could not figure it out either. What motives did they attribute to us? Were they laughable? Just as the Vietnamese often baffled us, we were an enigma to them. We mystified them. A central question that confounded them was why we were willing to expend our lives and our treasure for them. They wondered, I am sure, whether America's hidden agenda was to rule Vietnam, as the French had done.

In spite of the uncertainty and isolation I experienced, I wrote my family that I liked what I was doing, and truly I did: "In spite of all this I'm enjoying my tour and am thinking seriously of coming back here or working in an area of the world with similar conditions. It's interesting, honest and necessary work, but most important I'm good at it and I enjoy it."

Macao The U.S. Army had a policy that allowed advisors to take up to fourteen days of vacation in Bangkok or Hong Kong. Imagine being able to take a vacation from a war. It struck me as bizarre then, and it still seems strange. It was almost as though my war was not serious. I spent March 12 to March 19, 1963, in Hong Kong. Air travel (on chartered U.S. commercial carriers after I had hitched a chopper ride to Saigon) was arranged and paid for by the army. Upon arrival in Hong Kong we were warned not to go to mainland China, because China was an ally of the North Vietnamese. Ten hours after leaving my jungle base, I was loose in fabled, cosmopolitan Hong Kong. Try to imagine what it was like after six months in the jungle for a twenty-four-year-old with a pocket full of money to have seven carefree days in such an exciting city. I shopped and went to museums, of course!

The army had installed a powerful radio system that was linked through regular telephone lines to the hotel room. In order to speak, one said "over" and paused, then the party on the other end did the same, so the radio-relay operators along the way could forward the conversation much as ham radio would today. It was cumbersome, long before the days of touch-tone international dialing, but it worked, and I was able to call my mom on March 17, Saint Patrick's Day.

While in Hong Kong I hired a Chinese junk and crew to take me to Macao. I took with me an old Chinese woman as my cook. She carried a charcoal oven, wok, and food, all balanced on a pole. Also included in my entourage was an old Chinese man who played a vertical, single-string instrument with a large gourd on the bottom for resonance. A lovely "Asian flower" accompanied me as my guest. We were to make a night passage, spend the day in Macao, and return the following night. Lieutenant Dockery was going to Macao, and Macao was Portuguese territory. I did not think there would be a problem.

As the junk pulled out of Hong Kong harbor, the harbor police/customs officials boarded us. The Asian flower and I were below deck en flagrante delicto, don't you know. A heated exchange between my entourage and the harbor police was in progress when I arrived on deck. My people became quiet when one of the policemen asked in a crisp English accent for my passport. The police, upon seeing my diplomatic passport with its photograph of me in military uniform, refused to let us proceed, saying that I would be detained or kidnapped by the Red Chinese government. I protested, but they were adamant. Much discussion followed. I stopped protesting when they made the boatman give the money I had paid for the passage back to me. The policeman said the boatman knew the danger for me and should not have agreed to take me. There was some discussion about compensation for the Asian flower. I found out later that, although Macao was a Portuguese colony, the Red Chinese controlled egress and ingress. I have often wondered what would have happened if the harbor police had not turned me back.

Saigon 1963 In the field, at the cement plant, and in the lesser cities of the delta, I was always under scrutiny. I was stared at, pointed at, and reported on. I had no privacy and no personal space. Both were sometimes necessary. So too was an occasional change of circumstance and scenery. At least once a month I made my own way to Saigon, by hitching a jeep or truck ride to an airfield in the vicinity. It was always a last-minute rush, after learning of an imminent arrival over the military radio, to catch a supply or reconnaissance aircraft that was making a quick stop on its way back to Saigon. Airfields were usually just dirt strips, some with a one-story building with a tin roof occupied by a squad of soldiers. Other airfields were cleared areas, deserted until a plane landed, at which point children and adults would appear and then a jeep would arrive, either with a departing passenger or to pick up an arrival. It often seemed that the villagers knew of an incoming flight before the military did; they would always show up out of curiosity, looking for a windfall hand-out or as intelligence gatherers for the Viet Cong. Occa-sionally I would get a chopper ride to Saigon with returning colonels. I'd ask, "Do you have room for me? Hey, wait while I get my stuff." There were no scheduled flights, but all sorts of people, American and Vietnamese, military and civilian alike, would often show up unannounced and unex-plained. Sometimes there were no flights at all and, disap-pointed, I would retrace my steps to the battalion determined to try again soon. I went when I wanted to go. There was no one's permission to ask.

Saigon was known as both the Pearl of the Orient and the Paris of the East. It was special, and it promised and pro-vided anonymity, which I wanted and needed. The city had something for everybody. Every whim and every vice could be satisfied. There was entertainment available and things for sale and barter that could test any man's moral code. Saigon was a place to decompress.

Cho Lon, the Chinatown of Saigon, teemed with activity and shocking treats. Cho Lon translates as "Big Market" and indeed it was, as was the rest of the city. Men and women, young and old, transported food, cooking braziers, construc-tion material, water, charcoal, and other items of commerce in twin baskets balanced on a pole resting over the shoulder. Some of the people were merchants, others teamsters. Some carried Viet Cong contraband concealed in their baskets. They walked bent over for balance, with one hand on the pole and the other on a hip, and swayed rhythmically from point to point with mincing steps under loads that weighed up to eighty pounds. Without breaking stride, these heavily laden porters transferred the pole from shoulder to shoulder by lowering the head and rotating the pole on the back of the neck. They stopped often to adjust, rest, and hawk their wares.

It was an open city for Americans; everything was possible and every rumor was a fact. Rumors had swift legs, and essential "facts" changed quickly. A morning rumor would be contradicted by afternoon but reaffirmed by evening. Cyclo drivers, merchants, soldiers, and bar girls freely confided their "information."

Saigon had numerous street markets and stores, which offered, among other things, every imaginable American product. Young and old squatted on their heels hawking their goods in singsong voices. The products frequently were counterfeit or, if legitimate, were illegally obtained from the U.S. Army post exchange (PX) and sold profitably, first by the corrupt American connection at the PX, then by local merchants. There were sidewalk cafes, fashionable riverside restaurants, a few quality hotels, and hundreds of *khach san,* small, local hotels that ranged from respectable to nefarious. There seemed to be a pagoda in every neighborhood, and monks in saffron robes were on every street praying, begging, or leading antigovernment protests. Colorful funeral processions wound through the streets, the wealth and importance of the deceased evident by the drums and the cries of the paid mourners. Also in the streets were cyclo races, a zoo of sorts, a racetrack where scrawny horses ran clockwise, bomb explosions, countless Vietnamese servicemen and military vehicles, the mixed smells of incense and charcoal fumes from innumerable fires, and everywhere sex— sex for sale, to earn, and even get gratis. Beggars, both adult and children, would suddenly grab my arm as I walked, and plead for a handout. Other petitioners would solicit for gambling houses, cockfights, opium dens, sex shows, and always, women. The city teemed with thieves and thousands of Vietnamese draft dodgers. Dozens of bars with names such as Blue Moon, Starlight, New York, and OK Corral catered exclusively to Americans; the hostesses, gloriously perfumed offerings from the East, wore high heels, jewelry, and often little else. In contrast, elegant and beautiful young women, graceful and feminine, going to work or school on motorbikes and bicycles, traveled the streets with their lovely, long black hair and *ao dai* (traditional women's dress) panels flowing in the breeze.

An old colonial capital, Saigon had broad, tree-lined streets in its center and narrow ones, without trees, in its neighborhoods. Fragrant flowers of various shapes, colors, and sizes dressed the shops and sidewalks. There was a palace, a parliament building, office buildings, slums, a cathedral, exotic architecture, and almost 3 million people. Saigon offered a chance to wash off the war and the mud, actual showers and sheets, and the equal opportunity to travel from mild adventure to unlimited depravity. Roaming alone often led to back alleys and dead ends, but the crush of people and cyclos in frenetic movement also often generated interesting and unexpected situations and events. How and where the night would end was always a surprise.

This was a city in a war, not a city at war. People here raised their families and earned a living. Entrepreneurs of all stripes and persuasions catered to the tastes and desires of the city's citizens and its "guests." The poor and those displaced by the war in the countryside sold whatever they had. My U.S. dollars made me as rich as a king. There wasn't anything I couldn't afford, I was accountable to no one, and there was a cure for everything.

The city was full of Americans. Of the 16,000 American military in country in 1963, only 2,000 were actually engaged in the field in combat roles. Colonels, majors, sergeants, and civilian employees of the State Department, the Pentagon, and the Agency for International Development crowded the major cities, primarily Saigon. Some even brought their wives. It was an agreeable location for them, with guards, house servants, and preferential access to the best and most prestigious places and people. Although there were many Americans in Saigon, I knew none of them. Who were these Americans, walking, posturing, and strutting, I wondered. They ignored me and passed me by. Didn't they know I was the Delta Fox and conducting a war? What were they doing? Did they have jobs? Were they writing reports or just reading them? They were Saigon commandos. I felt superior and resented the bureaucracy and desk jockeys of Saigon. I was the warrior; they were the pencil pushers. I harbored resentment against these fellows. I liked coming to Saigon, but I didn't want to be in Saigon full-time. What I wished was that the Saigon commandos could be in the field full-time where they might do some good. I thought, how can they contribute to the war effort by just talking to one another all day long? But I knew that my reaction to, and feelings about, the rear-echelon guys was a bit unfair. Some of them must have had important jobs.

The Rex Hotel was in the middle of the city on Nguyen Hue. On the top floor of the Rex, and the adjacent roof, was the main American officers' club, where barbecued steaks and cold American beer, exotic treats for field advisors, were always available. Saigon commandos with their Vietnamese girlfriends vied for tables with advisors in from the field and visiting Pentagon brass. At night, artillery flashes from engagements miles from the city could be seen from the roof, but they were dim and the rumble was delayed and faint. I wondered about those people who gathered to watch and talk, and in these situations I always had the eerie feeling that I was watching them watch a movie that I was in. They seemed to consider the flashes a light show to talk about and not destruction and suffering to comprehend. The Rex was popular, so popular that in the late sixties, after large-scale American intervention, the club rules were changed to allow only full colonels, generals, and equivalent rank civilians and dignitaries and, of course, their lady friends. The club, large as it was, could not accommodate all the officers assigned to the top-heavy command structure of the U.S. Army and billeted in Saigon. Lower-rank officers were banished to the growing number of less distinguished clubs around the city.

Vietnamese police, soldiers, and security agents were everywhere. They were armed, as were the Americans. There were stories of shootouts and standoffs between the Vietnamese and the Americans. Some of the stories must have been true; so much testosterone. The White Mice, unkindly named by Americans, were both traffic police and Diem's street security agents. They were on every corner in their obvious white uniforms and white hats and carrying .45-caliber pistols. Usually they were the people who had to sort out things that went wrong between Vietnamese and Americans on the streets. Disagreements often escalated into arguments, then into incidents. The White Mice administered simple justice on the spot, and separated the Americans from the merchants, cyclo drivers, petty thieves, and prostitutes. It was not easy restraining armed, arrogant, and frequently drunk Americans, civilian and military alike. The mixture of sensitive ethnic and national pride, machismo, adrenaline, and alcohol was potentially nuclear. God bless the White Mice.

The Cercle Sportif, a tennis and swimming club in Saigon that provided sport for the aristocracy, was another prestigious and exclusive location that opened its doors to all of us early in the war but closed them later. Its members were French, privileged Vietnamese, and Americans. In 1963, for combat advisors visiting Saigon from near and far, it was a mandatory stop. Bikini-clad women—Vietnamese, Eurasian, American, and French—and gin fizzes at the bar and around the pool were the main attractions. I went there only once. I preferred to swim in the local seas: the city and its people.

I was captivated by Saigon and its exotica. The city was stupendous. It churned and fermented. The air was electric. I could not get enough of it. But after two to three days in Saigon, I always made my way back to my battalion. I had to. It was my job. I was anxious to return to my troops and concerned that I would miss something. I wanted to keep faith with them. Morality in that little war was personal; it is in any war. I strove to keep it so.

Generally within a day of leaving Saigon, I was back with my battalion. However, if the battalion had moved in my absence it took longer. I had to find it. I went from the excesses and comforts of Saigon to the stark and primitive countryside where my battalion was located. Chaotic Saigon was quite different from the quiet and orderly hamlets and paddies of the delta. So too the conservative peasants, who in many ways were unlike their countrymen who lived in the city. As for me, Saigon was necessary. As Augustine said, "Within me was a famine." God knows, I was young.

What Would Washington Say? For field advisors, the greatest single disease risk was intestinal sickness, transmitted mechanically (food, feces, fluids, fingers, and flies) from the sewage of infected persons to the mouths of advisors.

I lived with the battalion for eight months, the only American for most of that time. Slept where they slept. Ate what they ate. Drank the water. Used their privies. I suffered constantly from stomach cramps, diarrhea, and fevers. In April 1963 helicopters landed at the cement plant with two U.S. colonels from MACV, Military Assistance Command Vietnam. When Captain Beng brought them to my dark hut, they found me on my cot under the mosquito net, too weak to get up. I was wearing the black cotton shorts favored by the Vietnamese peasants. My body was covered with the signature red welts of traditional Chinese pain remedies. These colonels had a mess hall, electricity, hot showers, and real mattresses and beds back at their Saigon billets. I heard one comment, "What would Washington say if they saw this?" and "He's got a skin disease." The other colonel said, "He's gone native." Well, yes.

I left with them; they gave me no choice. Soon I was hospitalized in Saigon. Later I was evacuated on a stretcher and flown to Clark Air Force Hospital in the Philippines. I weighed 121 pounds, 40 pounds less than when I had arrived in Vietnam. I was at Clark for a month. While there I was treated for malaria, infectious hepatitis, amoebic dysentery, skin fungus, and worms. The first days I was hallucinating and, according to my ward mates, speaking Vietnamese in my sleep.

I have come to believe, without any proof, that Captain Beng reported my condition to his superiors and they informed MACV, which sent the colonels to get me. It was too much of a coincidence that they arrived on an inspection visit when I needed them most.

Seven

BACK TO THE USA

Our joys as winged dreams do fly;
Why then should sorrow last?
Since grief but aggravates thy loss.
Grieve not for what is past.
—Anon., The Friar of Orders Gray

The Rose Lieutenant My hospital ward at Clark Air Force Base contained thirty men of different rank, some wounded, some sick. After a week I felt well enough to talk to those around me. One afternoon the ward door burst open and a rather large orderly came skipping down the aisle to my bed, crying out as he came, "Roses for Lieutenant Dockery, roses for Lieutenant Dockery." In his arms were a dozen red roses from my mother. With great delight the entire ward joined in the cry. Being less secure than I thought, I immediately sent the roses to the maternity ward. For the rest of my hospital stay, I was called the Rose Lieutenant. I wrote to my mother, "Thanks for the flowers. Please don't send anything else."

I spent four weeks in bed, eating, sleeping, and taking medication. The doctors and nurses were attentive and took good care of me. Gradually, as I felt better, I became bored lying in bed. I kept sane by reading. Twice a week a library volunteer would wheel a cart full of books through the ward. I looked forward to these biweekly visits. She brought James Bond books, solace, and a flirtatious affection.

The hospital had a practice of allowing patients who were nearing recovery the freedom to go out each day, with the requirement that they not leave the base and be back in bed by 9:30 each evening. Like an injured animal that had been caged while healing, I was being released on a trial basis into the wild. The first day out, I found the library. The volunteer was there. I was feeling stronger. A responsive friend is the best medicine. I neglected to go back to the hospital that evening. Consternation was evident upon my return the following morning. The colonel in charge was upset. I should have listened more carefully to the rules. After some meetings and a verbal reprimand, they took away my furlough privileges.

The Wedding Feast The army maintained a golf and vacation resort at Camp John Hay near Baguio, the capital of the Philippines. It was a beautiful place high in the rugged mountains of Luzon and about two hours by train from Manila. The cool, sunny weather, the beautiful, tranquil setting, and standard American facilities made it a perfect place for American servicemen stationed in Asia to vacation.

At the end of World War II, Baguio was the last redoubt to which the Japanese withdrew and where it is thought they buried a large cache of gold. Rumors persist that President Marcos or General MacArthur, take your pick, later found and kept the gold. To this day it remains a subject of speculation.

Late in June, my prior rule breaking forgotten, I was sent by train to Baguio to recuperate for ten days before returning to Clark Hospital for release and return to Saigon. The two-hour train ride was interesting, because the track went through mountain areas controlled by bandits and the communist guerrillas known as Huks. Armed soldiers were stationed at either end of each car.

I had been on my back for weeks and was looking forward to a vacation. The resort was a beautiful place, but after two days I'd had enough of the officers' club and manicured lawns. So, on a Sunday afternoon I called a taxi and told the driver to take me to the nearest local nightclub.

The sign at the door, requesting patrons to check their guns, did not alarm me. Of course not; I was back in my element. Shortly after I arrived, more than a hundred well-dressed Filipinos arrived for a wedding reception. I was included in the festivities. At one point in the evening, I heard voices raised in anger and saw a table containing the wedding cake overturned and two men facing each other with pistols drawn. They had disregarded the sign's instruction. Everyone scampered to get out of the line of fire. The bride, in her flowing white wedding dress, stepped between the gunmen and somehow made peace. The guns were pocketed, and people rushed to salvage the cake. The party continued. What fun.

Unfortunately I played too hard at the reception and at other entertainment, had a relapse, and was readmitted to the hospital. There you go. Five days later I was given another convalescent leave, this one to Manila for six days. Manila in 1963 was an interesting city. This sure beat life at the cement plant.

New Orders In April 1963 I filed papers requesting a six-month Vietnam extension and assignment to the U.S. Special Forces in the Central Highlands of Vietnam. I wanted to stay in Vietnam, but I wanted something different. In spite of eight months of frustration, a certainty that South Vietnam was going to lose, and qualms about the righteousness of U.S. involvement, I still had not had enough. This contradiction can be explained by the fact that Vietnam and the advisor experience were extremely seductive. I was driven by the danger, the excitement, the need to contribute, and the desire to see this little war through to its end. Oh, and also I did not want to leave a certain friend I had in Saigon. The experience was seductive for many reasons, but I think the main reason was that I had more freedom than I, or most men, had ever known. Everything I owned fit in a duffel bag, and I was not responsible for, or to, anyone. I had more freedom then than I have today, for sure.

While on my back in the hospital I received new orders. My request for a six-month extension and assignment to the Central Highlands was denied. Instead, I was ordered back to Saigon to serve as the executive officer for the advisors' detachment working with the ARVN IV Corps. Then on August 28 I was to leave Saigon to give a lecture about my experiences as an advisor at a U.S. Special Forces facility in Oberammergau, Germany, before returning to the United States. With these orders, on July 7 I returned to Saigon, where, despite my lofty title, I had few official duties other than to prepare my lecture. I had become a Saigon commando. Today I chuckle at my letter home, which disingenuously cites "loose ends" for not returning to hospitalization in the States: "I had a chance to be evacuated to Walter Reed Hospital in D.C. when I first became sick. I had too many loose ends in Saigon to leave so suddenly—so I said no."

The hand of fate had plucked me from a rice paddy. Some computer or army personnel officer had selected me to carry the word. I wondered what they expected me to say in Oberammergau.

The orders specified that after the lecture I was to report for duty at Fort Meyer, Virginia. I was assigned to the Old Guard Regiment, which included in its mission ceremonial tasks in Washington, D.C., and at Arlington National Cemetery. In hospital beds on either side of me were career officers—graduates of West Point who, after examining my orders, asked how I got them. "Who do you know?" they asked. They explained that my assignment to the Old Guard was a plum much sought after by career officers.

Nuptials In Vietnam it was difficult to meet women who were available and educated. Educated women came from wealthy families and were forbidden by their families to socialize with American soldiers. Kim Ahn was educated, witty, sophisticated, and beautiful. She told me she was nineteen years old, which is eighteen in the United States, because the Vietnamese count a baby as one year old when it is born. She was also a mystery. In addition to Vietnamese, Kim Ahn wrote and spoke French and English. I met her in October 1962 on a trip to Saigon. She was having lunch at a French restaurant with girlfriends. We spent the afternoon together. Before leaving me, she said I could always get in touch with her when I came to Saigon by asking for her at the registration desk of the Caravelle Hotel. It seemed like an unreliable way to make contact, but it worked rather well. Three weeks later I followed her instructions, and she arrived in the lobby within half an hour. Kim Ahn was dressed in a lovely blue and white silk *ao dai,* the graceful national dress of Vietnamese women. Wearing a slight smile, she greeted me as *Trung úy Doc,* Lieutenant Dockery. After that day I managed to get to Saigon at least once a month. Only once was I unable to find her. Those were wonderful and memorable times. Her presence activated my senses. Every pore received her.

I never met Kim Ahn's family or, except for that first time, any of her friends. She would not tell me what she did or where she lived or anything about her family. Curiously, she told me that her brother was a Viet Cong captain. I did not know why she told me that. Perhaps she was warning me. She wrote to me at the cement plant, but I could not write to her. There was no return address. Her letters arrived via ARVN post. She did not use the Vietnamese postal service. Captain Beng, with merriment and some ceremony, personally delivered her letters to me. He wanted to know how and why she had access to ARVN mail service. So did I.

At that time and under those circumstances, I was able to accept our relationship on her terms, and in point of fact I found it appealing. I loved her and the idea of it all. It was not a commercial relationship. She enjoyed my company and asked to visit me at the cement plant, but I did not think it was a good idea.

The first thing I did upon my return to Saigon from the Philippines was to meet Kim Ahn at the Caravelle. I intended to explain my absence. But before I could, she asked how I was feeling and said she knew I had been hospitalized in the Philippines. She said she had been afraid I was not coming back. When I pressed her to explain how she knew, all she said was that a friend told her. For the next seven weeks we lived together in a house that belonged to one of her friends. We did not have to pay rent, she said. A ten-foot-high concrete wall, topped with broken glass, enclosed the house and its small yard, which had a fishpond. The house was furnished, but there were no clothes or personal items in evidence. In the main room against a wall stood a small ancestral altar, which was decorated daily with fresh fruit and flowers. Every morning Kim Ahn took a cyclo and went to wherever she went. Most weekdays I took a cyclo to my office to prepare my lecture. We both returned home in midafternoon. Kim's servant woman, who lived with us, cooked, cleaned, and did the laundry.

I had told Kim Ahn that I had orders and would soon return home to the United States, but she did not comment. One day she asked me to put my suit on because monks were coming to the house. In response to the obvious question, "Why are monks coming?" she answered, "You shouldn't worry because there won't be any paperwork." At 5 P.M. that day, Kim Ahn and I, both in our best clothes, stood on either side of the altar before two Buddhist monks dressed in saffron-colored robes. They prayed, bowed, and waved burning incense sticks. She knew the prayers and said them. The monks coached me on how to respond. When the ceremony was over, the servant woman served a meal to the four of us. That night Kim Ahn said it was okay for me to return to

America because now we would be together forever. The ceremony might have been a blessing of some kind or perhaps Buddhist nuptials. Confusion is the mother of love.

I had many unanswered questions about Kim Ahn, this girl I loved. Who was she? Who was her family? How did she know I had been in the hospital in the Philippines? How was she able to use the ARVN mail service? Was the Viet Cong "brother" her father? Her lover? Her husband? It crossed my mind that I might be at risk. But I had been living on the edge for eleven months and accepted the uncertainty of this relationship. I trusted her and was happy with her, and that is why I accepted it. The fact that she was beautiful did not affect my judgment.

One thing was certain, she was hiding me. I was inconvenient. Probably I was an embarrassment. Possibly I was endangering her. Kim Ahn's father was most likely a high government or military official. Her family must have had doubts about which side was going to win. They certainly respected the ability of the Viet Cong to strike at will in Saigon against the families of government officials. Her family would have thought that their daughter's relationship with an American lieutenant had no future and would only invite Viet Cong reprisal.

My last chance to find out about Kim Ahn was years later in 1968. Out of the blue, after no word or contact since I left Vietnam, she telephoned my father's tavern in New York City and asked for Martin Dockery, which was also his name. She had looked up the name in the telephone directory. After the confusion was cleared up, she told my father that she was an Air France stewardess named Kim Ahn, my good friend from Saigon, and was in New York. He learned more about her in one telephone conversation than I had in one year. He would not give her my phone number and told her I was a married man with a son and should not talk to an old girlfriend. Days later he told me all this with a big grin on his face. "I told her for you," he said. A silent understanding passed between father and son. I was disappointed, but of course he was right.

Given the chance, I would have stayed in Vietnam. I tried to stay. But it was over. It was time to leave. I was going home on schedule, one year after arriving. Captain Beng and my battalion were still at the cement plant or somewhere in the delta pursuing the elusive Viet Cong in an endless chase across rice paddies, into tree lines, and through canals. I said good-bye to Kim Ahn. I had mixed feelings about leaving. It was great to be going home, but I was leaving the girl I loved and the people I cared about in what I thought was a danger-ous and desperate situation. Soldiers do that.

The Dueling Colonels I left Saigon on August 29, 1963, via Military Air Transport Service. The United States military has a presence throughout the world. Military Air Transport ferries supplies, mail, military personnel, depen-dents, politicians, and U.S. government officials. Seats are assigned on a priority basis. My priority from Saigon to Germany was stand-by (the lowest priority), which meant I had to wait at the gate and hope that my name was called. If there was space, I would get on. The secret to this kind of travel is to take any plane with space that is going in your general direction. Sometimes one has to backtrack, but one keeps moving. I landed in twelve cities on this journey. It took me nine days and thirteen different flights to reach Germany via Thailand, India, Pakistan, Saudi Arabia, Libya, Spain, and Morocco. I arrived in Oberammergau on Sep-tember 7, exhausted.

I had prepared my lecture in Saigon and asked the colonel in charge of intelligence at MACV to approve a written draft. He made some changes that softened my negative observa-tions and opinions, but he would not be there to hear what I said. I was surprised that he did not delete from the draft the sentence that read, "I do not share the optimism of General

Harkins who has said the war will be over in one year." At the time, General Harkins was the commanding general of all U.S. forces in Vietnam. Junior officers do not publicly disagree with their commanding general. After the changes were made, the colonel approved the lecture I was to present in Oberammergau, but he instructed me (bless him; he must have had a premonition) to begin the talk with a statement to the effect that what was to follow were my views and opinions and not the army's and that I was a junior officer with limited experience and had no real knowledge of the current situation in Vietnam except concerning the battalion to which I was assigned. I agreed.

My lecture was given in an auditorium to approximately three hundred career soldiers, all of whom suspected that they would eventually serve in Vietnam. The audience was mine. I began with the "I am only a lieutenant" statement and continued with a description of my experiences, of Viet Cong strengths, weaknesses, and strategies, of ARVN successes and failures, and of new weapons being field-tested. My disagreement with General Harkins's "one-year" statement was mentioned. I told them how inept and poorly led the ARVN was and of the rampant corruption. My talk lasted an hour and was well received.

The customary question-and-answer period followed the lecture. This was what the audience was waiting for, and there were numerous serious questions. I answered each question directly and honestly, even though I knew that certain honest answers could get me into trouble and were beyond the agreed-upon limits. I felt bound to tell it how it was, although it would have been safer to just mumble decisively. In response to a question, I stated that it was a civil war that the South Vietnamese were not capable of winning on their own, and even with a huge increase in American troops, the war could go on for ten years and even then we might not win. I began my answer to a question about how could the

Viet Cong possibly be winning given the overwhelming ARVN superiority in soldiers and equipment by saying, "Guerrillas have been winning ground wars since, oh, the Minutemen." I suspect that some of my other answers were a bit sarcastic as well. Irony and disagreement with the "company line" are not appreciated from a first lieutenant in the United States Army.

A bemedaled colonel at the front of the audience rose to his feet. He challenged me and my remarks. He demanded to know who had authorized me to make them. A colonel in full stride can be intimidating to a first lieutenant. In response I repeated my "I am only a lieutenant" statement and kept to myself the old cliché "a mind is like a parachute, it's only good when it is open." Luckily for me, the colonel in charge of the facility engaged the offended colonel and said something like, We brought him all this way to hear what he had to say. The lieutenant might be right, so we had better listen to him.

I would not have called it full support, but it was enough to get me out of the auditorium with my first lieutenant bars still on my shoulders. Little did any of us know that, even with wholesale American involvement lasting thirteen years, the North Vietnamese would eventually prevail.

My lecture ended shortly after the flare-up with the colonel. I received a standing ovation, which I suppose could have been because they liked what I had to say or because they were enthralled by the sight of the dueling colonels and the rogue lieutenant. The angry colonel was nowhere in sight when I left the podium, thank God. The tension caused by my words and the reaction they elicited from the colonel would be mirrored in the United States in the years that followed.

I had a moral obligation as well as a sworn oath as an officer to tell the truth, and I believed then and I believe now that the truth is not a variable to be tailored to one's audience or other circumstances. In his defense, the offended colonel was more than likely a veteran of World War II and Korea and viewed my statements as disloyal to the army, the government, and the country. He probably viewed them as aid and comfort to the enemy because I was publicly disagreeing with my military and civilian superiors and, in the process, undermining the morale of the army. But I was right, the venue was right, and it was my duty. Ah, duty, an old-fashioned word. I have often wondered how many of the soldiers in the audience later served in Vietnam and whether my lecture informed or influenced them in any way.

Home Leave On September 16 I left Germany for London and a planned stop on the way home. I had purchased an Austin Healey sports car at an auto dealership in Saigon and arranged to pick it up at the factory in England.

I drove the Healey from the factory to the London docks for shipment to the States. At that time under U.S. Customs law, the drive qualified the car as used and, therefore, no tax was due upon arrival in the States. In August 1964 I sold my beloved Healey to pay for my first two years of law school, the beginning of wisdom. Jonathan Swift wrote about the wisdom of practicing law in his poem "Helter Skelter":

> Now the active young Attorneys
> Briskly travel on their journeys
> Looking big as any giants
> On the horses of their clients.

I don't think it's possible to find the lawyer I became in the lieutenant advisor of long ago.

It was easy for Dorothy in *The Wizard of Oz*. She only had to click her heels to return to the real world. I had two trips to make: one from Saigon to Germany to New York, and the other from the extremes of Vietnam to the sanctuary of home.

After visiting relatives and traveling in Ireland, I returned to the United States on October 10. I landed at McGuire Air Force Base in New Jersey and went directly to my Dad's tavern. In full uniform I walked in the door. Dad was behind the bar. He squinted, paused, and said my name. Customers, some of them veterans, surrounded me, shook my hand, and patted me on the back. Dad and I embraced. He bought the house a drink; although Dad did not drink alcohol, he made an exception and had a sherry. Soon I left to take the train to White Plains to surprise my mom. But Dad had called to say I was coming. He thought it best to give her a warning. She had a warm greeting for me. It was wonderful to be home.

During my ten-day home leave, my parents had a party for me. Friends and neighbors came to the house on a Saturday night. Mom asked me to wear my uniform, which I did for a while. It was great fun, but it was frustrating because none of my parents' friends understood. They had no idea what was happening in Vietnam. I knew things they did not know, things that some of their sons and brothers, in time, would learn. Returning soldiers feel this way. My reaction was not unique.

Dad's Prayer Worked My parents lived their lives according to a deep religious conviction. God, country, and family were what mattered to them. Today, these are the things that matter to me.

Letters home from me were important to my family. Some were addressed to my dad at his tavern and some to my mom at home, and at the end of most days one of them would say, "Yes, I heard from Martin and here is his letter."

I received many letters while I was in Vietnam, some from family and some from friends, but only one from my dad. His letter is the only one I saved. My father was a deeply religious man who looked to his faith for answers both temporal and spiritual. Excerpts from his December 16, 1962, letter evidence his belief and trust in God.

A few lines in answer to your frequent and newsful letters, which we look forward to. I am glad to learn you are getting along O.K. and I pray every day that God and His Virgin Mother may continue to watch over you, preserve you from sin and harm and bring you home safely to us at the end of your assignment.

We are all fine at home T.G. preparing for Christmas. Needless to say its happiness will be dimmed by your absence.

As I know you are in constant touch with the rest of the family and informed of the newest news, I will now conclude praying that God and Mary will Bless you with a Holy and Happy Christmas and preserve you in faith and health and from all harm.

> I Remain Your Loving Father
> Martin Dockery

For thirty-eight years I have been enchanted by this letter and a little numbed that my father signed it with his full name. And indeed, I did come home safely.

Diem's Death From 1954 to 1963 the United States supported Diem and provided him with military and economic support. We cultivated him and believed that he could establish and lead a government that would prevent the spread of communism to South Vietnam.

During the early 1960s, Diem lost the confidence of the Kennedy administration (another suspect Catholic politician) because of political and military ineptness, corruption, and lack of reform. The American media's relentless coverage of these failings and Diem's antidemocratic practices contributed to the undermining of U.S. support for him. Most of President Kennedy's advisors came to believe that the war against the Viet Cong could not be won with Diem in power. In a military coup instigated, or at least sanctioned, by the United States, Diem was shot to death on November 2,

1963. There was a sense of relief in the United States that Diem was gone and a belief that a new Vietnamese president would emerge who would solve the problems undermining the attempt to establish a government supported by the people and able to defeat the Viet Cong.

Replacing Diem did not produce the desired results. In the years that followed, coups and countercoups were common, some with U.S. approval, some without. None delivered meaningful land reform, effective anticorruption measures, democracy, or an efficient military.

The Old Guard In October 1963, after taking home leave, I reported to Company B, 1st Battalion, 3d Infantry (the Old Guard). The Old Guard is a ceremonial unit whose duties include service at the Tomb of the Unknowns, Arlington Cemetery burials, parades, ceremonies for arriving and departing dignitaries, and funerals of high government officials.

On occasion, courageous lieutenants of the Old Guard were called upon to perform escort duty, a dangerous but coveted assignment. Bachelor officers were assigned to escort women who were invited to diplomatic functions and affairs of state but had no escort. The officers of the Old Guard did this duty to the best of their ability and without complaint. Indeed, I volunteered.

The contrast in assignments was striking. At the whim of the army, I went from a grass hut and jungle fatigues that even Martha Stewart could not improve to the most spit-and-polish ceremonial outfit in the entire U.S. Army.

The Old Guard is a proud unit steeped in tradition. It was formed in 1784. Its uniform displays unique badges, braids, and symbols evidencing its prior assignments and current status. It is well known that the honor of burial in Arlington Cemetery is reserved for military heroes, high government officials, and, it has been reported, friends of and contributors to presidents. Cemetery burials were an everyday event and, although conducted professionally, with sympathy and dignity, were (and probably still are) irreverently referred to by the soldiers of the Old Guard as "plantings," as in, "I've been assigned to three plantings today." The burial ceremony, which was carefully scripted, followed the arrival of the burial detail: an officer, a sergeant, eight soldiers with rifles, the casket, and the grieving family members. A chaplain would say a prayer followed by rifle salutes. The flag draping the coffin was then removed, folded, and presented to the wife or mother of the soldier. Mourners threw flowers and mementos into the grave after the casket was lowered. The dead were of all religious and ethnic and racial backgrounds, and the burial ceremonies and the reactions of family members at the grave site reflected this diversity. At some burials, grieving relatives were emotional and demonstrative. On occasion, the wife or mother, overcome by grief or perhaps a sense of betrayal, would refuse to accept the flag.

President Kennedy's Funeral President Kennedy was admired by the military. He was one of us. He had experienced the terror and uncertainty of the war in the Pacific during World War II and returned a hero. He had bested Nixon and Khrushchev. He was our leader.

One of the traditions of Veteran's Day is for the president to lay a wreath and make a speech at the Tomb of the Unknowns at Arlington Cemetery. On November 11, 1963, the Old Guard was on duty during President Kennedy's wreath-laying ceremony at the tomb. Kennedy was at the top of his form, and I saw him that day as virile, intelligent, and wise. He spoke of the ultimate sacrifice the Unknowns had made for the country. He made sense and he was ours. The country believed that President Kennedy would lead us through the dangerous times to come. No one could imagine what was to happen eleven days later.

In addition to its ceremonial mission, the Old Guard together with other military units is responsible for the defense of the Capitol District. In the event of insurrection or attack by foreign forces, the Old Guard is assigned to defend and protect government buildings and government officials. Each battalion spent three weeks of the year in the field at Camp A. P. Hill in Virginia training for this mission. Camp A. P. Hill was named in honor of a Confederate general. Curiously, many army posts are named after generals who fought for the Confederacy during the Civil War. Training included small-unit tactics, weapon placement, and crowd control.

On November 22, 1963, my battalion was returning by bus and truck convoy to our barracks at Fort Meyer. Our field training at Camp A. P. Hill had just concluded. Somewhere in northern Virginia a private in the front of the bus left his seat, walked down the aisle to me, and said, "Lieutenant, the president's been shot in Dallas, he's near death." I angrily criticized the soldier for joking about a serious subject. He was speaking the unthinkable; it had to be untrue. I told him to return to his seat and be quiet. He did, but not before handing me his portable radio so I could hear the awful news for myself. Later, the private graciously accepted my apology and told me he understood my reaction.

President Kennedy was assassinated in Dallas that day. The secretary of defense distributed the following announcement to all members of the U.S. armed forces:

23 November 1963

I have the sad duty of announcing to the Armed Forces of the United States the death of John Fitzgerald Kennedy, The President of the United States, who was the victim of an assassin's bullet Friday November 22. The World has lost a gallant spirit whose championship of freedom and opportunity will be recognized by history.

All members of the Armed Forces, whose welfare was

his concern, can pay no better tribute to his memory than to carry on in the tradition which he shared and of which he was so proud.

Colors shall be displayed at half-mast for 30 days, beginning November 22 west longitude date.

Signed Robert S. McNamara

The funeral was memorable for all Americans and, it seems, for much of the world. I, as a member of the Old Guard, was assigned a personal, if solemn, involvement in the historic rites.

The funeral of a fallen head of state, especially a young, charismatic, assassinated head of state, is not only a sad event but an important and historic event. President Kennedy's funeral was that and, as such, meticulously planned and choreographed.

The funeral Mass was celebrated on November 25, 1963, in Saint Matthew's Cathedral, Washington, D.C. The night before the funeral, I was ordered to secure the church the following morning. I thought this was an unusual assignment, but I proceeded to the cathedral as ordered with a contingent of thirty enlisted men. A full complement of Secret Service agents had already arrived and was taking up positions in and around the cathedral. Upon arrival, I found that the people who had attended the 8 A.M. Mass were refusing to leave the pews. They informed me that they were going to stay for President Kennedy's funeral. It was necessary to lift some of them from their seats and deposit them on the street. We also had to remove people who were hiding in the confessionals and in other recesses of the cathedral. The Secret Service agents were diligent about finding the people who were hiding, but they wanted no part of moving them to the street.

The White House had sent color-coded, numbered invitations to heads of state, high government officials, and diplomats. Every seat was taken. Unknown to anyone, the pastor of Saint Matthew's, an elderly monsignor, had issued his own signed, handwritten invitations, styled "Admit One to Church," to clergy and friends. I was assigned to the door of the cathedral together with a Secret Service officer and the protocol officer from the State Department. There was great consternation when the protocol officer would not honor the handwritten invitations. Indeed, there was a confrontation between the protocol officer and a rather irate monsignor who kept referring to "his church" and "his invitees."

Many people tried to talk their way into the cathedral, especially police and sheriffs from neighboring states, "to help with security," they said. The nine members of the U.S. Supreme Court, dressed in their robes, arrived with their wives at the church by limousine. As they came up the cathedral steps, a young woman followed them. The Secret Service officer, assuming she was an interloper, refused to let her in the cathedral until she pointed to Chief Justice William O. Douglas (age sixty-five) and said she (age twenty-four) was married to him. Amidst some nonjudicial snickering from the rest of the court, Justice Douglas confirmed their relationship and she was admitted.

My job at the door of the cathedral was to assign ushers to everyone who had received an invitation. The protocol officer accepted the invitations, checked them, and turned to me to assign an usher to take the invitees to their seats. The ushers were senior enlisted men from the army, air force, navy, and marines. All went well until it was time to seat President Johnson.

There was one special usher, an air force lieutenant, whose sole job was to escort President and Mrs. Johnson to their seats. The protocol officer made it clear to the lieutenant and me that the president must sit in the outside seat of the first pew on the left side of the cathedral's center aisle. He told the lieutenant that Mrs. Johnson was to go into the pew first and that President Johnson was to enter the pew after her so he would be on the outside. When President and Mrs. Johnson arrived, I sent the lieutenant to them. Mrs. Johnson took his arm and they followed the president up the aisle. President Johnson entered the pew first followed by Mrs. Johnson, contrary to protocol. The brave lieutenant spoke to his president and told him he was in the wrong seat and explained why. Thereupon Mrs. Johnson got out of the pew, President Johnson got out of the pew, and Mrs. Johnson got back into the pew, followed by the president, so he was then in the correct seat. Before the lieutenant returned to the rear of the church, the president turned to the lieutenant, looked him in the eye, and said, "Lieutenant, if you're going to usher, learn how to do it right."

The lieutenant was sure his career was ruined. I applaud the young officer for his courage. I am not sure I would have told the president of the United States, especially President Johnson, that he was in the wrong seat. I could easily have rationalized that the president could sit any damn place he wanted and the protocol officer was a pipsqueak of little consequence.

Most of the activities surrounding the funeral were carefully planned and well thought out except for the parking of the limousines belonging to the dignitaries attending the funeral. They were parked at various locations and could not be brought to the cathedral quickly when the Mass ended. As a consequence, I stood next to the Kennedy family and numerous world leaders while they waited and waited and waited. They stood inside the door of the cathedral next to one another (and me) for forty-five minutes. I could have reached out and touched Robert, Edward, and Jackie Kennedy and her children, Caroline and John Jr., as well as de Gaulle, Haile Selassie, Prince Philip of England, and many others. I remember that de Gaulle was furious for being delayed and expressed his outrage to all within hearing in a stereotypically haughty, Gallic manner.

Mrs. Kennedy had invited Irish army cadets to attend the funeral as a guard of honor. The cadets, future officers, were seventeen years old. They stayed at Fort Meyer in the barracks of Company B, to which I was assigned as executive officer. There was concern that because of the relatively young age of the cadets, they would be taken advantage of by the more experienced U.S. enlisted men. As a precaution we moved all the enlisted men from the third floor to the first and second floors, and the cadets were installed on the third floor. I hoped that there would be no difficulties. However, the Irish cadets were too trusting, and cameras and other valuables left on their beds were stolen while they were at President Kennedy's grave site.

My final assignment relating to the funeral of the president was to escort the Irish cadets and their officers to Dulles Airport for their return flight to Ireland. They were to leave at 6 P.M. on the plane with Eamon de Valera, the president of Ireland. Eamon de Valera was born in the United States of an Irish mother and an Italian father. He grew up in Ireland and was a leader of the Irish War for Independence. He was eighty-one years of age, infirm, and nearly blind. He had already been escorted to his plane and was waiting for us. I was new to Washington and left it to the bus driver, an army private, to take us to Dulles after he assured me that he knew the way.

Many things went wrong: The driver took us to National Airport instead of Dulles, the cadets had to push one of the buses around because the reverse gear was broken, and we got stuck in rush hour traffic. I had to hire a taxi driver to lead us to Dulles Airport. The driver wanted payment up front, and after he got my money (twenty dollars), he promptly disappeared. Finally I flagged down a Virginia state trooper. When he heard my story and understood whom I was escorting and who was waiting for us at Dulles Airport, he turned on his siren and took us over back roads and through a restricted entrance onto the airfield and directly to the airplane. We arrived just at 6 P.M. and I bade farewell to all, sure that when I returned I would be severely criticized for lack of planning and leadership. However, the bus trip was never officially mentioned, which I attribute to the fact that no complaints were made by the Irish officers. To the contrary, see the kind reference to me in the following excerpt from a letter written by the chief of staff of the Irish army to the commander of the Old Guard.

> I should very much like to express to you and to your officers and other ranks, my warm appreciation of the attention, kindness and courtesy extended to our officers and cadets during their stay with your Unit on the occasion of President Kennedy's funeral in Washington. From all concerned I have heard nothing but praise for the way they were received and treated by everybody they met in Fort Meyer. In this regard you personally have been singled out for special mention. Likewise Capt GROVES, B Company, who went out of his way to be helpful to our Detachment. In Capt BURCHELL the officers and Cadets found a friend who was always on hand to advise and assist. With Lieut DOCKERY a valuable entente cordial was for obvious reasons readily and firmly established.

The words "obvious reasons" in the last sentence refer to the fact that my parents were born in Ireland and my dad had been an officer in the Irish Republican Army during Ireland's fight for independence, both of which were conversation topics during the exciting ride to the airport.

The assassination shocked the nation. It saddened and frightened us all. Our young and personable president had been killed in front of our eyes. How could it happen to us? Could our country be destroyed as quickly? Kennedy's death raised questions, and the funeral served as a catharsis. The funeral was a sad event, conducted with dignity and solemnity. In a strange way it brought us together; it united us in bereavement. All of us, from those days, remember John John's salute, the tragic widow, the solemn caisson, and the riderless horse with all of its epic and mythic implications. We were involved in a historic moment. There was also, for many, a deep and disquieting sense of foreboding.

The death and funeral of John Kennedy brought forth the tears of the nation. They also evoked a sense of national pride and unity. To this day, for those of us who were there, and indeed all Americans old enough to recall it, the remembrance of those moments, or a reviewing of the films of the funeral, rekindles all of the old emotions and feelings. I hope Americans will still feel some of these same reactions of unity, pride, and resolve a hundred years from now, when they also see those films.

In death, President Kennedy was a symbol of a still idealistic America, an America that "would bear the burden" to help the people of the "huts and villages" of a less fortunate world. History may judge some of these attempts as misguided, even foolhardy, but not, I believe, basely or meanly intentioned.

Kennedy's assassination, which followed by twenty days that of President Ngo Dinh Diem in Saigon, marked the end of my "personal" Vietnam. Or did it? I returned to civilian life in January 1964, worked in a bank, and traveled in Mexico until I started law school in September 1964. I was out of the army, but I was not "out" of Vietnam. I had a stake in Vietnam. I had invested a part of me there. I found it hard to watch a gradual and ineffective U.S. escalation to 550,000 soldiers in that ill-starred war. Over the next years, the pace of escalation on both sides, and the pace of escalation of our domestic problems, matched one another in a dark choreography.

I had been an advisor, and the Vietnamese were real people to me. I cared for them, and I cared for our own soldiers. They were all taking the terrible brunt of the war, and I knew that none would be winners. And I was not there.

Army Exit The military and civilian life are separate and different societies. The military has its own medical facilities, laws, regulations, judicial system, jails, protocol, educational institutions, commercial stores, and, yes, values. Some sectors of civilian society, such as academia and other self-described intelligentsia, speak and write of the military with suffocating contempt. For its part, the military regards civilian society with suspicion because of society's disregard of traditional values. The military abhors the seemingly willful gross mistakes concerning the maintenance of the military made by civilian leaders during peacetime that have resulted in unnecessary casualties in wartime.

The army is a wonderful institution; honor, integrity, and patriotism are values that are required and prized. Most soldiers understand that patriotism without virtue is not acceptable. Perhaps one day the military will serve as a wellspring, a reservoir for the values and ideals of our nation, values that our civilian society seems to have abandoned. I enjoyed the camaraderie of men from many different backgrounds and prized the experience and the exceptional things we did.

The army is insular and hierarchical but not rigid. It is a serious place. It changes slowly: People, ideas, and equipment have to be tested and proven before they are accepted.

Most of the career soldiers I met were fine men—ethical, honest, intelligent, and professional. They were dedicated to family and country. The military holds its people to standards higher than civilian society requires of its members, and, for the most part, service members and their families comport themselves accordingly. The foregoing reflects how I felt when I left the army and how I still feel today. I do not think I am an old veteran merely romanticizing after thirty-eight years.

Soldiers know they will eventually return to civilian life. They leave the military upon retirement or at the end of their obligations. The return to civilian life is the subject of frequent discussions and much planning. I knew I was not going to make the army my career; it was not the place for me. I did not think I would advance very far in the army. I felt I would have more opportunities in civilian life. One December morning shortly after President Kennedy's funeral, I submitted my termination papers. In January 1964 I became a civilian. At my farewell party, the officers of the Old Guard signed and presented me with a scroll containing the following humorous good wishes.

The Old Guard
1st Battalion (Reinf), 3d Infantry

1st Lt. Martin J. Dockery
On 20 October 1963, the 1st Battalion (Reinforced), 3d Infantry (The Old Guard) was awarded another Combat Infantryman's Badge. Tagging along behind the CIB was a small dark officer, a bit under the Old Guard optimum height, who identified himself as 1st Lieutenant Martin J. Dockery, fresh from hospitalization in the Philippines and the steaming jungles of Vietnam.

Your time in the Battalion was to be short due to your decision to return to civilian life. We are told that you made this decision the same day that your Company Commander sent you down to Camp A. P. Hill to look over that pleasure spot. Surely it is not as bad as that.

The officers of Bravo Company will long remember their three weeks there with you. Each morning they awoke to find you shaving in your Saigon Squat. And as Mess Officer and Cash Collection Sheet Guardian you did a masterful job of tracking down every officer after each meal. You even followed them up to the firing line on the ranges.

The State Funeral of our Commander-In-Chief was your first ceremonial assignment. None of us were inside the church so we cannot testify for certain whom you ushered where, but the confusion when the dignitaries came out seems to indicate that all may have not been correct. You also took good care of the Irish Military Academy Cadets during their visit. All went well until you left to escort them to meet their plane at Dulles Airport. How much did you have to pay that taxi driver to lead you out there? Is it true that Esso road maps don't have a declination diagram?

You were once seen observing a chapel casket transfer from the parking lot but is it really true, that during two months in the Old Guard, you have never seen the inside of Arlington Cemetery?

Who is Miss Phan-Thi-Mai? We are told that she returned your letter rather than paying the 1-cent postage due. Maybe she no longer lives at 484 Phan-Dinh-Phung in Saigon, or perhaps the letter was missent to Miss Heidi Krautsenfum in Hanau, Germany.

We of the Old Guard have enjoyed your brief stay with us and trust that in your civilian life your tour will be filled with success and happiness. Signed by the membership, the 10th day of December, the year of our Lord one thousand nine hundred and sixty-three, the first year of mustaches in the Old Guard, the fourth day of Captain Pond's honeymoon, the forty-second year of the Irish Revolution, the first year of the green beret in the Cemetery, the one hundred seventy-ninth year of the Old Guard, and the one hundred eighty-seventh year of the United States of America.

Since my arrival at Fort Meyer, I was concerned about my health. I was not feeling well. After my farewell party and days before my discharge, I checked into DeWitt Army Hospital, Fort Belvoir, Virginia, for a series of tests. On December 12, I was on my back in a ward with other soldiers and feeling sorry for myself. An army captain appeared at my bed and announced, "Lieutenant, you were terminated from the Army yesterday. You are not in the Army anymore and we cannot treat you here unless you reenlist. You have to take the oath of office right now. I'm here to administer it."

I was shocked. I was ready to get out. I definitely did not want to extend my service obligation. The captain explained that my reenlistment was only until I was released from the hospital. With great uncertainty, and having no real choice, I took the oath to extend my service.

Days later, the discharging physician told me he had bad news and good news for me. The bad news was that because of the hepatitis, I might have a liver problem when I got older. The good news was that if my liver began to fail, I was entitled to treatment at a Veterans Administration hospital. I was released from the hospital with a qualified clean bill of health. I started a new life, but a connection to the old one remained.

Inexplicable The dead were Vietnamese of different ages and sexes. It was a fresh kill. All dead. No wounded. I stepped over corpses covered by swarms of droning black flies. There were no jungle noises. The smell of gunpowder filled the air. Jungle growth blocked the path I was on. I parted the vegetation and stepped onto an empty beach. It was long, crescent shaped, and pristine. The wide, sandy beach sloped gently to the water. Coconuts rocked in the surf, and tide-line creatures moved to and fro. My jungle boots left a distinctive imprint in the sand. Close to the sea and in the middle of the beach, I sat on the warm sand with my submachine gun by my side. Fatigues and bush hat protected me from the sun. I could hear the gentle sounds of birdcalls, the rustle of bushes in the breeze, and the rhythmic crash of the waves. I contemplated the watery horizon and was content. I was alone, safe, and relaxed.

Soon, I sensed others and saw two individuals, one on my left and the other on my right, walk from the jungle and sit equidistant between the end of the beach and me. In geometric progression, others walked from the jungle and occupied the sand, always keeping equal space between them. Quickly, every bit of sand was covered with boisterous and argumentative people: Americans, Vietnamese, men and women, young and old. They were shoulder to shoulder. They crowded me. I was no longer alone, safe, relaxed, and content. My solitude was broken and I was angry, anxious, and irritable.

I turned my weapon on those nearest to me and in a sweeping motion I shot their neighbors too. I killed everyone at the seashore that day. They fell in grotesque postures, screaming, crying, squirming, and moaning. When it was done, I sat again and watched the surf, hoping to regain peace and solitude.

In time the beach emptied. Soon the beach was quiet and empty, save for me. But where before the sand was white and warm, now it was splotched bloodred and cold. There were no pleasant sounds or fragrances. Stomach contents and bloody flesh flavored the air. I was alone again, immobile and catatonic.

These confused and distorted images stayed with me as I left the beach and walked into the jungle on the same body-strewn path. I made my way up the path walking on the dead. Soon I was walking alone through the pathless gray jungle.

I had this dream while in Vietnam and for many years afterward. It was a source of conflict and anxiety because of the violent, depraved images and because I had not experienced anything like these scenes from my subconscious. The dream occurred sporadically, and as far as I could tell was not stimulated by events in my life at the time. Dreams supposedly contain information and meaning and tell us things about ourselves, about our emotions, but these inexplicable images and thoughts serve to hide the truth, and that is fine. I have avoided learned sources; no couch and free association for me. I know enough about myself and am content with what I know.

Eight

REFLECTIONS

'Tis with our judgments as our Watches, none
Go just alike, yet each believes his own.
—ALEXANDER POPE, *"An Essay on Criticism"*

The Advisor Program In theory, the advisor program was a great concept. United States support would be given if advisors were attached to Vietnamese military units. The field advisors were to ensure that the aid was properly used to conduct numerous and effective operations. Although advisors would provide tactical advice and coordinate U.S. support, they were not supposed to lead troops or engage the Viet Cong. Although some advisors to ranger and airborne units developed successful relationships with their counterparts, on the whole little advisor advice was accepted (at any level), and advisors, at least at the battalion level, regularly engaged in and sought out combat.

It was truly arrogant of the United States to expect Vietnamese officers to accept and follow the advice of American officers, even those with years of experience. American officers had different interests, different experiences, and a different view of the world. Upon arrival in Vietnam at age twenty-three, I had no idea what to advise these officers about and had little knowledge of or expertise on the country and its people.

Although the selection of highly motivated volunteers and the preassignment training were positive factors, the program's unrealistic objectives and failure to take into account the realities of human nature doomed it to failure. Due to the remoteness and relative inaccessibility of my battalion, I had little supervision by senior American officers in my chain of command. I was young and inexperienced and had little to offer beyond energy and aggressiveness. These facts plus the entirely human reaction of Captain Beng to my presence significantly reduced the possibility of my success as an advisor. But I did wave the flag, and although my achievements as an advisor were limited, I benefited in many ways from my time with the battalion.

It was never possible that advisors alone could change the ARVN into an effective fighting force with enough energy and aggressiveness to defeat the Viet Cong. Nevertheless, the American effort in Vietnam from 1960 to 1964 was to a great extent dependent upon the advisor. We were the major instruments of the U.S. military effort, and I was part of it. I helped, suggested, coaxed, and hectored. I lived under extremely primitive conditions and put myself in danger, all the while being ready to protect myself. Advisors, myself included, became personally involved. I wanted to help the Vietnamese. It was an exciting adventure.

Determination, patience, and perseverance were the most important virtues demanded of advisors, including me. These virtues were more important than the ability to face danger with confidence and resolution. I lived and fought in the bush with a battalion led in an inferior manner, and learned early on the importance of these qualities. I was often confused and misunderstood, and my patience and humility were continually tested. Frequently I was ignored. I developed a thick skin but also a highly tuned sensitivity. Both have served me well these many years. I persevered for one year and the United States persisted for another twelve years, but the Viet Cong and the North Vietnamese persisted longer and won the war.

In spite of the difficulties I faced, good things happened to me. I achieved a deep, personal satisfaction from the sense of identification with the ARVN soldier and developed a self-discipline and comprehension that came from living and fighting with strangers. I came to believe that I could do anything I decided to do. The advisor experience was a major influence on my life and a profound rush. It shaped me in a multitude of ways, some of which are evident to me only now. Life seemed so real because of the exhilaration that came with being an advisor and, sadly, the misery of others all around me.

Many advisors early on recognized that the advisor program was doomed to fail because the war was a civil war, which they came to believe the South Vietnamese would lose sooner or later. Advisors were constantly frustrated. The last sentence of my January letter home is uncannily prophetic.

> The military situation hasn't improved any since I've been here. As a matter of fact the good guys are just about holding their own. I can't envision a change for the good until the present government is replaced.
>
> I'm enjoying my work very much. It's hard, honest and rewarding but also very frustrating. The Vietnamese have no sense of urgency about this war—or anything. Suggestions are carried out slowly, if at all. The communists will be just as strong ten years from now.

The communists were stronger in 1973, but not for the reason I had anticipated. They were stronger ten years later because of the unqualified support of North Vietnam. The North Vietnamese involvement in the war changed in 1965 with the dispatch of the infantry battalions and supplies to the south by way of the Ho Chi Minh Trail. It was understood then that the Viet Cong could not defeat the ARVN, so the northern leaders sent to the south soldiers of the North Vietnamese Army (NVA). Although the NVA was defeated in battle by U.S. forces at every meeting, they overwhelmed the ARVN three years after the United States withdrew from the conflict in 1972.

The following paragraphs are from a March letter to my parents. Now, thirty-eight years later, I have no reason to change a word of it.

Most of the Americans are disappointed and disgusted with the whole aid program. The Vietnamese are more than willing to accept our money, but not our advice. It's very frustrating. I've seen little progress since I've been here. The local government is definitely not winning the war, contrary to newspaper reports. Don't believe the Viet Cong casualty figures that are printed in the papers. Most of them are false.

Currently, much of our money is being misused or made ineffectual by graft and corruption. I've seen U.S. wheat, which we have given to Diem, being sold to the peasants. I've seen an instance where a province chief (similar to U.S. governor) was given a large sum of money to pay the peasants working on public works—i.e. roads, bridges, canals—and instead of doing this he kept the money and made the people work for free. I really think that in a short time our government will have to completely reevaluate our aid program, both military and economic.

All too frequently corrupt officials, political and military, siphoned off our aid. A sure sign of a corrupt officer or politician in that poor country was a gold watch. More than once I saw high-placed officials wearing a gold wristwatch. Corruption at all levels was rampant and blatant, and it severely undermined the government's legitimacy in the eyes of the people.

Of course, the reason for the loss of Vietnam to communism was not the failure of the advisor program or of the subsequent American military effort, but the inability of the South Vietnamese government to effect real and meaningful political, social, and economic reforms. Land reform and political reform would have gone a long way toward winning the support of the people for the government. Reforms did not occur; possibly South Vietnamese government leaders did not think they were necessary because America was committed and the Viet Cong would be defeated by America.

The Peace Movement By the end of 1963, there were only 16,000 U.S. troops in Vietnam. No one imagined then what this curious little war would become. It split our country. Those against U.S. involvement in Vietnam organized a peace movement.

The peace movement did not outrage me. Our system, thank God, allows for dissent. It encourages debate. It allows us to influence and change our government's policies and actions. Protest is permitted, unless dangerous to persons, destructive of property, or actually treasonable.

Students, the media, academia, the political left, and a sizable percentage of the U.S. population supported the peace movement. The war was described as wrongheaded, foolish, imperialistic, racist, and immoral. The U.S. government could not satisfactorily explain why it was in the vital interest of the United States to fight a war in Vietnam.

At the beginning, the public overwhelmingly supported the war and our soldiers, but as the bodies of young men were returned home and the war went on year after year with no end in sight, a majority of the public came to oppose the war. People took to the streets of our major cities to express their view. The United States and its institutions were being overwhelmed by internal disputes. The situation was like that in Vietnam but on a different scale. We, too, were at war with ourselves.

President Kennedy, the media darling, had committed thousands of U.S. soldiers, including me and other advisors, to Vietnam. President Johnson, the media goat, escalated U.S. involvement and mismanaged the war to a fare-thee-well. In time, he and his cabal of advisors knew (or should have known) that Vietnam was a mistake and we should withdraw. President Nixon, the media villain, for most of his term in office tried to disengage from Vietnam on terms that preserved U.S. honor and South Vietnamese sovereignty. But honor is an unjustifiable goal when young men are dying in a lost cause. Honor and morality are not the same concept. Honor is singularly subjective. We should have gotten out earlier. Nixon tried diplomacy, negotiation, bombing North Vietnam, mining its harbors, invading the Cambodian sanctuaries of the communist troops, and large-scale U.S. military operations. American troop strength rose to well over half a million in 1969. But the north insisted on conditions that would leave South Vietnam in a weak position. Through it all we continued to encourage and threaten the South Vietnamese military and political leaders to improve. But to no avail; it was now our war. Our forces were successful against the North Vietnamese in every engagement. The U.S. weapons, tactics, and soldiers prevailed on the battlefield, but we could not force them to accept our terms for ending the war. We could only win by doing things our government rejected out of concern for Soviet and Chinese reaction. The United States was like a porcupine without quills.

The peace movement was instrumental in forcing the United States out of Vietnam, but contrariwise it contributed to the length of time it took to end the fighting and negotiate our withdrawal. The domestic pressure brought on President Nixon by the students, media, and political left to end the war strengthened the resolve of the North Vietnamese, and they increased their demands and conditions.

Young men struggled with their consciences and ambitions. Many thought the war was unjust and immoral; out of principle they risked jail by not reporting for the draft. They were noble. Other less principled young men (a future president included) seized on the arguments of the peace movement to justify avoiding military service and they, by any means, let others go in their place. It was not an easy time for anyone.

A Corrupting Influence Another reason for the peace movement's success was the unfair and corrupt system used for selecting men to fight in Vietnam. It has been estimated that only one-third of the eligible (draft age) U.S. male population served in the military during the Vietnam War. One-third of those who served were assigned to units in Vietnam; of this one-third, 15 percent were involved in combat.

Many men manipulated the draft system to avoid serving. America has a history of its men avoiding the draft. Vietnam was not unique. At that time military service was a variable in every young man's life. It was an uncertainty they had to deal with. At the age of seventeen, all males were required to register with their county's selective service draft board. The draft board, after decreasing its pool of men for approved exemptions and deferments, would select names by lottery. The men thus selected received "Greetings" from the government ordering them to report for duty at a specific time and place for a specified period of time, two years in the 1960s and 1970s.

Legal exemptions from the draft fluctuated depending on the military's needs and included exemptions for conscientious objectors, marriage, fathers, clergy, felons, and homosexuals and for medical reasons. No women were drafted, and I feel they will be exempt the next time too. The military wanted perfect male specimens with no known problems, so exemptions for medical reasons included many minor ailments and imperfections, such as flat feet, skin rashes, poor eyesight, abnormal blood pressure, and antisocial behavior.

Deferments were granted to complete an education, for teachers, and for jobs considered essential to the defense of the country. Deferments could be successive; that is, a four-year college deferment could be followed by a three-year graduate school deferment followed by a strategic job deferment. Piling on deferments, one after another, until at twenty-six one was beyond draft age was a successful strategy.

With the help of cooperative doctors, psychiatrists, clergy, deans, parents, influential friends, and employers, a determined man with resources could avoid the draft. Among those who were drafted, some resorted to taking drugs that would induce symptoms of high blood pressure and other unacceptable medical conditions so they would fail the preinduction physical. Some just ran. It is estimated that 20,000 young men fled to Canada to avoid being drafted.

The draft that sent men to Vietnam was outrageously unfair, more unfair than past conscriptions except perhaps for the draft law in effect during the United States Civil War, which among other injustices allowed the wealthy to pay others (mostly poor immigrants) to take their place. During the Vietnam War, many, including the rich, well connected, and opportunistic, manipulated the system to avoid service. To a large extent, the poor, immigrants, minorities, and those without opportunities, resources, and connections filled the draft quotas. But for most young men it was not a simple choice between duty and avoiding military service. Most struggled with their options. In spite of the unfairness of the draft, more than 3 million Americans served in Vietnam from 1962 to 1975. Heroically, they reconciled their qualms and ambitions with their duty to serve, no matter how much they disagreed with the war.

Although unfair and corrupt, the draft and its administration were not a miscalculation. The draft reflected political choices. Our elected leaders put it in place to lessen opposition from the influential parts of our society and to protect their own sons. If the draft had been fair, if there had been limited exemptions and deferments, perhaps the public debate over our involvement in Vietnam would have been concluded much earlier.

In an attempt to heal the country, President Jimmy Carter granted amnesty in 1977 to those who had left the country and to all others who had illegally avoided the draft. I supported the amnesty. It was the right thing to do and it was for the right reason. No draft-dodging trials ad infinitum. I think it was the high point of Carter's presidency.

Brother Emmett My brother Emmett thought the United States was foolish and wrong to be involved in Vietnam. He resented his three years in the navy and missing out on the first eight months of his first son's life. He served as a navy supply officer aboard the USS *Iwo Jima,* which included tours off the coast of Vietnam, one in 1967 and another in 1968.

The *Iwo Jima* was the command center for various landing assaults. My brother recalls the detailed preparations for these coordinated attacks. After steaming independently, seven or eight ships would congregate on the morning of a landing. The beach would be heavily bombed and strafed until the moment when the first small boat landed its marines. As the wave of beached marines moved inland, opposition would be hit with air strikes. A new wave of marines would be airlifted to landing zones behind the enemy's lines. As helicopters continued to transport an entire battalion, including artillery pieces and small tanks, returning choppers would bring out the dead and wounded.

The *Iwo Jima* had a series of operating rooms, and my brother recalled teams of surgeons working around the clock. He related that these landing operations were an awesome demonstration of power but generally achieved mixed results. Of the six operations he was involved in, three met no resistance. One featured "a landing in the delta by a jovial battalion of South Vietnamese marines." Two were considered moderate successes in that they temporarily drove Viet Cong from contested areas. A landing on South Vietnam's northern coast proved costly. A battalion of U.S. Marines suffered heavy casualties when it encountered an entrenched force of North Vietnamese regulars. The marines had to be withdrawn. Emmett still remembers the prelanding optimism and has the memo sent by the aggressive marine colonel to his battalion the night before the operation. It states: "If we receive fire, let's draw blood. I don't like a report that states: Quote, Negative Results, Unquote."

As a reluctant participant, Emmett recalled the excitement of these large operations and a sense of bewilderment at why the United States was doing these things. He spoke of the surrealistic experience of shooting home movies, which he still has, of these landings and of just-wounded marines being helicoptered back to his ship for surgery. He felt more an observer than a combatant. To this day he believes that we were in Vietnam to help the French maintain their semblance of an empire.

Sister Una My sister Una also served, although not in the military. In 1967 she was a flight attendant for Airlift International Airlines. She flew on charter flights once a week from San Francisco to Saigon with full loads of 165 soldiers to and from the war. She remembers taking loquacious, adventure-loving boys to Saigon. The return flights were void of youthful high jinks. Weary, spacey, mute, and inattentive men were on the return flights. Una's last flight to Vietnam was during the Tet Offensive, conducted by the North Vietnamese Army and the Viet Cong. Her plane landed at 11 P.M. on January 31, 1968, at Tan Son Nhat airport by the light of flares; the airfield landing lights were out, to prevent the Viet Cong from destroying her plane. Her words describe that moment: "From the cockpit, I could see battle fires in the distance and technicians up close on the tarmac, guiding us to a stop. With my heart racing, we quickly deplaned the troops. I whispered 'good luck and God Bless,' and in that moment vowed not to participate in this airlift again. We departed immediately, with a full load, back to Bangkok and the U.S. At that point in time, I understood the old eyes of young soldiers."

After the Tet Offensive, Una did not want to participate in the war anymore. Many Americans came to the same conclusion. The Tet Offensive was the turning point of the war, but not in a military sense. It was planned and directed by North Vietnam. The North Vietnamese knew that the offensive was suicidal, but it encouraged the Viet Cong to believe there would be a general popular uprising in support, which did not happen. Although the Viet Cong suffered tremendous losses, the North Vietnamese gained an invaluable psychological victory. Their ability to mobilize nearly 70,000 soldiers and launch surprise attacks against more than a hundred cities and towns amazed and troubled the American people. Our government told us that our opponents were insignificant and we would soon win. They told us that victory in Vietnam was a light that could be seen at the end of the tunnel. Our leaders were wrong, and it was obvious that they were misleading the people or had no idea what the real situation was. Whatever the reason, many Americans came to believe that their government was not to be trusted, and that the enemy was a formidable foe capable of engaging America in a protracted and costly struggle. The American public was shocked by those events, and many who had supported the war joined the peace movement.

Cousin Pat Most of the U.S. soldiers who served in Vietnam were draftees and, for the most part, did what they had to do. The war affected the lives of all of them and of all Americans, those who served and those who did not.

The war affected the life of my first cousin Pat Mulvihill in a somewhat unusual way. Pat emigrated from Ireland to the United States in 1965 at the age of twenty. He stayed with relatives at first, then, after getting a job in a bank, moved in with friends. Pat was doing what countless immigrants did before and since have done: building a life for himself in America.

America has always drafted immigrants. It seems fair to me that anyone who wants to live here should be subject to the same obligations, including the draft, as citizens. Pat was aware of the Vietnam War but did not think he would be drafted into the U.S. Army. It never crossed his mind. Compulsory military service never existed in Ireland. Nine months after arriving in the United States, Pat received a letter from the draft board ordering him to report for a preinduction physical and an IQ test. The envelope contained two subway tokens, which friends told him was a good sign because the second token was for his trip home after the physical. My cousin was one of seven hundred men who reported at 7:30 A.M. for a four-hour IQ test to be followed by a physical. Pat did his best to fail the test, and he succeeded. That afternoon he and thirty other men who failed the IQ test were individually interviewed. After the interview, an officer told Pat he didn't believe his low test score and said he would be drafted in a month. Subsequently, Pat received an envelope in the mail containing one subway token and a letter of greetings from the president of the United States.

Pat had his own way of avoiding the draft. He was resourceful. He decided to return to Ireland, although he was criticized by some of his relatives in the United States for doing so. Pat said, "I should not be compelled to serve in the armed forces of a foreign country, especially when hundreds of thousands of young Americans were avoiding the draft by seeking asylum in Sweden and Canada or by remaining in school indefinitely."

Pat has no regrets for the actions he took all those years ago. He has a good lifestyle, wonderful family, and happiness in Ireland. Naturally my cousin wonders whether, if he had survived Vietnam, he would have achieved his American dream or, if not, whether his name would be on the Vietnam Memorial Wall in Washington, D.C.

The Dominos Stopped Falling United States involvement in Vietnam, from beginning to end, was marked by mistaken appraisals of the situation. Slowly, gradually, in fits and starts, as the situation worsened, we committed more men and treasure. But we could not win. The confusing combination of religious, ethnic, territorial, military, political, and ideological issues contributed to a crisis atmosphere month after month. These difficult dynamics overwhelmed South Vietnam. Our ally was weak and corrupt. We could not have lost without them. And we did lose but not on the battlefield. We were not beaten there but we lost nonetheless. But rarely are victories final or defeats forever. Life is a continuum and so is time, the great equalizer.

When the definitive history of the conflict between the Soviets and America, between communism and capitalism, is written, I believe it will state that the rising tide of communism was stopped in Vietnam. American sacrifice proved our intent to contest the communists everywhere. Thereafter, we prevailed: in Eastern Europe, in Afghanistan, in Central America, in Southeast Asia, and in the Mideast. Our ideas and economy won the day. Our losses in Vietnam were part of the price of our ultimate victory. But, and here is the sad part, we probably would have prevailed without becoming involved in Vietnam, because communism is a flawed ideology. Its basic tenets conflict with human nature and man's values and hopes. However, hindsight has no value unless it is used to allocate blame, and hypotheticals have no historical value at all.

In the end, the Viet Cong and the North Vietnamese won the war because they were highly motivated, they persevered, and they had the unquestioned support of a large portion of the population. They were willing to endure countless hardships and accept horrendous casualties because of their belief in their cause. We ignored Ho Chi Minh's statement to the French in 1953 that you can kill ten of my men for every one I kill of yours, but you will lose and I will win. We did not think it could happen to us.

The American people did not believe that the cost of the war, in life and treasure, was worth the goal. Our leaders made two fundamental mistakes. Pursuing the war without having overwhelming civilian support was a mistake. A large percentage of the population came to deny the validity of the domino theory and wondered of what possible interest it could be to the United States if South Vietnam went communist. That small country was 7,000 miles away. It wasn't worth American lives.

The second mistake was letting the war become our war. The unpleasant reality was that what had been a Vietnamese civil war became a war between a large portion of the Vietnamese people and the U.S. military. We went into Vietnam at the request of the South Vietnamese government to help them, not to fight their war. They took our supplies and equipment but not our advice. They were corrupt. There were few reforms. Their armed forces, at their best, were ineffective. The United States should have made the political and military leaders of South Vietnam take our advice, or we should have left. But we ended up fighting their war because our leaders had it fixed in their minds that Vietnam was part of the global struggle with communism. And it was. And we took on the challenge, and lost.

However, it can be argued, with some merit, that it was our war from the beginning and that the United States created South Vietnam in 1954 ex nihilo for our own purposes; to contain communism in Southeast Asia. Subsequently we invited ourselves in to save South Vietnam when its leaders proved unable to secure the support of the people or govern effectively. According to this view, it was not surprising that the ARVN, the army we had trained, clothed, fed, paid, and armed, performed so poorly. That army did not want to fight our war.

My War My tour in Vietnam was self-indulgent; it was quixotic. I was not driven by ambition. I volunteered not for patriotic or idealistic reasons but solely for excitement and adventure. The pursuit of truth and the respect of my fellow man did not enter into my decision. I do not recall pondering these issues. I traded principle for excitement and adventure. In a moral sense, I was a spectator of all that was around me; for that matter, to a great extent I still am. At best, I was amoral. My only explanation was my youth, although I was not just a kid. I wanted to be in the arena, and things happened there that I cannot explain today and need not describe to tell my story. Well, I got what I went for, and more.

What about our leaders? What can be said for the wisdom, even good faith, of our leaders? They were experienced and, one hopes, wiser than I. Some of them believed and some just went along. The first rule was self-interest. It almost always is. Later, in leisure, those who went along fashioned analysis that justified their actions. Time is their ally; they use it to distort the truth. They are shameless. Today these cardboard figures self-consciously publish their tortured explanations. They try to manipulate the past in order to secure bravos for themselves.

However, it is easy from this distance to sit back and criticize, to judge. I remember that I believed in the rightness and righteousness of our cause, but, based on my experience as an advisor, I wondered how we could win with the ARVN and the South Vietnamese government as our allies. Victor Hugo wrote, "Great blunders, like large ropes, have many fibers." But I was only a lieutenant and did not have the knowledge or influence that our leaders had.

I am only sixty-three years old and do not have one of those famed Ph.D.s, which apparently confer great wisdom.

But I do not think we can always avoid debacles such as Vietnam (and all wars are debacles). War is a facet of life, as is error. We are human and fallible. We make mistakes. Mistakes do happen and sometimes they are costly. Sometimes things go wrong and you lose.

All we can really learn from history are the mistakes we are going to make. We do not learn the correct course of action by studying the past, because knowledge does not equate with wisdom and virtue. Historic events occur through the interaction of human nature and circumstances. Human nature is not going to change, and it is difficult to control situations. Above all, the United States must stay strong and not trust anyone. To reject this view is to proceed at our peril. This is a sad, revealing philosophy, but when tested against what we know of man's nature, about his inhumanity to his fellow man, we must adhere to it, remain vigilant, and continue to ask the same old questions. When the canal that is supposed to be on the left is not there, and the rice paddy that should have peasants in it has none, it is appropriate, imperative rather, to ask, "What is happening?"

Nine

RETURN TO VIETNAM

Spring seedlings,
Fragile, small and meek.
Summer flower,
Showy, full and at your peak.
Autumn colors,
Tall and reedy, the garden queen.
Oh, wonderful Impatiens
Depart with the frost, the snowy mean.
—MARTIN J. DOCKERY, "Four Seasons"

A Twenty-two-Hour Flight Although I thought little before making my first trip to Vietnam, I spent thirty-seven years deciding to return. Once the decision was made, I looked forward with wonder. In January 1999 I contacted Mike Blackwell, my old army buddy. In 1973, after spending fourteen years in the army, Major Blackwell left active duty. His second tour in Vietnam was in 1969 when he served as a district advisor in the delta.

Mike and I decided to go back together, a couple of old soldiers, each over sixty, doing our thing. A lot of water had passed under the bridge, and although there was an awful outcome to our original mission, we felt the same old excitement. We two, who volunteered for duty back in the dawn of our history, were taking that old walk again. We were thrilled. Maybe we would find some old wanted posters of us. We joked about that, of course, but in 1963 it was literally true. Captain Beng told me I had a price on my head; the Viet Cong had distributed a poster with my name, description, and a bounty. I never saw the poster, but I wanted it to be

208

true. Today, it is romantic to think it was so. Mike saw his wanted poster, and I saw posters describing other advisors. It was a matter of dark humor, especially if the price went up, as it sometimes did when somebody thought we were accomplishing something. Depending on his mood and how he felt about me at the time, Captain Beng would tell everyone within hearing range whether he thought the price on my head was too high or too low.

I was determined not to get sick during this trip to Vietnam. In the weeks before leaving, with vivid memories of tropical diseases still in my mind, I visited a tropical disease clinic in New York City, where I paid $260 for a consultation and five vaccinations. Prescription medicine cost me an additional $320. I overdid it, but I was not going to take any chances this time.

I arrived at Saigon's Tan Son Nhat Airport on February 7, 1999, after a twenty-two-hour trip from New York City via Vancouver and Hong Kong, carrying excessive medical supplies and irrepressible excitement. A modern, new terminal building stood beside the crumbling, old terminal and the rusted revetments that had protected U.S. warplanes.

After leaving the plane, I passed through customs, manned by soldiers in military uniforms with the Red Star prominently displayed on their caps. The memory of a captured flag, with the same red star, residing in my basement flashed through my mind as I walked out of the terminal into a throng of vendors, potential guides, and drivers. I remembered my arrival thirty-seven years earlier, the bus ride into Saigon past the cemetery for the French legionnaires, and how much I did not know. The smells, sounds, and chaos of the traffic were familiar. The French cemetery was still there. Despite our agreement at the airport, the taxi driver I hired took me to a hotel where he wanted me to stay, not the one I requested. Most likely he was paid a commission for every American he delivered to "his" hotel. I convinced him in my gentle way that he had made a mistake and I was not going to pay him unless he took me to "my" hotel.

Mike and I stayed at the Mai Lan, a Vietnamese-style hotel, for sixteen dollars a night. Each room had a bath, air-conditioning, telephone, and TV and was large, clean, and quiet. The hotel was a great choice. The rooster in the back ensured that we would get early-morning starts. The extended family that owned and managed the hotel lived on the first floor.

Buildings in a Vietnamese city, including stores and hotels, have no doors in the western sense. Often the entire front is open to the street, and at night a large iron gate is manually slid across a metal track for security. So too with the Mai Lan. The hotel itself had no lobby, just a small ground-floor area for a check-in desk, a few tiny tables, chairs, an ancestral altar, and some potted plants.

The street was the lobby. In the evenings, after returning from dinner (the hotel had no restaurant), we would sit in the folding beach chairs on the sidewalk, drink tea or the strong, espresso-type Vietnamese coffee, and watch the passing scene. The hotel family and neighbors often joined us and were alternately curious, questioning, shy, and eager, especially to learn English and hear about us, our families, and America. On the street before us, a constant stream of cycles, motorbikes, pedal bikes, and motorcyclos, loaded far beyond their capacity, provided a fascinating panorama of city life in today's Vietnam. The overwhelming impression here, and we were to find it true throughout the delta, was of incredible business, movement, and freedom.

Tet We arrived in Saigon six days prior to Tet, the Lunar New Year. Large and small banners proclaiming *Chuc Mung Nam Moi,* Happy New Year, were hung from and between buildings and across streets. It was indeed a Happy New Year for me; I had returned to this land of many memories. Tet, which lasts for three days, is the most important holiday of the year. It is believed that the first part of Tet determines one's fortunes for the rest of the year. It is a religious and family-oriented holiday of great importance. People return to their families, pay their debts, forgive one another, buy new clothes, clean house, give and receive gifts, visit temples and ancestral graves, and make offerings to spirits. Flowers and fruit trees decorate homes and businesses.

Saigon 1999 Almost 8 million people crowded present-day Saigon. Traffic was bumper to bumper. In the business districts everyone seemed to have a cell phone. Just as in the United States, the phones were a nuisance in restaurants and dangerous to everyone in the vicinity when used by someone on a motorbike or motorcycle. The streets and sidewalks were busy and full. Minicafes, made up of small, scuffed tables, folding chairs or stools, and charcoal braziers, interrupted pedestrian traffic on many sidewalks. Old women, seated on strategic street corners, filled flat tires from noisy air compressors for pennies. From their carts, vendors sold sugarcane, lottery tickets, drinks, fruit, vegetables, and sweets. There were no uniformed police in sight. The White Mice (our term in 1963 for the Vietnamese police) were long gone. I saw no pregnant women, and no women smoking, but every man smoked incessantly.

I could not help but think of Saigon in 1963 and the things that had happened then. It was not difficult to make a comparison between then and now, even after thirty-seven years. Beggars were still plentiful and beautiful women too, although more women now wore tight-fitting western clothes rather than the traditional *ao dai*. But both the curious and the various entrepreneurs were more discreet, and we drew less attention as we walked and browsed. The bars, with fragrant hostesses catering to foreigners, were still there. The Rex Hotel still had an exclusive restaurant on the roof, and steak and cold beer were still on the menu, although the clientele was different. Civilians, most of them Westerners, and predominantly French, now dined and drank high above the Vietnamese street. The colonels were gone, and there were no dim artillery flashes in the distance.

My powers of observation, my tolerance, my stamina, and my willingness to act contrary to my sense of right and wrong are different today than they were in 1963. I am different. What was ordained and necessary in those days seems wild and irrational today, and I neither sought nor experienced those places and activities that so characterized Saigon for me in 1963. I was never surprised at how or where the night ended. The war and the Delta Fox are no more. God knows, I have gotten older and wiser.

Mike had made various business appointments in Saigon. After a meeting with the number-two men at an important government department located in Saigon, the official asked me whether this was my first trip to Vietnam. On learning that I had been here as a soldier, he informed me that he had fought on the "American side," then proceeded to relate that his opportunities were therefore limited. He said that because of this history and the fact that he was a southerner, he would never achieve a top position. After the meeting we were told that a family member who had been a Viet Cong, a not unusual circumstance, had secured this man's position for him. At other meetings with other businessmen and government officials, former Viet Cong spoke without boasting of their individual role in the war. It was humbling to hear them speak of their hardships and losses.

Many of the people we met had in dangerous times cast their lot with us, and we had abandoned them. Many of them were the elite of Saigon society, and they lost everything; some spent years in reeducation centers. Now they were entitled to the losers' share. They were a difficult ally, and we were foreigners involved—at their request, we said—in their civil war. I detected nostalgia for the old days and resentment at their losses, but I did not feel anger directed at the United

States or me. There was a sense of common experience. Perhaps their true feelings have been masked by twenty-five years of wearing the loser's cap.

Delta Drive We made arrangements to rent a van and driver for a trip through the Mekong Delta. For four days we retraced our steps of long ago and revisited places and relived events. We drove through the delta and to the cities we knew: My Tho, Vinh Long, Can Tho, Rach Gia, Ha Tien, Tri Ton, Chau Doc, Long Xuyen, and Sa Dec. Each city and the countryside revived memories of people, places, and things. The rural delta, except for infrastructure development projects such as building roads and bridges, had not changed much.

The prices (for everything) were negotiable. We never paid more than twelve dollars per night for a large room with a bath and balcony. In Vietnam there is a two-tier price system, which I found annoying but is the custom. It is possible—actually necessary—to bargain, and with a little Vietnamese language from long ago and a few smiles and general good humor, we could improve the deal, but a foreigner always pays more than a local. Vietnamese pay one-third of what foreigners pay for everything, including food, hotel rooms, and clothing. The identical room in the same hotel for our van driver each night was four dollars or less.

Road and bridge construction slowed us the length of our trip. Everywhere, we saw building projects. Narrow bridges were being replaced by wider ones, ferry crossings were being replaced by modern bridges, and electrification along the main road appeared complete. Houses were much the same as before—brown thatch, bamboo pole, dirt floors, open front—but many had the incredible addition of a TV antenna. We saw new canals under construction and a tall silver-colored statue of Uncle Ho in a people's park in Can Tho. Ho, looking grandfatherly and benign, was seated with small children on his lap. This old revolutionary and architect of the communist takeover of all of Vietnam surpassed his dream. He has passed into myth as the father of his country.

Vietnam was an agricultural society, as before. About half the delta was under cultivation. In some rural areas we saw rice husks spread out on woven mats to dry by the side of the road. In the countryside, sugarcane and stalks of grain were neatly placed in the road so the weight of passing cars could mash them and assist in their processing. Most people produced, transported, or sold food, or sold and repaired the transport vehicles. Nothing appeared to be thrown away. Everything was eaten, fed to animals, saved, recycled, or burned for fuel. In this regard, nothing had changed since 1963, or probably since the long distant past.

The Far Point The far point and for me the high point of the trip was a visit to the cement plant that my battalion guarded in 1963. Except for the limestone mountain that was being leveled to make cement and the canal between my old quarters and the cement plant, I recognized nothing.

The cement plant village of 1999 was a busy town. The town was built up, and there was substantial evidence of industry as well as debris. The mountain, reduced by decades of incursions by digging men, still dominated the landscape. The plant itself—bigger, busier, and more modern, with numerous additional support and outbuildings—was still the governing man-made feature; and the canal, silent and constant, still pointed dramatically to the horizon and the Gulf of Siam.

The plant, which was completed in 1964, was producing 1.5 million tons of cement a year by 1999. All the infrastructure of a large industrial complex, together with supporting industries, was in place. Wharves, docks, electric power plant, water treatment facility, sewage disposal facility, worker housing, maintenance yards, and a small city stretched from both sides of a well-maintained paved road.

In one sense, my objective in 1963 had been achieved. The communists never managed to destroy the cement plant. Back then they probably knew that eventually they would own it, so why destroy it?

The various structures hissed, belched, and vibrated. We could have been astride the New Jersey Turnpike. All homes and businesses in the immediate vicinity were permanent structures; there were no bamboo and grass huts and no dirt floors. The changes were so great that I could not with certainty locate the site of my thatch hut of yore. I was disappointed that I recognized so little and was in awe of what had been accomplished. But images and memories of people, incidents, and violent things (and sweet things too) came to mind. I remembered the confusion, the isolation, and the turmoil. It was hard to imagine that I had been part of this place. I recalled and knew that it was a good thing that happened to me so many years ago. Indeed, it was.

Cement plants are built where clay and limestone are plentiful. The area around Ha Tien has abundant clay and numerous isolated limestone mountains. They rise singularly out of the rice paddies. The third ingredient, a type of iron, arrives by boat from Malaysia. The improbable mountain that had been in front of my hut was reduced by a third, and large pits from which clay for the factory had been gouged dotted the area. The plant owners believed that the area contained enough limestone and clay for twenty-eight more years of cement production. When these raw materials were exhausted, the cement plant would be shut down. Of course, by then that beautiful, pristine place on the Gulf of Siam would have been transformed into an ecological eyesore. Environmental damage would appear before long, I feared. All this under the watchful eye of the Vietnamese communist government, in pursuit of the export dollar. For me, my cement plant was no more. From now on, it would exist only in my mind.

The Mystery Inspectors Before leaving the United States, Mike and I had arranged to visit the cement plant. Upon our arrival, the plant director, a serious Swiss man, who proceeded to give us a full-blown presentation, including overhead projections, charts, and graphs, met us at the gate. The plant was now owned by a joint venture between a Vietnamese government–owned company and a Swiss company, which had invested $350 million. There were four hundred Vietnamese and ten foreigners working at the plant. It was intended, and the plant director expected, that the Vietnamese, when fully trained, would gradually replace the foreigners.

Upon completion of his twenty-minute presentation, the director leaned over the table and asked, "Who are you guys?" After we told him we were just a couple of old soldiers retracing our steps of long ago, he relaxed and explained that he had received two letters on our behalf: one from the Vietnamese Embassy in Washington, D.C., and one from the chairman of the board of directors of the joint venture that owned the plant. The high status of the letter writers caused him concern about the purpose of our visit. The plant director asked me for a description of the locale in 1963. My description was not what he asked for. Instead of a physical description, I described events of long ago and how it felt to be so isolated, so alone. He said his workers occasionally found unexploded ammunition around the plant.

Toward the end of a delightful lunch attended by several expatriates and their wives, the director excused himself, saying that the French ambassador was arriving in fifteen minutes for a tour. It seemed that, in one respect, activity at the cement plant had not changed; the inspection visits continued. I wondered whether the current inspections were as meaningless and foolish as the ones I had had to stand ready for.

Changes There were physical changes in the delta: The

cities were larger, with more buildings, and the roads were vastly improved. New bridges were being built over the many Mekong tributaries and canals. The population of Vietnam had more than doubled since 1975 to 75 million. Half the population was born after 1975, so most of the people had no memory of the war. The delta was the most populated area of the country and was crowded. People were on the move—on foot, on bicycles, in cars, on buses, on motorbikes, in carts, and astride animals. Produce and animals destined for market were on the road. Pigs, chickens, ducks, goats, and dogs, some alive, some gutted, were tied to vehicles or carried on shoulders, in sacks, and on poles by men, women, and children of all ages. It was busy.

The Vietnamese have been influenced and changed since Europeans arrived in the 1600s. However, the war, globalization, and foreign investments have brought new and accelerated cultural, technological, and industrial changes to Vietnam. Although family, religion, and ancestor worship still have paramount importance, traditional Vietnamese culture is being challenged. Television antennas are ubiquitous, and televisions are visible from the street in almost every home. Cell phones, Honda girls (prostitutes who solicited pedestrians and other motorbike riders while riding around the streets on a Honda), plastic flowers, Tet Santa Clauses, and the chase for the quick buck are indicative of the changes wrought by foreigners. Just as traditional western values in the United States have given way to modern ideas of propriety, morality, and ethics, there is concern within Vietnam that the values of their traditional culture will dissipate and be replaced by modern western values.

The Farmers Prevail The delta is so fertile and the peasants are so industrious and skilled that prior to 1975 Vietnam was an exporter of rice. The Vietnamese maintain that you can throw a handful of rice in the delta and come back in six months to harvest enough rice to feed your family for a year.

After the North Vietnamese won the war in 1975, the government confiscated all the land and introduced collectivized farming. The landowners were not compensated. The peasants, to whom the Viet Cong had promised ownership of land, got none. The peasants toiling in the rice paddies no longer paid a share of the rice crop to an absentee landlord, but they benefited little from their labor. Under collectivization, the share paid to the government was larger than the share paid to the former landlord. For all his labor the peasant realized only enough to live on, not enough to improve his lot. The farmers did not think this was progress. What followed was predictable. The peasants started producing only as much rice as they needed for their families. Rice production fell. Between the years 1976 and 1986, Vietnam had to import rice to feed the people. Only after collectivization ended in 1986 did Vietnam again become an exporter of rice. Today Vietnam is the number-two rice exporter in the world, second only to Thailand.

No Reunion It never occurred to me that I would have a reunion with Captain Beng or others from the battalion. And I did not. I had no way to locate these people. That is not to say I have not wondered about the fate of Captain Beng and the other officers and men of the battalion. I can see them all now. After I left Vietnam in August 1963, they had twelve more years of war, a war that grew steadily more intense, violent, and brutal. In 1973 the United States negotiated a withdrawal of its troops and the release of American prisoners of war. We got out of Vietnam and left the South Vietnamese to fend for themselves. In 1975 the north launched large-scale attacks that overwhelmed South Vietnamese resistance. The South Vietnamese government surrendered on April 30, 1975. Vietnam has a long history of violence and reprisals against its own people. It was no different this time. I don't know whether Captain Beng survived the war. If he did, he was probably sent to a reeducation camp. More than likely he is dead now and I am the one left with these memories.

Hanoi and the North We returned to Saigon by following the great Mekong as it flowed past Chau Doc, Lap Vo, and Sa Dec, all cities from our past experiences. I then flew to Hanoi and Mike returned to his home in Hawaii.

Hanoi is a beautiful city, more than a thousand years older than Saigon. The bread was French, the girls were stunningly beautiful, and the atmosphere was old world. I stayed for four days in a fifteen-dollar-a-day hotel room with bath and balcony in the French Quarter, and I visited cultural sites, which surprisingly helped me better understand my former foe.

The northerners won the war after twenty years of fighting and millions of casualties, and now they rule the southern cities and provinces. The north decides all policy, business, and government issues affecting the south. There is little local autonomy. In the south, communists hold the top position in all agencies, cities, departments, and private companies. Southerners are bitter toward the north because it controls all aspects of political, religious, and economic life in the south and because they believe that the north intentionally directs investment away from the south to the north in order to limit economic growth in the south. In return, northerners protest that the south is chaotic, unreliable, unruly, and disorganized and therefore impossible to govern. I found it interesting that in 1999, as in 1963, the south was ruled by northerners and resentful of it.

The Temple of Literature The culture, psychology, and ethics of Vietnam, China, and other Southeast Asian countries have been shaped to a great extent by Confucianism, which is a philosophy, not an organized religion. A strict moral code, together with an emphasis on obedience and on a personal duty to family and society, are intended to produce stability, which is the goal of Confucianism.

The Temple of Literature in Hanoi represents the essence of Vietnamese/Confucian culture. It stresses the virtues of classicism, scholarship, and public service. The temple once housed the National Academy, which was founded in 1076 and is considered Vietnam's first university. The academy educated the brightest young men of the kingdom in Confucian learning and conducted examinations to appoint senior mandarins, who were the intellectual leaders of society.

The temple abounds with gardens, trees, and plaques. Eighty-two stone stelae resting on the backs of massive stone turtles contain the names and birthplaces of 1,306 doctor laureates of the 82 "examinations" held at the National Academy between 1484 and 1780. There are gaps as long as ten years between examinations because no one could satisfy the rigorous criteria that had to be fulfilled to achieve the distinction.

The importance of learning in Vietnamese society is evident from this inscription on the stone plaque erected at the temple in 1442. "Virtuous and talented men are state sustaining elements: The strength and the prosperity of a state depend on its stable vitality and it becomes weaker as such vitality fails. That is why all the saint emperors and clearsighted kings didn't fail in seeing to the formation of men of talent and the employment of literati to develop this vitality."

A culture that honors learning and beauty, that not long ago was America's implacable and ruthless foe, and that sacrificed millions of its people in the name of national unity, is not an inherent contradiction. This apparent dichotomy is part of the human condition. Mankind is capable of great and of awful things.

On February 20 I took a day trip to the Perfume Pagoda, which is located forty miles southwest of Hanoi. The pagoda is a complex of pagodas and Buddhist shrines built into the cliffs and caves of the Mountain of the Fragrant Traces. The one-way journey by car, sampan, and mountain trail took four and a half hours. It was tiring, but the place was so exotic and the scenery so beautiful that it was worth the effort.

My trip occurred during the Tet holidays, and thousands of Buddhist pilgrims seeking purification and cures and wanting to make offerings and give thanks to God traveled to the Perfume Pagoda the day I did. On the mountain path, traffic passed both ways, shoulder to shoulder. It was a festive trip with singing and chanting. Most of the pilgrims carried fruit, chickens, or other offerings. I was the only Westerner among them.

Eventually we retraced our steps and arrived back in Hanoi. After a long and fascinating day, I paid the driver the agreed amount and we said our good-byes. I was leaving Vietnam the next day. To my surprise the guide showed up at my hotel early the next morning wanting more money. His wife had told him he deserved it because he had worked extra hard.

I could not help but chuckle, to the bewilderment of the taxi driver, as I rode to Hanoi's International Airport to begin the long journey home. I had crossed a number of bridges, bamboo and otherwise, since those long-ago days with Captain Beng, but the same question remained. "What is happening?" True communication between two people of the same culture is difficult enough. Understanding between peoples of vastly different cultures is extremely difficult to achieve even when the words themselves seem clear. Something always gets lost in the translation.

And yet, and yet, not all of it. Whether through accident or design, I have been involved with these people from so far away for all of my adult life. They are part of me. Experiencing it was important. Understanding all of it is not necessary, important, or possible.

I was surprised at how I was affected by this trip; the experience was powerful and indeed emotional. Lots of memories, but I felt no danger and no cares this time. No *xin loi* (regrets) either, and no guilt. Everything was familiar. If there was one really strange thing about my trip back to Vietnam, it was that there was not anything really strange at all. I got some goose bumps and some déjà vu, but mostly it was wildly interesting and strangely comfortable. There were neither ghosts nor devils. It was just hello again, no apologies given or expected. And for the Vietnamese too. "Hey, you GI, hello again, you come back Vietnam. Hello." The door of where I used to live is open.

AFTERWORD

Paradise isn't where you end up, it's where you have been.
— ANON.

Three American presidents served during the long years of the Vietnam War, and I crossed paths with each—just. I supervised the ushers at President Kennedy's funeral Mass and the seating of President Johnson in the cathedral. And in 1967 I began working at Richard Nixon's law firm.

In September 1964 I enrolled in law school at Catholic University of America. In high school and college, I was at the bottom of my class, but in law school I excelled. A Wall Street law firm (Nixon Mudge Rose Guthrie Alexander & Mitchell) hired me upon graduation in 1967. The firm had among its partners Richard Nixon and John Mitchell. As a young associate lawyer, I met both of them and worked for Mr. Mitchell on several occasions. I soon developed respect for Mr. Mitchell as I learned that he was a man of integrity and loyalty. Mitchell even told one of his partners, "I reviewed Dockery's work and I agree with it and if it's wrong it's my mistake." However, our first meeting did not go well.

On my second day at the law firm, my phone rang and the caller identified herself as Mr. Mitchell's secretary. Without thinking, I said, "Who's Mr. Mitchell?" Her terse response was, "Look at the letterhead. He's a name partner." Mitchell wanted to see me in his office that afternoon and was seated at his desk, leaning back and smoking a pipe, when I arrived. Vietnam was on his mind. He wanted to know about my experience there and my general opinion of the war. He told me he had been a PT boat commander in the South Pacific during World War II, as had President Kennedy. We moved onto other topics, and eventually he asked me if I wanted to work on his team. He was getting more legal work and his team needed help. He said that it was an interesting area of the law and I would prosper both professionally and financially. I asked him what his specialty was. "I'm a municipal bonds lawyer," he said matter-of-factly. I asked innocently, "What are municipal bonds?" Mr. Mitchell leaned forward in his chair. With his left hand he took the pipe from his mouth and with his right he slammed the desktop. "Goddammit, Dockery. I've been working on municipal bond deals for twenty years and you've never even heard of a municipal bond?" Memories of Oberammergau and the irate colonel came to mind. Though somewhat shaken, I immediately agreed to join his team of bond lawyers. It turned out to be a good decision. His notions of prosperity proved true.

Mr. Mitchell was then Dick Nixon's campaign manager and did not spend much time at his law practice. I did little work directly for Mitchell. Two new lawyers and I learned municipal law from the nine experienced lawyers of Mitchell's bond group. Municipal bonds are an important tool of local government; they are sold by states, cities, and other political subdivisions to finance the cost of roads, schools, hospitals, power plants, sewers, and other public projects.

After Nixon was elected president in November 1967, Mitchell became the attorney general. Before he left the firm, he called me to his office and asked if I wanted to work with him in Washington. I didn't. I told him I had been in New York only a short time and wanted to learn the law, start a family, and get established before moving anywhere. He was understanding and courteous and told me to get back to him if I changed my mind. I had made what turned out to be a fortunate decision. Other young lawyers from the firm joined the new administration, and some of them were caught up in the widening Watergate scandal.

At Mr. Mitchell's invitation my wife, Meliora, and I attended the inauguration ball in January 1968. He invited his bond lawyers. The ball was held at several locations because there were so many invitees. We met President and Mrs. Nixon when they visited the ballroom we were in. A platoon of eager, vigilant, tuxedoed secret service men chaperoned the president. No chopsticks, black pajamas, thatch roof, or dirt floors there.

On June 17, 1972, there was a break-in at the offices of the National Democratic Committee, located at the Watergate Hotel in Washington, D.C. At that time, Mr. Mitchell was the director of the Committee to Re-elect the President (with the unfortunate acronym of C.R.E.E.P.). As the scandal began to envelop the administration, Mr. Mitchell resigned his post as attorney general on July 1, 1972, and returned to New York to resume his law practice. He left Washington amid rumors that he had authorized the break-in. Every day the newspapers carried stories about him and spoke of his potential involvement and possible grand jury indictments.

One afternoon I was in Mitchell's office while he was reviewing a contract I had prepared. His secretary came to the door and said that the White House was on the phone, and the president wanted to talk with him. I got up to leave the room but he motioned for me to stay. I heard one side of what was a three- or four-minute conversation. I don't recall any pleasantries, but I do recall hearing statements such as, "I don't remember anything like that," "There's going to be enough heat for everyone," "That's a problem," "Do what you have to do," and finally, "Good-bye, Mr. President." Mitchell said nothing that revealed to me exactly what they were talking about. It could have been anything, including Watergate. After he hung up he looked at me for a few seconds, then without commenting on the conversation he gave me guidance on the contract and told me how to proceed. Not long after that call, Mitchell resigned from the firm. Eventually he was found guilty of perjury and obstruction of justice relating to the Watergate burglary, and was sentenced to jail. Years later I saw him at a Washington, D.C., restaurant and went over to his table to greet him. He seemed glad to see me and asked how the municipal bond practice was doing. He also said he was fine, but plainly he was, by my reckoning, a good man who was paying dearly for a mistake.

I met Mr. Nixon several times at the law firm but never did any work for him. When he was elected president and moved to the White House, the firm kept his office exactly the way it was when he was there. Photographs and mementos from when he had been vice president were on the walls and tabletops. It was a shrine to which clients and potential clients were taken to remind them of how close the firm was to the president.

In reality, the president was upset with his former partners. He thought he should have received more money from them after his departure than the partnership agreement provided for by contract. Under the partnership agreement, a withdrawing partner was entitled to receive only his capital contribution to the firm. Nixon wanted more in recognition of clients he had brought to the firm and from whom the firm would surely benefit after his departure. The partners wouldn't agree because they didn't think it looked right for his old law firm to make a payment to the president of the United States that was not specifically required by the partnership agreement. Representing clients before federal agencies could conceivably be challenged on ethical grounds, and other partners upon leaving the firm might demand similar treatment. However, the partners did not want the president angry with the firm, because that wouldn't be good for attracting or retaining clients either. So $200,000 was placed in trust and the president was asked to name a charity to which the money would be donated. The firm was saying, "It's not the money, Mr. President, it's the principle." Ah, "principle," his long suit.

In 1974 I became a partner in the firm, and the chairman told me the details of this story and about the money held in trust. Nixon, either out of pique or simply because he was preoccupied with the Watergate scandal and with trying to extract the United States from Vietnam, had never designated a charity, and under New York State law the money in the trust had to be distributed to a charity that very year. Eventually it was donated to a nonprofit group that provided free legal services to the poor. Nixon was right to be preoccupied with Vietnam and Watergate. In time they would destroy his presidency.

I have practiced law for thirty-four years and can state with certainty that the law has been an exciting, stimulating, and rewarding career. Having come on the heels of my military service and duties in Vietnam, my law career may seem to an outsider to lack the same level of intensity of the career that preceded it. However, like those often gut-wrenching experiences in Southeast Asia, my career has enabled me to gain deep and particular insights into the souls of both my fellow man and myself. The law, like military conflict, is human interaction writ large. Both are governed by rules that can be logical and absurd at the same instant depending upon the consequences exacted upon each participant. As I grow older, my experiences of childhood, work, and family blend rather than diverge, with seemingly disparate parts becoming bound inextricably into the tableau that is my life. It is as it is. It can be no other way. On the whole, I have done the best I could to make bad situations better and to avoid repeating mistakes I made along the way. Sometimes my efforts have met with success.

This book, for the most part, is about a personal, intense period in my life. Vietnam and my advisor experience left an indelible imprint on me. They had a profound and durable effect on my life and my evaluation of the relative importance of things. For me it was a positive experience. But I have not been able to let go of Vietnam. It is part of my life, a large part. It is at my core, never far from my thoughts, and to a large extent defines who I am. Vietnam did not harm me; it was good for me. I returned to the States confident, capable, reflective, and with the knowledge that at times there is a middle ground between right and wrong. Vietnam was an experience that makes difficult an unqualified belief in absolute moral values.

Today, I am in good health and everything still works, everything. I have been married for thirty-five years to Meliora, a Latin word meaning "better." I tell her she is *optima*. We have two sons: Martin, a struggling playwright, and Tim, a struggling attorney. I, the struggling husband and father, am justly proud of all three of them. I have had the good fortune to be continuously employed since graduating from law school.

Although I keep my distance from and travel the circumference of every circle to which I belong, life has been good to me and mine. It has certainly helped to be born male, white, and in the United States. How to make life good for everyone is the most difficult question. I do not have that answer, nor apparently do others.

I began writing this book in February 1999 while on my visit to Vietnam. It was an exercise that presented me with the opportunity to examine on a personal level my values and beliefs in light of my actions of long ago. But hindsight is a difficult tool to use. It is not balanced, because it is impossible to accurately gauge the intensity of distant passions or give sense to distant motives. I cannot reconcile all of those actions with my values and beliefs. There are contradictions, but those were decisions made and actions taken

long ago under circumstances far different from those of today.

Many American combat soldiers who came to Vietnam after I left had different and much more dangerous experiences. Many of them returned home with lifelong problems.
I recognize my luck and God's grace.

APPENDIX A

Myths

There are many festivals, at least one a month. The following are a few of the customs and taboos that are observed by some of the people, but not by all. They are based on old legends long forgotten. Some of the superstitions have no known reason why they exist.

You may see a mirror attached to the front door in some of the houses. That is so that a dragon, trying to get in, will see the reflection and think that there already is a dragon in there and go away.

Village affairs and gossip are "top secret" and not to be divulged to outsiders. Severe penalties are sometimes inflicted on violators of their code.

Conservative women do not dance western dances in public, but might do it in the privacy of the home.

The Vietnamese resent direct questions from Westerners they don't know, especially concerning their names. To give your name is to expose yourself to evil. Hence, the Vietnamese has a secret name, known only to himself and parents, which he does not give to anyone, not even his wife, lest it give them power over him. Children are named according to rank in the order of birth and never called by their name outside the family.

Girls are under the close scrutiny of their parents. They do not date or go out without a chaperone.

The people are shy and will avoid even looking at you in

the beginning. After they get to know you, you will find out that they are kind and friendly.

They do not shake hands (according to custom) but most of them have the western habit by now. In some areas it is considered barbaric. Don't shake hands with a woman unless she first offers her hand. That is a basic etiquette here. The people live simply: Don't appear surprised or shocked at some of their ways that may seem crude or unsanitary to us.

Help civilians with their problems when the occasion offers. They have a long history of oppression and fear of the military.

They believe in a force, inherent in all nature, called "tinh." It is a sort of spiritual power. The Emperor, tigers, whales and dolphins are full of "tinh."

The building of a house or boat requires quite a bit of sorcery and ceremony because of the spirits involved. The sorcerer knows all the rules for the governing of the spirit world.

There are many taboos on things intimately concerned with life, sex, birth, marriage and death. For instance: a man should not be surrounded by his children at his last hour. A woman should not go out of the house during her "period," or go around holy places, and sexual relations are forbidden. Never express admiration for a baby. The devils might hear it and covet and steal the child (not too generally observed).

Poverty and the injunctions against killing account for the low meat consumption among the Vietnamese—probably poverty more than anything else.

The tiger is dreaded and his name is never used. He is called Ong Ho or Ong Cop—the "ong" means "mister." Offerings are sometimes made to him before entering the forest. Viets say the tiger is tuned into mental telepathy. If you plan a tiger hunt or think long about it, he will have all the plans. The only way to get him is decide on the spur of the moment or run into him by chance.

Vietnamese wear white for mourning and go to great expense for elaborate funerals.

They believe that all people have a "vital fluid" in them that is either good or bad—a sort of Joe Spfltz [*sic*] of Dogpatch fame—and it is bad luck to have any contact with such a person.

Here are a few taboos, not heard of by all: Don't tap anyone on the shoulder—the genie resides there and might be disturbed. Don't touch anyone on the head—it is considered a sacred part of the body and the spirit resides there. They have a belief, too, that if a person is beheaded his spirit will roam forever without a place to rest. Never serve one bowl of rice and one set of chopsticks; always at least two (one bowl is for the dead). Never light one lamp from the wick of another—bad luck. Do not have one set of chopsticks touching another set at table; never hand anyone a toothpick, nor use a relative's towel; never buy one mat or pillow—always two or more. Don't cut nails at night. Bad luck to beat both sides of a drum or overturn musical instruments; try to arrive at a performance before it starts—bad manners to be late.

The Vietnamese admire honesty but don't practice it too much. They will tell you what they think you want to hear, whether it is true or not.

They are given, at times, to brutality and high emotionalism. Also they are very credulous and will believe almost anything. That is why communist propaganda can gain such headway.

The Vietnamese are law-abiding when it suits their purpose. They are very broadminded when it comes to the interpretation and application of laws to themselves. To get around a law against killing pigs on a certain day, they will stick the pig under water and claim that he fell in and drowned and that they bled him so as not to waste the meat.

If a relative dies during a period of espousals, they are

supposed to put off the marriage for three years. So, they delay publishing the death until after the marriage.

The Vietnamese customs and taboos are based on the idea that spirits are more powerful than humans, but less intelligent and easily duped.

The above list of customs and taboos does not pretend to be all-comprehensive, and many of the Vietnamese that have had much contact with the westerners look upon them as silly superstitions. But, there are some who believe in some, if not all of them. It is good to know that they exist. The best rule of thumb to get along with other people is "always be a gentleman, i.e., hurt no one." Just don't be a bull in a china shop where your relations with strangers are concerned. Be quiet, kind and considerate of others' feelings, and you will get into no trouble and will be a credit to your country.

The Vietnamese are poor but they are very proud. They love to be hospitable and will invite you to dinner. It may be necessary to borrow to be able to pay for the entertainment, but do not pretend you know about it. They really enjoy the opportunity of being a good host. Do not offer gifts that they could obtain themselves. That would be a reflection on their status. Gifts of cigarettes, liquor, American candy are acceptable because they could not obtain them at any rate; and, therefore, is not a reflection on their means. If you give any candy to a number of children, make individual gifts. They will not divide one large gift. American sweets are much sweeter than native candy. If you get into a habit of giving candy to children, be sure you will be able to continue it. Don't expect women to wear hats in church—they don't.

APPENDIX B

Role of the Advisor

1. General

This section covers the role of the advisor from a practical, day-by-day viewpoint. Some points expressed here may be more pertinent to one advisor than to another who is assigned an entirely different job. Most of these are so indicated. Some points covered here may be repetitious or may cover "old ground" for more experienced personnel. The main purpose of this section is to offer advice to those who need it and to renew the thinking of personnel more experienced in this field.

2. The Role

A. The advisor performs as an individual and as a member of a team.

B. As an individual, the advisor takes upon himself the responsibility to get out and see what can be done to accomplish his mission, i.e., he generates most of the work towards that end through his own efforts. He tries in every way to advise and assist the Vietnamese so that they accomplish their work in a proficient manner. He is concerned about every problem that the supported unit or activity has, whether it be in the field of administrative and tactical operations of a military unit or whether it be morale, living conditions in dependent quarters, pay and allowances, postal service or general sanitation. Even if the responsible Vietnamese does not recognize the problem, still the advisor must attempt to improve conditions which hinder or prevent the unit or activity from attaining combat readiness.

C. The advisor diligently and willingly carries out the tasks assigned by superiors, abides by policy and guidance of superiors and keeps superiors informed about his work. It is his duty to inform his superior when things are not going too well, or when assistance from higher echelon is required. He coordinates with other advisors, units, or agencies when they are involved, thus completing the teamwork.

3. Rules of the Game

A. Establish good relationship with the unit or activity supported and the counterpart that you advise.

  (1) Develop a genuine interest in the welfare, customs, ethics, and beliefs of the military and civilian community.

  (2) Demonstrate your desire to pitch in and help to get things done—don't mind getting your hands dirty.

  (3) Volunteer to assist in every way possible on "Do-it-Yourself" projects, such as:

    (a) Design and construction of ranges for small arms, automatic weapons, mortars and grenades (particularly anti-guerrilla terrain-fire-type ranges for remote civil guard/self defense corps units and training sites).

    (b) Design and construction of training areas for teaching principles of ambush, counter-ambush, raids, patrols, compass courses, etc.

    (c) Prepare and conduct training. In this regard, it must be emphasized that many advisors, particularly those who go to remote civil

guard/self defense corps sites, will be without benefit of interpreter. It is even more important to develop and utilize training aids
so that the advisor can communicate ideas
and teaching by demonstration. Such devices—sketches, models, match-stick layouts, cardboard mock-ups, sand table layouts,
demonstrations with personnel and/or equipment—can accomplish required training.

(d) Prepare prototypes to sell ideas for improv-
ing living conditions, e.g., improvised bath
shower, pit latrine, waste disposal sump, water purification device, etc.

(4) Demonstrate, and assist in supervision of maintenance of weapons and equipment.

(5) Participate in athletics. Teach new games. Learn
old games. Help build facilities for sports and assist in obtaining athletic equipment.

(6) Assist in design of security system and in improvement and execution of security plan. Report
to next senior advisor when required security is
beyond local capability.

(7) Avoid offending Vietnamese by showing dislike
for their food, their customs, their way of life in
general.

B. Dig into the status of the unit or activity supported so
that you find out those things you need to know in order to give constructive advice and assistance.

(1) Determine status of personnel, facilities, equipment, weapons, ammunition and ammunition
storage, communications, state of training, administration, and morale.

(2) Determine what has been done or needs to be
done to remedy shortages or to secure necessary
resources—follow through Vietnamese channels

and keep next higher advisor informed on assistance required by personnel.

(3) Develop an intimate knowledge of the organization, chain of command, communication system, source and system of supply, and intelligence net.

(4) Determine the needs of the military unit or activity supported and its dependent community from the standpoint of medical, adequacy of housing, food, and clothing, etc. Work towards self improvements. Submit recommendations for assistance in improvement of conditions to next senior when such assistance is beyond local capabilities.

C. Find out what you can do to aid the local populace under the civil actions program, through things you as advisors can do or through actions the unit or agency you are advising can put into effect.

D. Take care of yourself.

(1) Take care of your body; you only have one.

(2) Make your living quarters as sanitary as you can.

(3) Be alert mentally and physically, always think of security measures and fit them into the accomplishment of your mission.

E. Adhere to chain of command.

(1) Become thoroughly familiar with command channels, teach and sell chain of command to the unit or agency you are advising and assist them in effecting coordination and obtaining support through proper channels.

(2) Strictly adhere to advisory channels. Do not make promises or otherwise go out on a limb offering support, such as helicopters, on your own initiative. Senior advisors will support you insofar as their resources allow, but you must coordinate with them or their authorized representatives before you commit such support.

APPENDIX C

Dos and Don'ts

Dos

Maintain your sense of humor; you will discover that the Vietnamese also possess a sense of humor.

Approach the subject under discussion from a different direction and with different words until you know that your ideas are understood.

After "planting" an idea, let the Vietnamese take the credit if it is accepted and put into practice—your satisfaction is in the net overall result obtained.

Keep abreast of what is going on in the unit, keep in close contact with commanders and staff officers to obtain information, and constantly follow up on leads obtained.

Transact business directly with your counterpart. Do not permit the commander or his staff to subordinate you or your position.

Keep your personal appearance and conduct above reproach. Remember that the Vietnamese are careful to follow correct protocol at ceremonies and social events.

Keep a running account of major events—this is useful when it is necessary to render reports, establish the history of a subject, or follow up. A good filing system is a must; a suspense file is also essential.

Accept invitations to Vietnamese dinners, cocktail parties, ceremonies, etc. You will find that most of them are considerate and understanding as to menus and drinks served. By exercise of reasonable precaution, your health will not suffer.

When using interpreters, speak in phrases and short sentences; do not expect the interpreter to remember long speeches. Have it clearly understood with the interpreter that he will ask you and/or the Vietnamese to repeat what has been said rather than to translate incorrectly. On written translations from English to Vietnamese, always have the interpreter read back from his Vietnamese copy to ensure correct translations. Remember, the Vietnamese vocabulary is limited.

Study your counterpart to determine his personality and background; exert every effort to establish and maintain friendly relationships; learn something about the personal life of the Vietnamese with whom you work, and demonstrate your interest—it pays dividends.

Always exercise patience in all your dealings with your Vietnamese counterpart. Never expect the job to be done at the snap of a finger.

If you find it necessary to make a suggestion or recommendation that might imply criticism of existing Vietnamese policy or procedures, do so in private, never in the presence of superiors or subordinates of the Vietnamese commander.

Appreciate the work-load of the Vietnamese commander. He will be unable to spend the entire day with you although he will probably never call this to your attention. Make yourself available at all times but let him have sufficient time to run his unit and do his paper work.

Respect the Asiatic custom and desire of "saving face."

Local conditions involving the national economy, customs, and educational development often dictate procedures that are considered inefficient and uneconomical in our Army. Avoid an arbitrary attitude towards these procedures. Try to understand them before recommending changes.

Maintain the same moral and ethical standards in Vietnam

as you would at your home station in the United States. Moral degeneracy and weakness are indications of national decadence to the Vietnamese.

Try to anticipate the Vietnamese problems that your counterpart cannot foresee because of inexperience, and appraise him of the situation in time so that he can make proper and timely decisions.

At every opportunity stress the chain of command and its use by commanders at all echelons.

Stress at every opportunity maintenance of equipment, supply consciousness and the filling of school quotas with qualified personnel.

When advice is rendered, be sure you are on firm ground and be certain that it is within the capability of your unit to carry it out.

Be truthful in everything you say and do, as the Vietnamese appreciate and admire one who speaks the truth.

Encourage your Vietnam associates to widen their horizons by explaining U.S. customs, by discussing world affairs.

Use your English classes to put your ideas across. For instance, Field Manual 22-10, Leadership, is an excellent textbook for intermediate reading.

Make a special effort to keep physically fit.

Always praise at least some part of what the Vietnamese do or plan to do. Then if you have criticism, couch your suggestions in tactful terms as a modification to their plans.

Set a good example in dress, posture, conduct and professional competence for the Vietnamese officer.

Present your suggestions carefully, in detail, with adequate reasons. The statement that the United States Army does a certain thing a certain way is not generally sufficient for the Vietnamese to be confident that way is the best.

Continually stress the mutual advantages of good military-civilian relations to avoid the pitfalls of military arrogance, which easily irritates the civilian populace.

Constantly encourage the strengthening of unit esprit de corps. This may well sustain the unit in the face of other difficulties.

Be able to explain or discuss basic U.S. policy. Continually formulate in your mind how you will answer inevitable questions on current topics of the day such as racial integration, etc. However, be careful to avoid being drawn into a heated argument on the subject.

Encourage initiative and inventiveness by all commanders and officers. This trait is especially valuable in an Army of a "have not" nation that can never expect to receive all the outside material support it wants and needs.

Participate actively in the military, social and athletic functions of your units.

Avoid underestimating the ability and capability of the Vietnamese officer. He may not have the U.S. Army touch but he knows his own country and terrain and has been fighting on it for centuries. He and his men can be formidable opponents on their own home grounds.

Treat the Vietnamese with whom you work as you would a fellow American—equal in every aspect.

Always remember you are an advisor and have no command jurisdiction.

Shake hands with all Vietnamese officers in a room when entering and leaving.

Exchange amenities with Vietnamese officers prior to discussing official matters.

Request copies of directives issued by the commander subsequent to your submission of a recommendation to determine if your ideas are being bought and promoted. A responsive commander will not hesitate to publish a good idea over his signature block.

Observe your contemporaries carefully, particularly those in key slots or with whom you have constant contact, for any indications of hostility or resentment. When such individual feelings exist, your problems are compounded.

As time progresses you may think or feel that you are doing all the "bending over backwards." If you observe carefully you will find that this is not so and that the Vietnamese are meeting you halfway.

Stress teamwork and coordination.

Emphasize the importance of doing things on time by being punctual yourself. Many Vietnamese have a very casual attitude toward time.

Take every opportunity to visit other parts of Vietnam. A knowledge of the terrain will help you understand Vietnamese military problems and will be invaluable in case of war.

Show an interest in Vietnamese customs, language, history and people. Your ideas will be more readily accepted if you show an understanding of theirs.

Keep U.S. officers at higher levels advised of conditions of which you are aware.

Keep in mind the seriousness and urgency of your mission.

Develop the commander's efforts towards organized troop discipline.

Develop a recognition of the importance of sanitation and police.

Teach by example wherever and whenever possible.

Maintain close contact with the commander to whom you are advisor. Tactful aggressiveness on the part of the advisor is essential.

Use highly qualified interpreters on important matters.

Persuade Vietnamese personnel to pass information automatically—up, down, and laterally.

Poke around in corners and buildings and you will find usable equipment and training aids that have not been used or even made available.

Spend maximum time in your units so that the troops get to know you and trust you.

Encourage staff officers to get out and see other regiments and other battalions train. They can't have all the good ideas. This should encourage a better parent unit esprit as well as better training.

Develop a sense of responsibility toward the unit being advised to the degree that you can feel a personal gratification for a job well done.

Try to instill, through a progressive program, U.S. methods and practices approved by ARVN.

Consider the age and experience of commanders and staff officers at each echelon.

Think—be imaginative. The lack or absence of initiative and imagination is the only deterrent to a successful tour as an advisor.

Don'ts

Don't forget for a single minute that you may have to go to war with your unit. Any opportunity for preparation lost now may be fatal in case of war.

Don't relax your standards even though the Vietnamese standards may be lower and you are far from U.S. supervision. However, don't flaunt your higher standard of living.

Don't forget that the Vietnamese are basing their opinion of 160 million Americans on even your most casual words and actions.

Don't forget that a careless word or action of yours can cost the U.S. very dearly in goodwill and cooperation, which have been built up here at the cost of billions.

Don't hesitate to point out faults, especially when they pertain to neglecting the welfare of the troops or wasting U.S. aid.

Don't assume that the U.S. school solution is the only one for the Vietnamese.

Don't try to sell a U.S. method with the sole argument that it is U.S. An explanation of the advantages will be more effective.

Don't condone a Vietnamese officer's attitude that officers are a privileged class without equivalent responsibilities.

Don't stimulate Vietnamese appetite for more intricate and complicated equipment by boasting about superior equipment available to U.S. units.

Don't underestimate the Vietnamese people. They achieved independence from both the French and the Communists against incredible odds.

Don't lose a single opportunity to learn about SE Asia, especially guerrilla fighting and security in rear areas. It will be valuable to you the rest of your military career.

Don't be discouraged. Suggestions and advice you have given may appear to have been disregarded and then be implemented.

Don't drink to excess in Vietnamese company. They are a people who use alcohol moderately.

Don't ridicule the Vietnamese in conversation with other Americans. Many Vietnamese understand much more English than they admit.

Don't refuse invitations to quasi-military functions. The presence of American advisors adds prestige to many occasions.

Don't summon a Vietnamese by shouting, whistling or hand motions. Catching the individual's eye and a head gesture will produce more effective results.

Don't criticize an individual in the presence of other Vietnamese. Always use private constructive criticism.

Don't discuss Vietnamese politics with Vietnamese personnel.

Don't fail to recognize military courtesy. Vietnamese personnel render courtesies to officers in a variety of ways unfamiliar to Americans.

Don't take offense at what sometimes appears to be abruptness and even actual discourtesy at times. It is part of the job to overlook these attitudes while at the same time doing everything possible to create goodwill and mutual understanding.

Don't accept a "yes" answer at its face value. "Yes" may mean only that the person to whom you are talking understands what you have said, but it may not indicate that he "buys" your suggestion.

Don't expect the Vietnamese commander (or staff officer) to accept all of your suggestions; he is the commander, not you.

Don't present too many subjects at one time or prolong unnecessarily the discussion of any one subject. It is better to have another conference at a later time.

Don't make promises that you cannot or should not carry out.

Don't show an air of superiority, regardless of rank of officers you are dealing with.

Don't endeavor to give advice until you have made friends with the Vietnamese officers.

Don't be afraid to get your hands and clothes dirty when giving advice in the form of a demonstration.

Don't compare relative pay scales of the American and Vietnamese Army.

Don't give advice that conflicts with directives from higher echelons of command.

Don't do the job yourself. Persuade the Vietnamese individual responsible to do it.

Don't let Vietnamese personnel substitute your chain of command for theirs.

Don't hesitate to begin a project because you won't be in

Vietnam long enough to complete it. Get it started and sell your successor on completing it.

Don't give up your efforts to analyze training because it is conducted in Vietnamese; get an interpreter and find out all the details.

APPENDIX D

Tips to Advisors

1. Professional Duties and Interests

Sell in-place training, once units return to posts. One thousand inch (approximately 25 meters) firing is ideal for small posts to fire weapons.

Spend maximum time in your units so that the troops get to know you and trust you. Keep abreast of what is going on in the unit, keeping in close contact with the commander and staff.

Encourage frequent command inspections by the commander. Many often show a reluctance to inspect, relying solely on correspondence and reports to evaluate the effectiveness of the unit.

Continually stress mutual advantages of good military-civilian relations to avoid the pitfalls of military arrogance, which easily irritates the civilian populace. The development of a proper soldier-civilian relationship is civic action at its best.

Constantly strive to raise the standards of your unit to your standards. Guard against lowering your standards to those of the unit you advise.

Keep training standards high enough so that the unit is ready for an inspection at all times. This saves the wear and tear of preparation for inspection and the disappointment that follows when it's cancelled. Do not use training time for housekeeping matters. Discourage the idea that the two of you can conspire to "eyewash" inspectors; it must be permissible to "eyewash" you.

An advisor should have sufficient knowledge of all aspects of U.S. aid programs to counter insurgent propaganda depicting this aid as interference into the affairs of the people.

Constantly observe for signs of fatigue. There is a marked difference between American and Vietnamese stamina. Pushing at peak performance will cause a long-term decrease in efficiency.

2. Techniques

An advisor must constantly bear in mind that he is an advisor and not a commander. He is not in Vietnam to fight or lead troops.

Avoid rushing your acceptance by your counterpart. Overselling yourself will arouse suspicion and delay acceptance. Time spent developing a healthy relationship will pay large dividends later on.

Advising works both ways. Set an example for your counterpart by asking his advice; you will get many good ideas from him.

Avoid giving your counterpart the impression that each time he sees you, you are interested in asking for status reports, etc. You will soon find him avoiding you and information increasingly difficult to get.

Transact important business directly with your counterpart for assuring full understanding of difficult subjects. Work from the soft sell to the request for official information.

Don't present too many subjects at one time or prolong unnecessary discussion of one subject; it is better to have another conference at a later time. Don't speak rapidly or use slang. By the same token don't speak too slowly; it will insult his intelligence.

Correct the most important deficient areas first. When you

arrive you will see many things you will want to correct immediately. At all costs avoid the impression that everything is all wrong.

Avoid making recommendations that lead to decisions. Leave sufficient room for your counterpart to exercise his prerogative. One of his greatest fears is that he will appear dependent upon his advisor to his troops. Carefully choose a time and a place to offer advice.

Use your subordinate advisors to lay the groundwork for new ideas at their level.

For successful combat operations do your homework thoroughly. The amount of advising done during combat operations is small. The advisor does most of his advising in preparation for combat, based upon his observations or those of his subordinates, during past operations; hold a private critique with the commander upon completion of an operation.

Don't be afraid to advise against a bad decision, but do it in the same manner you would recommend a change of action to an American commander for whom you have respect and with whom you work daily.

Approach the subject under discussion from different directions and with different words, until you know that your ideas are understood. The Vietnamese seldom admit that they do not understand. Don't accept a yes answer at its face value; yes may mean that the person understands but does not mean that he buys your suggestion. It may also be used to cover a failure to understand.

Always exercise patience in your dealings with your Vietnamese counterpart. Never expect the job to be done at the snap of a finger—and don't snap your fingers.

Information from your counterpart cannot be accepted in blind faith. It must be checked—discreetly and diplomatically, but checked.

After planting an idea, let the Vietnamese take credit for it as if it were his own idea.

3. Personal Attitude and Relations

Getting accustomed to the native food and drink presents a problem, in somewhat varying degrees, to the advisor. You will not lose face if you eat and drink with your counterpart; conversely, you will gain face.

Don't become discouraged. All of your advice won't be accepted. Some of it will be implemented at a later date.

Don't forget that a careless word or action can cost the U.S. very dearly in goodwill and cooperation, which have been built up with great effort and at considerable cost.

Don't discuss Vietnamese policy with Vietnamese personnel. It is your obligation to support the incumbent government just as you do your own. This is U.S. national policy.

Study your counterpart to determine his personality and background; exert every effort to establish and maintain friendly relationships. Learn something about the personal life of the Vietnamese with whom you work, and demonstrate this interest.

Set a good example for the Vietnamese in dress, posture, and conduct as well as in professional knowledge and competence.

Develop a sense of responsibility toward the unit being advised to the degree that you can feel a personal gratification for a job well done. Do not become so involved with the unit that you cannot readily recognize failures.

Vietnamese desire appreciation, recognition, and understanding; they seek security and attention, they like to feel important, like to contribute and like to belong. In brief, they react to these things as we do.

Accept invitations to Vietnamese dinners, cocktail parties, and ceremonies. Shake hands with all Vietnamese in a room when entering and leaving. Exchange amenities with officials prior to discussing business matters.

Don't summon a Vietnamese by whistling or shouting.

You will note that Vietnamese summon each other by a wave of the hand, similar to our farewell wave.

Don't fail to observe and recognize military courtesy.

4. Personal Qualities and Requirements

Based upon observation and experience, U.S. advisors returning from the Republic of Vietnam have pooled their thoughts on what it takes to be an effective advisor. No doubt each one of us is most anxious to do our best in assisting our Vietnamese allies expel insurgency from their country as soon as possible. For this reason it is felt that you will welcome the opportunity to examine what these U.S. advisors have to say on the subject of advising. It is hoped you will give them attentive consideration; and to the extent indicated by introspection, make them a part of your personal attributes prior to and during your tour in Vietnam. These qualities and requirements, along with a general summation of desirable advisor traits, are set forth in the following paragraphs:

Persevere in implementing sound advice, exercise patience and tact, display a pleasing personality, be adaptable to environment and changing situations, be honest, maintain high moral standards, be understanding and sincere, present a sharp military appearance, evince devotion to job assignment, keep in good physical condition, acquire ability to demonstrate effectively, know your job, know thoroughly the unit you are advising as to organization, equipment, and tactics, know thoroughly your own branch and have a good working knowledge of other branches, know your counterpart's problems and demonstrate your awareness of them to him.

Advisors are restricted in their operations because they are not authorized to exercise command in accomplishing advisory functions. They must rely on their ability to sell the most indefinite commodity which is represented in the individual himself. The traits of an advisor encompass all the traits of leadership plus the ability to adapt to his environment. This environment changes with the locality or area in which the advisor is assigned. If he is in the Far East, he must remember that arrogance and dogmatism are all the more taboo, for the religious and philosophical background of the Asian strongly opposes this type of personality. To sell one's self, you must prove your value—an advisor must present a favorable personality in the eyes of his counterpart. This can be accomplished in due time by a gradual demonstration of your capabilities in an unassuming but firm manner. Be positive, but not dogmatic, in your approach to any subject. However, if you are not sure of the subject matter, it is better to say so and take timely measures to obtain the correct information. To attempt to bluff through a problem will only result in irreparable loss of prestige.

A most favorable trait is persistence, tempered with patience. If a problem area is discovered, continue efforts to solve it, recommend appropriate measures to be taken, and then follow through, again remembering that patience is of utmost importance. But, the matter must be continually brought to your counterpart's attention until he is sold on taking the measures necessary to solve the problem or correct the deficiency as the case may be. The ultimate in good advising is to advise your counterpart in such a way that he takes the desired action feeling that it was through his own initiative rather than yours.

Possibly the most desirable traits you as an advisor can possess are knowledge of the subject, ability to demonstrate your capabilities in an unassuming but convincing manner, and a clear indication of your desire to get along and work together with your counterpart and other associates—however, not to the extent of obsequious behavior nor acceptance of abusive treatment. These traits, along with leadership ability and desirable character traits accepted in our own society, will usually lead to a successful and satisfying advisory tour.

He wouldn't kill for his country, but that didn't mean he wouldn't die for it.

MEDIC!
The Story of a Conscientious Objector in the Vietnam War
by Ben Sherman

Ben Sherman was a carefree college student when he was drafted. As a medic, Sherman wouldn't carry a gun, but he would clean the bodies of American GIs for shipment home, barely escape being beaten to death by a deranged private, and walk in more blood than most people see in a lifetime.

Accompanying platoons deep into enemy-infested territory, descending into raging battles to medevac the wounded, saving lives on the jungle floor—Sherman did it all, often under a hail of screaming bullets, mortars, and rockets. This is his story: unflinching, honest, and unforgettable.

Published by Presidio Press
Available wherever books are sold

At last, the full story of Khe Sanh—from acclaimed Vietnam War historian
EDWARD F. MURPHY

THE HILL FIGHTS
The First Battle of Khe Sanh

While the seventy-seven-day siege of Khe Sanh in early 1968 remains one of the most highly publicized clashes of the Vietnam War, scant attention has been paid to the earlier battles of Khe Sanh, also known as "the Hill Fights." Based on firsthand interviews and documentary research, Murphy's deeply informed narrative history is the *only* complete account of the battles, their origins, and their aftermath.

"[A] VALUABLE ADDITION TO THE MILITARY HISTORY CANON . . . Murphy, who served in the Vietnam War, tells his story forcefully and with empathy for the American fighting men on the ground."

—*Publishers Weekly*

Published by Presidio Press
Available wherever books are sold